BATH

Ace of Clubs

BATH
Ace of Clubs

BRIAN JONES

The Breedon Books
Publishing Company
Derby

First published in Great Britain by
The Breedon Books Publishing Company Limited
44 Friar Gate, Derby, DE1 1DA
1993

Photographic Acknowledgements

Photographs supplied by *The Bath Evening
Chronicle*, Reg Monk and Stuart Nolt. Cover
photographs by Neil Elston and Steven Bardens.

ISBN 1 873626 45 2

Printed and bound by The Bath Press Ltd, Bath and London.
Covers printed by BDC Printing Services Limited of Derby.

Contents

Acknowledgements

MY thanks go to those at the club I consulted about this book, including the Bath secretary Clive Howard, the coach Jack Rowell, and others including some former club captains. Over the years of watching Bath, I also heard the views of countless others in the Bath crowd, some of them friends, but also including many whose faces have become familiar but whose names I do not know. But their lively opinions, garnered in past seasons, have helped to inform the pages that follow. Kevin Coughlan's statistical records of Bath's matches in recent years also helped save many hours of my time.

I thank them all, but opinions in this book about clubs, games and players, except where otherwise attributed, are my own. So are the statistics; so, I fear, are any errors.

Finally, my thanks to the *Bath and West Evening Chronicle* and its editor Paul Deal for the many photographs used in this book; to Dick Douglas-Boyd whose good idea it was; and to David Foot who suggested I should attempt it. I hope it does them — and Bath — justice.

Brian Jones
June 1993

Dedication

To Jack Rowell, the players,
and all who have helped Bath Football Club,
past, present and future,
from those of us who stand and cheer and criticise but mostly admire.

Introduction

AS STUART Barnes aimed his vital kick at goal in the closing moments of the Twickenham Final, the Bath supporters in the crowd could scarcely believe their eyes or their luck. His kick went wide — and Bath had won the cup. An earlier drop-goal from Bath's England international fly-half had been decisive.

No aberration: simply a glance back to the 1984 Twickenham Final, the first that Bath won, with the drop-goal coming from John Horton. It was against the favourites Bristol, whose fly-half that day was Stuart Barnes.

Eight years later, Barnes's other more famous and more difficult shot at goal, a drop-kick from all of 40 metres in the closing seconds of extra-time, was memorably successful and Bath had beaten Harlequins in the classic Twickenham Final of 1992.

There were three other survivors from that first cup triumph in the 1992 side, prop Gareth Chilcott, scrum-half Richard Hill and lock Nigel Redman. But if it was a remarkable enough achievement for one club in nine seasons to reach seven Twickenham Finals, the more astonishing feat — probably beyond hope of repetition — was that they won every one. They beat Bristol, London Welsh, Wasps (twice), Leicester, Gloucester and Harlequins.

And while they were winning cups at Twickenham they were four times winners of the Courage Clubs' Championship, Division One, in its first six seasons. Twice in those six seasons they also achieved cup and league 'double.'

This is the story of those years — from Horton to Barnes — when the game enjoyed, honoured and occasionally snubbed the most successful club side in the history of Rugby Union in England, and maybe in the world. It tells of the players who sweated and starred and sometimes suffered, and of the man who, more than any other individual, made it all possible, a coaching genius from West Hartlepool, Jack Rowell. It should perhaps be called The Team (or teams) that Jack Built.

Trophies

Bath's Winning Decade
1984-1993

John Player Special Cup		**Courage Clubs' Championship**
		Division One
Winners	1983-84	No competition
Winners	1984-85	No competition
Winners	1985-86	No competition
Winners	1986-87	No competition
KO Fifth round	1987-88	Fourth

Pilkington Cup		
Winners	1988-89	Champions
Winners	1989-90	Third
KO Third round	1990-91	Champions
Winners	1991-92	Champions
KO Third round	1992-93	Champions

Bath Football Club Officers

May 1993

Past Presidents

Sir Robert S.Blaine, F.W.Forester, J.Stuart Goold, J.H.Colmer, R.Scott Reid, S.L.Amor, Arnold Ridley, Sir James Pitman, L.D.Wardle, B.C.Barber, W.S.Bascombe, C.H.G.Beazer, H.J.Crane, J.F.Bevan-Jones, D.M.Smith, Mrs Molly Gerrard, G.S.Brown, H.L.Bradford, W.J.F.Arnold, H.J.F.Simpkins, J.W.P.Roberts, N.P.Halse, A.O.Lewis.

President
(1992-93)
L.A.Hughes

Vice Presidents

W.J.F.Arnold, R.J.Barber, J.F.Bevan-Jones, G.Bramall, T.R.H.Brinkworth, G.S.Brown, A.H.Burcombe, F.Carey, F.Cottle, D.P.R.Curran, B.Davis, S.G.Dickinson, H.T.C.Ferguson, A.F.Foster, D.J.Gay, G.George, N.P.Halse, C.K.Hamon, G.W.Hancock, N.Harris, J.Hawkins, F.W.Haywood, R.J.Hedley, R.G.Hillman, J.P.Horton, C.D.Howard, J.M.Jeffrey, L.D.L.Jones, J.S.Kay, P.V.G.Lang, A.O.Lewis, C.G.Malcolm, A.J.Meek, L.J.Newton, J.A.Palmer, D.J.Parsons, B.Perry, L.St V.Powell, J.W.P.Roberts, D.G.Robson, J.Rowell, C.Smith, T.H.Smith, W.J.Stevens, F.J.Thomas, W.Walworth, W.Zalek.

Chairman
J.Gaynor

Secretary: C.D.Howard. **Assistant Secretary:** B.Shaw

Treasurer
C.S.Gale

Fixture Secretary: G.W.Hancock. **Assistant Fixture Secretary:** T.D.Martland.
Membership Secretary: T.K.Selley. **1st XV Secretary:** B.Shaw.

Sub-committee Chairmen
Selection: J.Rowell. **Grounds:** R.A.Seaman.
Bars: L.D.L.Jones. **Fund-raising:** D.G.Ryder.
Match: J.R.Allen. **Social:** P.Beechinor.
Coaching: J.Rowell. **Under-21:** A.G.E.Clarkson.
Youth: M.Robinson. **Juniors:** J.Mack.
Mini-rugby: G.P.Grimshaw

The Beginning

THE team that Jack Built — that, I suppose, is the theme of this book. Perhaps it should also be its title, because Jack Rowell was the prime architect of the decade that brought Bath success unprecedented in club rugby. It is that achievement which this book is intended to celebrate.

Along the way, Rowell had gifted helpers on and off the field. Not all of them may be included in the pages that follow, but the players are there. And not only those who have 'done the double' or celebrated a third successive league championship. Some talented players won nothing — other than many matches — during their time at Bath.

But the running game introduced, at first tentatively in the late 1960s by Peter Sibley and Phil Hall, then honed in the 1970s by the talented Mike Beese and his contemporaries in time for John Horton to take charge, meant that the club — although it may not have known it — was ripe for the rich harvests reaped later under Rowell's husbandry.

A constant crop of trophies was visible testimony to the new standards of club rugby set by Bath from the 1980s into the 1990s, a season-by-season feast which other clubs would strive mightily to spoil or to emulate.

But as I've suggested, it is necessary to go back the best part of three decades to identify the seedcorn of later playing prosperity.

Most genuine Bath supporters of any seniority probably don't know when they consciously started cheering on the team down at the Rec. They just can't remember a time when they didn't. But some of us can pinpoint it to the very season. In my case it was the season that started (so I now discover) two weeks after Nigel Redman was born (in Cardiff) and nine months before Jeremy Guscott glided his way into the world in Bath.

Even the Avon, which now courses smoothly over Pulteney Weir beside the Recreation Ground, thanks to major river works, was different in those days — liable to flood the centre of the city at the drop of a torrent in the Mendips; pictures of rowing boaters cruising down Stall Street, to be seen on the front page of the *Evening Chronicle*, seemed startlingly apt for a city named Bath.

Perhaps that was why the Bath wicket, used one week in the year by Somerset, was so notoriously suspect. Certainly the Rec was better-known for its cricket in those days than for the play of Bath Football Club. But the often boggy pitch they played on probably didn't help.

Happily for me, I'd arrived in Bath in summer 1964 just as Bath cricket week, rather than the Avon, was in full flow. As I enjoyed a pint after work in the modest beer tent of those days, watching Bill Alley enjoying himself as the Bath Abbey bells rang out, I wondered where I'd been all my days. This, I thought, is the life.

Discovering the Rec for rugby came with the start of the next season. I could nip away from the *Evening Chronicle* offices — we worked a shorter day on Saturdays, honest — just 15 minutes before kick-off and easily find a privileged place to watch from the stand side, cheering an Ian Duckworth try or a Phil Hall tackle.

The size of the crowd was no problem — I could stroll about during the game and say hullo to colleagues from work such as former player Jim Cope from the process department, Ted Whitemore, the printing overseer, or Eric Cockram, the accountant, and wave to the young John Stevens in the press seats where he sat alongside the rubicund figure of 'Captain' Dick Ledbury; unless the visitors were from Wales or one of the big English city clubs they might be alone. Dick Ledbury was the local newspaper linage king of the day, whose latterday confusion about the laws of the game was a constant problem — he was still liable to 'score' four points for a dropped-goal, for instance.

Indeed, Bath in the so-called 'swinging sixties' was briefly better known nationally for its soccer than for its rugby. A rising manager named Malcolm Allison, with the Scot Charlie 'Cannonball' Fleming (whose career was largely past him) up front, and Tony Book (whose better days were yet to come) at the back, brought temporary fame to Bath City with a famous FA Cup run.

The same Malcolm Allison, nearly 30 years

later, was to return to Twerton Park, again briefly, to help the ailing Bristol Rovers, by then weekly, sometimes weakly, boarders in Bath. But that's a story for someone else to tell.

When I began researching for this book, and hunted among some old treasures, I came across a Bath Football Club programme ('Price 6d') for Monday, April 5 1965. The advertisements alone belong to what now seems like a more innocent world.

'Fishy' Evans (as celebrated, at least to Bathonians, as Harry Ramsden in Leeds) exhorted: 'After the Line Out, Tackle a good meal, Scrumptious Fried Fish and Chips.' More sedately, W.H.Smith (Bath) Ltd, saddlers, advertised 'all requisites for your Horse and Dog.' The Odeon Theatre 'three minutes from Bath Spa and the Central Bus Station' was 'warm and comfortable . . .just the place for an evening's entertainment after the match.'

The fixture list too belonged to less sophisticated times. Bath had lost away to Llanelly (*sic*) 35-3, beaten St Mary's Hospital at the Rec but lost the return match, won 41-3 against Old Cranleighans, lost 22-14 at Bridgwater, and thrashed Old Blues on Boxing Day 1964 by 51-0 — just as well.

The programme showed that of 37 games played up to April 3 that 1964-65 season, Bath had won but 10. Only one was against a club that might reasonably have been considered in the senior flight — Waterloo. (Bath beat Weston-super-Mare, twice, for example, but lost at Cheltenham and Devonport Services.)

That night's match was against 'our friends from Bristol (who) readily co-operated when the wintry weather made it necessary to postpone the Bristol game on 6 March last. Although both clubs are heavily committed this month, it was found possible to arrange the game for tonight. Our thanks are due to the Bristol officials for their amiable co-operation.'

Different days indeed — and not only in the gentlemanly pleasantries of respective committees. Bath expected to be duly beaten by Bristol — that was the nature of contests between the two.

Bristol that night included at centre the legendary John Blake (who died in 1983), Richard Sharp, already capped by England and inevitably misspelled in the programme, was at fly-half. John Pullin (also with his name wrongly spelled) and not yet capped for England, was at hooker, with another future international, Dave Watt, in the second row. Bath had one international, Geoff Frankcom, of the RAF and capped at Bedford, in the centre.

I report it simply as I knew it. The Bath team

The night it all began? Programme cover from April 1965 (complete with pork pies and paint) for Bath's first win over Bristol in ten years.

in those days was a cheerful enough band, but were expected to lose and they usually did. But we cheered them — and turned up in our modest hundreds for most games in the hope of seeing at least some exciting play from livelier opponents (from Gloucester we expected no excitement other than from a few punch-ups.)

Those were seasons too when a try scored only three points, a clearance to touch could be 'straight in' from anywhere on the pitch. (Gloucester's Micky Booth made a notable career from pushing his kicks and his pack line-out by line-out up the touchline.)

I should also explain that I'd abandoned play myself five years earlier, my game having progressed — regressed? — to Coarse Rugby even before Michael Green had officially christened it.

Like many Lancashire lads, I played Union at school and happily watched League in the holidays — the mix of the codes always seemed more natural there. I even saw Fran Cotton's father Dave (look, no teeth), playing as hooker in a great Warrington RL side. And both codes mingled in National Service.

I had played for Ilford Wanderers Extra 'A' team 20 years before Damian Cronin graced the club. Later, I was briefly at a similar lowly level with Heaton Moor, on the fringes of Manchester. Then I did something nasty to my knee one miserable day at Oldham, and in typical Coarse Rugby fashion was left to travel painfully to hospital by train, bus, sweat, and hobble. When I left hospital I was on crutches.

My redoubtable boss in Manchester, John Putz (who ten years later on his retirement moved to beautiful Wellow, only a few miles from the Rec), told me firmly that if I wanted to progress — at work rather than at rugby (he didn't know how bad I was at the game) — I should give up rough sports and take up chess instead. As I was only playing to keep fit, and successive injuries were making me unfit, I took his hint, and retired.

All this I mention simply to make clear that I am a spectator rather than a player, and a journalist who happens to be a Bath member. The book is not, cannot, be written from the viewpoint of the players, therefore, or the committee or the coaches. It is for all of them, but it is above all for the ordinary spectator and written from his or her point of view. That for the most part, has been mine, too, for nearly 30 years; a majority of the matches mentioned in the book I saw. And that includes — ah, yes — the memorable game against Bristol on the Rec that April night in 1965.

John Stevens (soon to reject overtures to do the rugby job on other, bigger newspapers) wrote with all the relief of an historic victory for Bath resonant in his summing up:

"At long last Bath have done it. For the first time in ten years they have beaten Bristol . . .many of the bitter disappointments of the season were forgotten in this moment of triumph."

John Mason, then of the *Bristol Evening Post* (but soon to accept similar overtures from the *Daily Telegraph*) was more specific:

"You have to turn the calendar back to 16 October 1954, to find a scoreline which . . .shows Bath defeating Bristol. Since that date Bristol have come off best in 20 successive matches."

The long wait was over. The score was 17-12, with tries for Bath by Frankcom, Bruford and Martland, with Blake scoring Bristol's only try.

Both reporters praised Bath's half-backs Jim Galley and Brendan Perry and the 'ferocious work' of the back row. A great occasion for Bath, then, and this team:

A.Gay; Margretts (capt), O'Mara, Frankcom, Bruford; Perry, Galley, P.Parfitt, Buckle, Smerdon, Armstrong, Marson, Martland, Heindorff, Hall.

Henceforward — although it seemed hard to believe at the time — Bath would increasingly become a tougher match for Bristol, Gloucester, and assorted Welshmen. True, it might not be until well into Jack Rowell's later stewardship that the surprise would be if Bath, rather than their opponents — any opponents — were to lose. But the better times just around the corner were about to be heralded by the arrival at the Rec of a wingman whose eyesight had cost him a Blue but whose vision of the game, backed by that same 'ferocious' back row, would provide the first firm step on Bath's stairway to success.

Sibley's Team

PETER Sibley was playing for 'the Club', Blackheath, then rather more celebrated than it has been in more recent years, and he enjoyed its style of running rugby. But he was 30 and thinking of moving gently down the scale with his local club in Sussex where he'd been invited to become captain. Instead, he was offered and accepted a job teaching at Monkton Combe, Bath.

Roger Berry, then Bath's team secretary, and later its chairman, invited him to join. It was the 1965-66 season. And after one game with the United side at Cinderford (and a massive hangover), Sibley was in the first team and stayed there until he retired — rather later than he had imagined. And if the crowd at the Rec in those days was rather smaller than gathered 20 years later, it was still a shock to Sibley.

"We were used to playing in front of 20 men and a dog at Blackheath," he recalled. "But in Bath there was an evening paper that devoted most of its back page to rugby — and two or three thousand people might turn up for a Bristol game. It was quite a change — even a bit frightening at first."

It was a change in more practical ways too. Sibley, who played many times for the university during his time at Oxford, never got a Blue: he had to leave his spectacles in the dressing-room. "I think they were worried that I mightn't see the ball on a murky December day at Twickenham," he said. Bath eventually, and quickly, solved his problem — lending him the money to buy a set of the comparatively new-fangled contact lenses (what would the RFU had said if they'd known?).

Someone else who didn't know was his former Oxford colleague Jim Glover, who was with Bristol. The famous story goes that one day against Bath, Glover wisely and cruelly, kicked deep across field to Sibley's right wing, expecting him either to see the ball too late or even drop it. Sibley fielded it and streaked away to score a winning try, thanks to the 'secret' lenses.

Bath was 'a lovely, friendly, family club,' according to Sibley. But it was also remarkably content with its modest attainments. "I remember in one game in my first season, against one of the Welsh clubs, I hardly got the ball. We lost about 6-3 on penalties, and the committee were pleased and thought we'd done well." Sibley thought they could have won with a bit of enterprise and said so. His comments didn't go down too well.

Once, too, he suddenly appeared in a game outside his left winger, who wasn't best pleased at such presumption. "What did you think you were up to?" he said to Sibley later, only less politely.

But when Geoff Margretts gave up the captaincy, he and flanker Phil Hall suggested Sibley should succeed him and put his preaching into practice. He led the team for three years, with Hall as his vice-captain. "They were the three best rugby years of my life."

Always a running back himself, he now encouraged the side to move the ball around a bit, and in spite of some doubters in the club, the players for the most part backed him. He cites the back-row of Tom Martland, Peter Heindorff, and Phil Hall in particular, and the young David Gay — capped for England at no.8 for the entire Five Nations' Championship of 1967 in his late teens and — shades of years to come — ignored thereafter.

Rule changes outlawing the 'straight-in' kick to touch outside the 25 helped, too. "They played into our hands, literally." Such players as Bob Orledge in the pack, Jim Galley and Mal Lloyd at scrum-half, Jack Thomas, the precocious Vaughan Williams, and the mature Terry Hopson from Gloucester, all seen at fly-half, added to the growing air of adventure down at the Rec. But wingers Peter Glover, capped three times for England, and the remarkable eccentric Ian Duckworth were extra attractions — Sibley would move into the centre to accommodate them if necessary.

Training was taken more seriously too, with moves and set-pieces practised, and old sweats like the celebrated Peter Parfitt joined in too — even

Pioneer skipper Peter Sibley, kicking for once rather than passing, nearly a decade before Jack Rowell's arrival in the late 1970s.

if he still stubbed out his inevitable Woodbine only seconds before he ran out on match days.

Duckworth was a character who seemed a throwback from a novel by Conrad or Somerset Maugham, a former Royal Marines officer out East, who had become a mature student, whose friends didn't always know what to make of him or even where to find him — he occasionally slept in unusual places, benches in the clubhouse, in caves, or in the woods near Bath.

On the rugby field he was a marvellous attacker who was a fast, dry run for the Trick yet to come, but with 'a tackle like a torpedo', as Peter Sibley has described one match-saving Duckworth display. He also won matches which the side didn't deserve to win simply by his brilliant running, and if it was certain Duckworth was playing then the news added a hundred or more at the gate (more shades of the Trick to follow.)

He was erratic in his appearances and his behaviour. There's the tale of how, irritated by the pipe-smoking (and only) committee-man on the coach to Llanelli one night, he threw the pipe out of the window. Shocked, the committee-man ordered the bus to stop and he, not Duckworth, got out. Skipper Sibley told Duckworth he'd better play well that night — it might be his last game for the club.

Bath lost hooker Alan Parfitt a couple of minutes after the start (no replacements in those days) but held a strong Llanelli, Phil Bennett and all, to only one score. Duckworth had a magnificent game, and the Stradey Park crowd gave the Bath side a standing ovation as they left the field. And Duckworth did play again for the club.

He may nearly have played for England, too.

In those days Bath met Metropolitan Police on the morning of an international, staying overnight at club secretary Jack Simpkins's favourite hotel at Roehampton. On the eve of the 1967

Wales match, Dickie Jeeps rang up and asked for Duckworth — there was an emergency and he might be needed for England.

Now rumour in the Bath camp had it that the unpredictable winger, who had declined to make the London trip, was variously reported to be unwell, or spending the weekend with his latest girlfriend, or that he'd acquired a new motorbike. Whatever the truth he clearly hadn't wanted to be in the company of the men of the Met. Jack Simpkins said Duckworth had 'flu — but Sibley was around, and would he do? Jeeps said something unprintable and put the phone down.

Instead, Keith Savage of Northampton, who had played on the Friday night for his club, travelled down to London and played against Wales. And Duckworth never did play for England. He probably had a good weekend, nevertheless.

But if Duckworth was comet-like in his brief and brilliant but finally burnt-out career beside the Avon, other stars were beginning to shine under the Sibley reign. A knee injury meant that the 1969-70 season was Sibley's last. But already Jim Waterman was an established favourite at the Rec, unleashed by the new laws as full-back, and Mike Beese in his teens was making his first appearances in the centre.

If Sibley pointed the way, Waterman and Beese were busily paving it adventurously. Soon, an impish playmaker would arrive to help fashion an even more exciting time for Bath.

Horton Arrives

MIKE Beese came to Bath from a soccer school, Keynsham Grammar School, his high promise as an attacking and tackling centre already evident from playing for Keynsham colts. It was the tag-end of the Sibley era. There was an adventurous spirit at the Rec, he recalled. "But the expectation was that we'd lose to the big clubs. And we usually did. It was a case of living off scraps, because we got very little possession."

An early lesson for the tall young centre was a scolding from flanker Phil Hall — for kicking the ball from hand. "Winning the ball from a line-out was often such a rare commodity he was furious that we had kicked away possession."

By the early 1990s, it may be difficult to imagine how much has changed within a Bath team of 20-or-so years before. But Beese was emphatic. The worthy packs of those days were stones lighter than their present-day successors, smaller men. And the team knew its limitations and its few strengths — speed and invention in the backs when they had the ball.

Beese has pointed to the enjoyable annual West of England Veterans' tournament in which he played for many years. There, the contemporaries of his day such as Bert Meddick and Derrick Barry, Chris Perry and Robbie Lye, would compete again against old rivals from Weston-super-Mare or Bridgwater, say, "Bath veterans versus Weston was a fairly equal contest — just as it used to be."

That put the achievements of the side he first joined in context of the game's and Bath's subsequent development. The present-day Weston players are divisions below Bath; then they were a match. Indeed, Weston were competing for the services of John Horton when he came to Bath at the start of the 1973-74 season.

Mike Beese, however, was an infrequent member of the Bath side during the early 1970s. He played for Liverpool for much of his six years at the city's polytechnic except for the 'year out' which brought him back to Bath, and during vacations. That could lead to some blunt rugby education. "I remember one Christmas holiday I played at Cardiff first for Bath, and then for Liverpool — we lost disastrously both times."

At Liverpool, like Bath a side that depended largely on its running abilities, Beese won his three England caps in 1972. Even at the time, preparation seemed peculiar — the day before the first match he was taught scissors move techniques and other variants for the first time, with colleagues he had scarcely met. Then, after damaging a cartilage in training while sidestepping, he needed an operation — and lost his sidestep. Thereafter he changed the style of his play to a degree, concentrating on positional play, direct running and tackling. Those attributes were still highly valued 20 years on by all who saw Beese at his incisive best.

One day in 1973, he called at Bath Technical College where his wife Christine was a member of the physical education department. He saw a familiar figure waiting in a corridor. "Don't I know you?" said Beese, after they had exchanged glances of mutual half-recognition. It was John Horton, about to take up a post in the same department. Horton joined Bath as well as the technical college. Robbie Hazard at Weston had written inviting him there. "But knowing Mike Beese from his time at Liverpool when I was also in Lancashire persuaded me to play at Bath. It seemed the obvious thing to do." By such coincidences were Bath set more firmly on the road to later success.

One person was the catalyst who set the backs running more constructively than before: John Horton. "He had the ideas," said Beese. "He could sidestep one way, and then another and then another. As a centre it was often difficult to read him — he was so unpredictable." His breaks were usually on the inside which could make it even more difficult for his centres to follow. But because Horton in those early years surprised his colleagues, the opposition was surprised too — and at least the Bath support was aiming in the same general direction.

Jim Waterman was one of the first of the running full-backs, liberated by the rule against direct kicks to touch except from the 25 (later 22). Defences had to become much more sophisticated, too, if they were to cope with the problems posed by Waterman's expertly-timed, unexpected runs, which set up new alignments for attack.

But such adventure was born of desperate necessity. For those Bath sides it was often very much a question of running with the 'wrong' ball. "We had to run with the one we'd got," recalled Mike Beese.

In spite of his international caps, he appeared as 'Breese' in the Falmouth programme for a National Knock-Out Cup (as it was then known) match in November 1974. Bath scraped through on the away rule in a 9-9 draw. One Barry Trevaskis was on the right wing for the Cornish side that day. Further to put those days in perspective, Bath went out of the cup — "We know very little about our visitors except that they must be a very good team . . ." said the programme engagingly — to Morpeth from Northumberland, in a game played in a high gale on Kingswood School ground — the Rec was unplayable. Fifteen seasons later, Morpeth were seven divisions adrift from Bath.

The Bath team: C.Perry (capt); Hicks, J.Davies, Beese, Gaiger, Horton, Lloyd, Pudney, A.Parfitt, Meddick, B.Jenkins, Plummer, Lye, Harry, P.Hall.

Results such as that illuminated the gap between the players' ambition and the team's achievement. Yet that season they also did the double ("No mean feat," said Jack Simpkins) over Bristol.

A major problem was the lack of line-out ball. Such stalwarts as Radley Wheeler, Brian Jenkins and Derrick Barry strove bravely. But there was no disguising the lack in weight and height, of real size, in the engine-room. Bath's packs of those days were made up of the same ingredient that had served them unspectacularly and solidly for seasons past — good honest clubmen. But competent opponents didn't need to be particularly wily to know that if they put paid to the Bath pack then the backs would starve.

But two of the better-travelled members of the side had already played against the future, without knowing it.

Beese for Liverpool, and Horton for Sale, both met Gosforth while with their northern clubs — a Gosforth side already flexing its considerable muscle towards Twickenham Finals later in the 1970s, and captained by a tall, fearless forward, Jack Rowell by name.

Enter Jack Rowell

AS WITH John Horton, so with Jack Rowell — it was work, not play, that brought him to the West Country.

"I was going to live in Bath, and a good thing about rugby is the social side, so I thought if I was going to live there I'd join the club and I'd meet a few people," Jack Rowell recalled. "So I wrote to Jack Simpkins, then the club secretary. He rang up and I wasn't there. So I rang, and it was, well, a friendly but somewhat faltering reply, I suppose. But I went down . . ." And to a training session.

Mike Beese took up the story: "I remember feeling immediately that here was someone who was going to do us . . .something good."

But to go back first a few years in Rowell's career before he came to Bath is to find him at Oxford University, and incurring serious injury, badly torn neck and back muscles, in a freshers' trial. At club level he played for Hartlepool Rovers (his home town), Middlesbrough, and then Gosforth which he captained and — after injury ended his playing career — coached in the days of Roger Uttley, Peter Dixon, Duncan Madsen, Richard Breakey and other luminaries.

He qualified as a chartered accountant and moved to Lucas Ingredients at Kingswood, Bristol, whose chief executive he was to become. At first he worked with Clifton who introduced him to the West Country rugby scene. But with his domestic move came the approach to Bath — and the greatest record in British club rugby.

All that though was some seasons away when Rowell came to the Rec. Tom Martland and Dave Robson, both former players, were prominent among those helping to coach the players. But within a year, Rowell took over. He said, "It was 1978-79, Mike Beese was captain and an outstanding captain — and it was a cracking season."

There were wins over Pontypool and Swansea, Gloucester and Harlequins, but defeats by Bristol (twice) and Leicester, in a season whose second half was disrupted by snow.

Rowell recalled: "There was a nice set of people there and some outstanding players behind the scrum — a young John Palmer was coming out

of teacher training and just getting involved, there was Beese and Waterman. Horton had that mercurial individuality that could win games. But teams playing Bath in those days would focus on the forwards and the other players wouldn't come into it. The side had an awful record against Gloucester and Bristol and Welsh clubs.

"We gave them an improved way of playing, a better balance. With the forwards there at the time, people like Geoff Pillinger, Brian Jenkins, Robbie Lye, we worked to improve their will and technique and working more as a unit, and — very important — more steel. The pack became more resilient."

Training also became tougher — Bath hadn't the greatest of reputations when it came to training. John Horton remembered sessions when the backs would have finished perhaps three-quarters of an hour before Rowell had let the pack depart. "He would spend hours with them on details of technique. He had great technical knowledge of the game."

Mike Beese said: "There was a new confidence born out of Jack's being over us. We took on an extra dimension as a team. He was someone we respected and he respected us and we were confident playing under his guidance."

Two players who came with Rowell from Clifton were the hooker Simon Luxmore, and lock Nick Williams. Like the pack Rowell inherited, they had Faust-like 'to sell their soul,' as one player put it, not to the devil but to Bath and be so committed that playing for Bath became a way of life, not an outing for a side of outstanding individuals.

But for the backs there was probably greater freedom. As Beese put it: "Jack was not particularly adept at coaching backs — he let them find their own abilities." With such entertainers as Bath possessed that was not too difficult. But with the improved technique and resolution up front, the moves that had too often petered out by half-way began to be more fruitful.

New backs arrived to complement the established names (who included the largely unsung John Davies who played in almost every position

Some of Rowell's raw material . . .a side from the late 1970s. Back row (left to right): A.N.Other, Beese, Hill, Pudney, Wheeler, Jenkins, Lye, Dunbar. Front row: Perry, Parfitt, Davies, Horton, Waterman, Norris, Pillinger.

behind the scrum and whose goal-kicking was a powerful aid to the side.) The exciting young David Trick from Dorset added real speed; the schoolmaster from Dauntsey's in Wiltshire, Derek Wyatt, offered strength and determination to his lock forward's build on the left wing.

In the pack there were new names too. The Dutchman, van der Loos, was winning the ball in the line-out. To Pillinger and Lye in the back row came grafting flankers like Gerry Parsons, and the fast, strong charges of Simon Jones ("He'd have done well in rugby league," decided Horton.) Young props arrived eager to learn, Richard Lee from Somerset, Gareth Chilcott from Bristol, and eventually two experienced back-row men in mid-career, Paul Simpson from Wiltshire and Gosforth, and Roger Spurrell, from the paratroops, Plymouth Albion and Cornwall.

That geographical mix was to recur again and again in the Rowell years and the successive Bath teams he built. He quickly realised that to draw solely on Bath junior clubs for future teams was to end in a comfortable cul-de-sac, and no more. The Beeses and Palmers were exceptional but rare local talent. A Horton (like a Rowell) was a happy accident of employment.

"Bath's not a conurbation," Rowell explained. "Conurbations have a head start, like Bristol, Leicester, and even Gloucester with a large catchment area." In going beyond the local 'combination' clubs, Rowell consciously spread his net to cover the South-West. "We recruited from a wide area. People from all over the region could identify with Bath as the club for the South-West. We went to Devon and Somerset and Wiltshire, and, of course, Cornwall. That's how we knew about people like Chris Martin when he was coming from Penryn to the university."

People who would once have gone to Bristol started coming to Bath (Chilcott was one.) Others like Nigel Gaymond and Barry Trevaskis came from playing in Bristol's second team to become significant figures in the first Bath cup successes. The Irish international lock Ronnie Hakin and utility back Charlie Ralston were experienced players whose jobs brought them to the area and added their skills to the ever-strengthening team.

Part of Rowell's philosophy was that the Bath club and its playing style should become so attractive that the best players living in or coming to the area would want to join.

But of all the arrivals, one had particular impact — on his teammates as well as opponents. Roger Spurrell was a leader who fired up his pack and expected them to be prepared to lay their life on the goal-line. He was prepared to show them how, first. "He had to be hard to take the kicks — and there were a lot of them," said Rowell. "He

Piratical Jim Waterman, 1981.

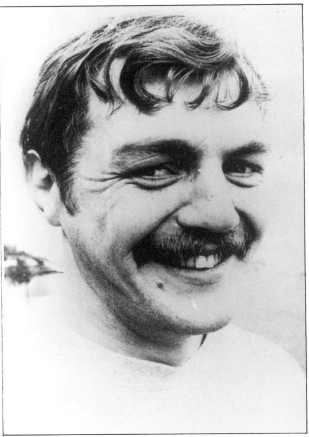

Irish prop Ronnie Hakin, now a Bath schoolmaster, 1981.

Nobbut a lad! John Hall in 1981 with Oldfield Old Boys.

was physically and mentally strong, a real motivator.''

As a leader of the side Spurrell was one of the outstanding captains in the Bath story. Not everyone at the club, or in the team, took kindly to his style — or occasional scarifying verbal scorn. But none could deny that he was a leader by example. Under his aggressive, motivational leadership the Bath pack was never again the comparative pushover of the past.

Who said he was a dour Scot? Hooker Rob Cunningham, 1981. His later coaching career with Bristol ended after the 1992-93 season in a dispute with the Bristol committee.

John Palmer in his early days with the club, 1980.

Mike Beese had come to the end of his career, but a game in which he played against his old club at Liverpool in February 1980 shows how the pre-Rowell names and those who had joined as his reign began overlapped from the Morpeth misery of five years earlier. In true programme tradition the remarkable Trick was named as 'Thick,' but, as with the winger and so many defences, I'll let that pass. Bath's team was:

Waterman; Trick, Beese, Palmer, Wyatt, Horton, Murphy, Meddick, Mason, Lee, Thomas, van der Loos, Parsons, S.Jones, Spurrell.

Eighteen months later against Bristol, although Waterman, Trick and Wyatt were absent, the transition was continuing — note the experienced hooker Rob Cunningham's young props. (As for Chris Bird in the centre, he was used to the corny jokes about Birds and Beese; his partner, another Chris, was making a rare appearance in that position):

Bath: Ralston, Simmons, Bird, Martin, Trevaskis, Horton, Lewis, Chilcott, Cunningham, Lee, Williams, Barry, Parsons, Patching, Spurrell.

When Beese bowed out to his last round of deserved applause, Simon Halliday, another bright spark — like Trick, from Dorset — arrived to complement John Palmer, brilliantly inventive in the centre. Steve Lewis was the last in a succession of scrum-halves — Horton reckoned he played with at least ten different partners in his years at Bath; another young Bath boy, John Hall, made up a new back row with Simpson and Spurrell.

The poise and pace of Trick was offset by the direct and record-breaking try-scoring of Trevaskis. Bath supporters began to wonder what they had done to deserve so entertaining and so exciting a side. The name Jack Rowell still meant little to the average watcher — some who heard his name thought it must be the former Leicester and England forward, Bert Rowell, and were a mite miffed to find they were mistaken.

But still the failures to make any headway in the knock-out competition rankled and suggested flaws in the frame. In season 1981-82, Bath failed even to qualify for the John Player Cup, finishing sixth in the South-West merit table for reasons too complex, and too daft, to delve into at this late stage.

Nevertheless the team was making many people in the rugby world aware that something unusual was happening beside the Avon.

Rowell said: "We were building and building and building, with continuous improvement and a year before we won anything I felt we had a team, and that's when the Rec filled up. There was always a big crowd, and by the end of the season Hill had arrived from Exeter University.

The Cardiff game said it all."

The Cardiff game Rowell mentioned was the last home game of the 1982-83 season played on a sunny day at a packed Recreation Ground. The team was unbeaten since losing at Leicester on New Year's Day. Llanelli and Swansea, Newport and Northampton had been among Bath's scalps since the New Year. Now it was to be Cardiff's turn, in the most successful season in Bath's history.

That many-capped Welsh forward Clem Thomas, now a respected commentator on the game, covered the match for *The Observer*, and encapsulated the playing reasons for that success:

"Bath's remarkable results have been achieved by delightfully balanced rugby. Yesterday against Cardiff a hardworking pack inspired by captain Roger Spurrell allowed the constructive back division, with John Horton as its mainspring, to unleash some brilliantly effective rugby."

The teams that day, with Bath's almost that which was on the brink of winning a trophy, were:

Bath: Martin; Trick, Halliday, Palmer, Trevaskis, Horton, Hill, Chilcott, Adams, Lee, Gaymond, Hakin, Hall, Simpson, Spurrell.

Cardiff: Goodfellow; Hadley, Barry, Ring, Cordle, Davies, Williams, Newman, O'Brien, Eidman, Scott, Edwards, Golding, Lakin, Charles.

The game was typical of that Bath side's often coruscating style. Thomas's report reflected it well. He mentioned, typically, 'a beautiful break by Palmer,' Trick 'running with superb poise' to score a delightful try, Trevaskis scoring his 32nd try of the season, a club record, and a Horton speciality:

'. . .a delightful piece of touch play by Horton created a lovely try. He chipped ahead and raced on to re-gather before giving to Simon Halliday who ran hard for the try.'

We remember it well . . .

That Cardiff game, indeed, was a spring celebration of the wonderful rugby the side had been playing. it was refreshingly free, and surprising— to supporters at least — that the exciting seeds sown in the days first of Sibley and Phil Hall and Beese had now taken such handsome root.

No surprise though that Bath's four tries to Cardiff's one in the 28-9 victory prompted Clem Thomas, like others, to mourn that because of the absurdity of the selection method Bath were excluded from the John Player Cup 'which in truth they had the capacity to win.'

Nevertheless that was also a bold claim, given the side's appalling cup record. For all the show of skills by Bath sides during the years before the great harvest of trophies, the return from

Golden (hair at least) age of Roger Spurrell, 1980.

involvement in the club' knock-out competitions was meagre enough for Mother Hubbard's cupboard.

In 12 seasons Bath were knocked out at their

Utility back Charlie Ralston, 1980.

first attempt (whatever the opening round may have been called technically) seven times, and — as Clem Thomas observed — failed even to compete in 1982-83's cup (thanks largely to the ludicrous qualification system which, in turn, had also dispensed with both Bristol and Gloucester on occasion).

The best Bath could boast was to have made the quarter-final in 1974-75 (the season they lost to Morpeth), and again in 1979-80. With that faltering record (a home defeat by John O'Driscoll's London Irish was a particularly bitter memory) it was perhaps no surprise that some of their opponents — Bristol included — discounted them as serious rivals for a place at Twickenham when the 1983-84 season kicked off.

But Jack Rowell's team was about to start writing a new chapter in rugby history more remarkable than even he had imagined when he had written that simple letter to Jack Simpkins a few years earlier.

First Cup Win: 1983-84

WHEN the 1983-84 season started, it was Bath's old rivals and neighbours who were again expecting great things. Bristol had just come away from the heady draught of that 1983 John Player Special Cup Final at Twickenham, when after being 3-10 down to Leicester, they came back to win 28-12. In the inevitable euphoria of the days following, it was understandable that coach David Tyler suggested that Bristol could only get better over the next five or six years.

Yet not only hindsight suggests that the danger for Bristol was quite the reverse. For such outstanding players as Rafter and Hesford and Morley and others, the 1983 triumph was to remain a highlight of their careers, and except for one bright flurry, their club was soon to play second best to Bath for some years to come. The pretenders from down the A4 were about to wrest the cup from the more fashionable Bristol side.

For Bath, it was to be the season when at last the promise of so many past performances would bear a tangible prize. Two players in particular added a freshness and a zest to their play that meant the side was at last near Jack Rowell's ideal for which he had been patiently striving. Richard Hill had joined just before the end of the previous season from Exeter University. Jack Rowell already knew what England were later to exploit. Hill had a quick pass that meant the Bath midfield would have vital extra seconds in which to make their play. He was also — in those early days — a scrum-half with a quick eye and quick feet for the darting break.

Another player, with strength and skills in and out of the mauls, who was now to come to his peak value was Paul Simpson, an ideal complement to the captain Spurrell and the emerging John Hall, in a back row whose consistent success, some would argue, has probably not been matched since the retirement of the former two and the injuries to Hall. (Two men named Clarke and Robinson will no doubt argue back.)

But the season didn't start too propitiously. In spite of two drop goals by Horton, and crunching tackles by Martin, Bath lost at Leicester on 10 September — their first defeat in a 24-game run stretching from the previous New Year's Day when they had lost to . . .Leicester. Three weeks later they lost at Aberavon, 25-16, with the pack often struggling — an inauspicious first appearance for 19-year-old Nigel Redman, a second-row forward from Weston-super-Mare.

But the better times were not far away. Ominously for Bristol, they were first evident in a rain-soaked day at the Rec when Bath won 12-10 in spite of the absence of Halliday (making his first international appearance that day, against Canada) and Hall, who was on the bench. Better still, two weeks later, Neath, leading the Welsh merit table and minus some key players, were astonished to lose 67-0. John Palmer, not always the most consistent of goalkickers, converted ten of the day's 11 tries of which he had scored two.

For Bristol, there was further indignity when for the South-West's game at their Memorial Ground in November, only one of their players — Harding — was originally selected, with Stuart Barnes, the Bristol fly-half being drafted into the centre for the injured Simon Halliday. Six Bath players and eight from Gloucester had been chosen. No wonder Bristol players and supporters were asking aloud who had won the cup so recently.

Halliday's injury was a bad break of the ankle, during a county match against Middlesex at Bridgwater (and where there were inadequate initial facilities for coping with such an accident.) It cost him his cap against New Zealand, due a few days later, and it was also the end of his season.

For Bath it was the loss of a key player and it was some time before they came to terms with it. The occasional over-elaboration to which the midfield players were prone, and which often irritated the home crowd, as another miss move to scissors ended in a dropped pass or loss of possession, was particularly evident in the home defeat by Harlequins just before Christmas.

But by 30 January and the John Player Cup round against Headingley, the team was coming on song again. The Yorkshire side were worthy opponents, and included the England flanker

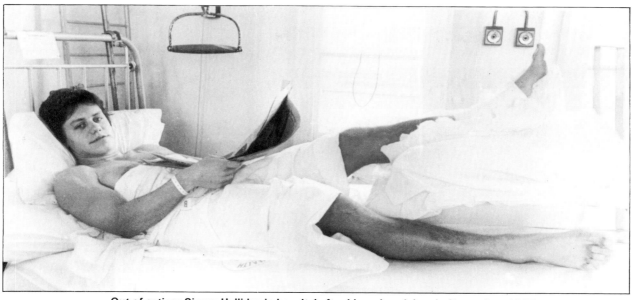

Out of action: Simon Halliday in hospital after his serious injury in November, 1983.

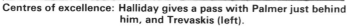
Centres of excellence: Halliday gives a pass with Palmer just behind him, and Trevaskis (left).

Under the hair, Simon Halliday, 1982, in his first season with Bath.

Peter Winterbottom who was to be on the losing side against Bath in even more important cup games in seasons to come.

Headingley pushed Bath hard and were only 7-0 down late in the game when the young spark Richard Hill burst through on a 30-metre break

Almost a lad: Chilcott, 1984.

Chris Martin at full speed against Gloucester, 1984.

deep into the Yorkshire defence. Remarkably Horton was at his side for the perfectly timed pass. But Horton at this stage of his career was not quite what the old Green 'Uns used to call 'a speed merchant.' His way to the line was blocked by three defenders, but he made it with guile, not pace. He sold a dummy, made a sidestep or two and the trio were left sprawling as they grasped for him in vain. One or two had recovered in time to follow Horton over the line beside the posts. Charlie Ralston converted and Bath were safely on their way to the next round.

If that try was evidence of a fizzingly fresh talent at scrum-half, it was also a sample of vintage Horton that can still bring a smile in the memory of all who saw it.

A satisfying win at home against Gloucester a fortnight later by 13-6 with the back row in particular outstanding, and Hall and Simpson combining to put Trick over for the decisive score. Meanwhile those two Bath forwards were being used as a Box and Cox arrangement by the England selectors, with Hall being chosen to replace Simpson as blindside flanker (Simpson was playing at no.8 for Bath, on the flank for England.)

In the next round of the John Player Cup, Bath were away to Blackheath in what was claimed as the first game between the clubs for 37 years. The London pack had a young Mickey Skinner on the flank: an older Mickey Skinner was to return there as coach after his career with Harlequins. In the second half Bath ran up 34 points to dash Blackheath's hopes, winning 41-12.

Bath were at home again for the quarter-final, and were embarrassingly outplayed in scrummage and line-out by Wasps. But Horton had one of his most inspired days in his control and vision, aided by the inevitable trio of Spurrell, Hall and Simpson grabbing possession from the mauls and the loose. Finally (including his second try, in injury-time) Trick outsped and out-tackled his opposite number, Mark Bailey.

Curiously the game was notable for each side losing its scrum-half and hooker through injury in the first half. But whereas Bath had specialist players as replacements, Wasps lacked a stand-in half-back when Cullen went off and the difference was inevitably crucial.

Meanwhile, back in the routine of club matches with nothing particular at stake, Gareth Chilcott, still comparatively unreformed, was sent off against Exeter for butting an opponent — a blow to Bath as well as to Exeter. His automatic suspension meant he would miss the cup semi-final at Nottingham, and also the first Twick-

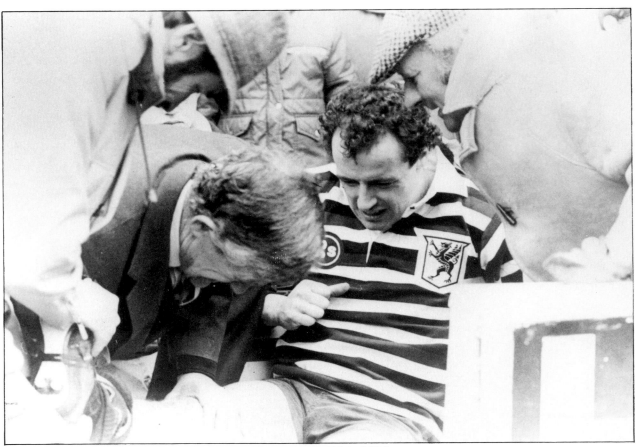

Treatment for Trick, 1984.

Words of encouragement at the line-out from skipper Spurrell.

John Horton, the young Richard Hill behind him, kicks ahead, 1984.

enham Final for many Bath players that season, Somerset against Gloucestershire in the County Championship Final. Yet curiously Chilcott's self-inflicted absence may not have been all bad for Bath, as it turned out.

First, because of bad weather, Bath's semi-final at Beeston had been postponed until the week after the county Final. At Twickenham on 31 March, Somerset held Gloucestershire to a 9-10 lead at half-time before capitulating 18-36, Alun Rees scoring the final try of the day for the losers. But the scoreline, though it did justice to Gloucestershire, may have proved dangerously misleading to Bristol — or at least to pundits who didn't study closely the team-sheets for the county Final. The teams were:

Gloucestershire: Cue; Mogg, Hogg, Knibbs, Morley, Barnes, Harding, Preedy, Mills, Blakeway, Fidler, Orwin, Gadd, Hesford, Rafter.

Somerset: Ralston; Trick, Palmer, Rees, Simmons, Horton, Stanley, Lilley, Bess, Lee, Hakin, Stiff, Hall, Simpson, Spurrell.

The tendency had been to assume the Final was almost Bath versus Bristol, which was nonsense. First it certainly wasn't Bristol masquerading as Gloucestershire. Instead it was a canny blend of Bristol's backs with only Mogg an intruder, and the Gloucester pack with Hesford and Rafter in the back row. Somerset (or Bath's 14 plus Peter Stiff of Bristol in the second row) were minus key players in Chilcott (suspended), hooker Rob Cunningham and scrum-half Richard Hill (injured), and full-back Martin and left-winger Trevaskis, who played their county rugby with

Spurrell in emphatic action.

Tongue out, ball in hand, a typical Palmer posture as he slices through a gap with (from left) Simpson, Trick and Hill on hand.

Cornwall. In sum a third of the regular Bath side was not playing for Somerset. And during the game they also lost Trick and Spurrell with injuries.

But there was more than a myth in the air that a Twickenham Final between Bath and Bristol would be a kind of re-run of the county Final.

Bath, though, still had a semi-final at Not-

tingham to win. They did so, by playing 10-man rugby — at the time a comparative novelty for Bath — which effectively stifled Nottingham's hopes of an expansive game, with Hill, Horton, and the back row controlling events.

If the manner of the victory disappointed the Nottingham crowd, there was at least a novelty in injury time when Chilcott's stand-in, Chris

Chris Martin in action for the South-West against the Australians.

Under the mud, Rob Cunningham in 1983.

Lilley, found himself with the ball in his hands in the Nottingham half. Remarkably he kicked judiciously into the right corner for Trick to gather and run under the posts for the game's only try. A few spoilsports pondered later whether Lilley should have been anywhere near the ball at the time. But he had no doubts. "I saw three men coming at me and just chipped it," he grinned after the game. And if the story of how Lilley ensured Bath's place in their first Twick-

Red-haired centre Alun Rees, 1984.

Record try-scorer of the early 1980s: winger Barry Trevaskis.

enham Final has grown a little over the years in the pub he now runs in Bath, the Rugby Arms, then it deserves an extra flourish or two. (The Lilley Trick may also explain why Gareth Chilcott was seen to try the same tactic once or twice thereafter.)

One other unsung stalwart also made a vital contribution to the semi-final victory. The useful utility back, Charlie Ralston, kicked two penalties and converted Trick's try when he came on as a replacement in the centre for an injured John Palmer. But Palmer was fit again for Twickenham, and Ralston, who was Rosslyn Park's stand-off in the side which lost to Gosforth in the 1976 Final, missed his chance on the replacements' bench because of injury.

Unluckier still was Ronnie Hakin, the experienced Irish lock whose speed about the pitch made such an important contribution to Bath's recent seasons. Injury and illness kept him out of the side on several occasions, however, and that helped persuade Jack Rowell to prefer the emerging Nigel Redman, for the rearranged semi-

final (for which Hakin was the original choice) and for Twickenham. "An awful decision to have to leave him out," Jack Rowell has said since. Otherwise, Halliday apart, Bath were at full strength.

Not so Bristol. Their influential no.8, Bob Hesford, was a late withdrawal because of injury (and another change, therefore, from that county Final line-up) and his place was taken by the relatively unknown David Chidgey. Chidgey was 30 but in his whole career played only 17 games for Bristol. Nigel Pomphrey in the second row was also short of match fitness. Teams:

Bath: Martin; Trick, Palmer, Rees, Trevaskis, Horton, Hill, Chilcott, Cunningham, Lee, Gaymond, Redman, Spurrell, Hall, Simpson.

Bristol: Cue; Morley, Knibbs, Hogg, Carr, Barnes, Harding, Doubleday, Palmer, Sheppard, Pomphrey, Stiff, Polledri, Rafter, Chidgey.

Referee: R.C.Quittenton

Bath hit Bristol from the start, and the contrasting confidence of the two packs was startlingly evident. Bath's back row imposed

First of the many: the Twickenham programme cover for Bath's first Cup Final win, 1984.

Skipper Spurrell hoists the John Player Special Cup aloft, 1984.

Shy winners: Hill (centre) flanked by Palmer (left) and Spurrell, with Hall, Redman, and Martin behind them.

immediate authority and Bath were 10-3 up before Bristol were properly awake. Even so John Palmer had missed four first-half penalties and a conversion of Simpson's 18th-minute try. Simpson scored after driving through from the back of a scrum, to add to John Horton's dropped goal in the fifth minute. A Barnes penalty was answered almost on half-time by a Palmer penalty.

In the second half Bristol began to show some of their best form with Barnes involved in most of their best chances. He converted Harding's try after a tap penalty, and watched as Horton (hints of a Twickenham Final yet to come?) only narrowly missed with another dropped-goal attempt. Barnes and Polledri also managed to stop Simpson from scoring when he was half over the line, which was more than the All Blacks had managed to do a few months earlier.

But in injury-time came that Barnes missed penalty mentioned in the opening chapter ("I misjudged the wind"). Referee Roger Quittenton said afterwards that if the tackle on Morley who hadn't got the ball had been five metres closer to the line he would have awarded a penalty try. As it was Trevaskis lived through a few awful seconds with John Hall staring him in the face and repeating one word, "Why?" But Barnes, to his own dismay, failed where so often that season

Now you've spilled the champers, Jack!
A bubbling Roger Spurrell with Jack Simpkins and the 1984 John Player Cup.

John Horton in his playing prime, 1981.

his kicking had carried Bristol to victory including the cup semi-final over Waterloo.

Nevertheless it had been a tension-packed last 20 minutes or so ranking among the best of local derbies — even if it was at Twickenham. Bath's inspirational captain Roger Spurrell had no doubt about how Bath had won: "Our front five easily held Bristol. We were so much quicker and more positive into the match." Jack Rowell returned the compliment: "John Hall and Paul Simpson live off what Roger Spurrell does on the ground."

So Bristol, cup holders and favourites, were outsmarted by the underdogs. But should Bath have been so unfancied? Even Bristol players conceded that on the day Bath had deserved to win. It seems that the pre-match predictions foundered on two crucial points.

Bristol, first, had not had a good season, even though they had recovered from a disastrous opening of nine defeats in 14 games, but they relied in key matches on Barnes's goal-kicking. But the second mistake, as I have already suggested, was to read too much significance into that earlier county Final.

Seven of the Bath winning side didn't play in the Somerset team. Simply, Bath's was a much stronger side than Somerset's. Bristol, without those Gloucestershire forwards — and Bob Hesford — were always likely to be outplayed up front. And Bristol knew it, even if some of the national pundits did not. Chris Ducker, Bristol's official historian, wrote in the club's 1988 centenary book:

"In truth, the game was probably lost in the dressing-room beforehand."

John Stevens writing in the *Bath Evening Chronicle* sensed the mood of 'arrival' felt by everyone playing for or watching Bath that day: the team, he said, finally emerged from the shadows cast over them for a decade by their big neighbours.

Jack Rowell, who missed the Final drama, and the last five minutes, wandering off into a Twickenham car park because of the tension, summed up the cup triumph similarly: "For so long Bath lived in the shadow of Bristol and Gloucester — now we are up with them."

Not even Bath's dedicated coach could then have realised that over the next few seasons, Bristol and Gloucester, by contrast, would have to learn to live in Bath's shadow.

The Cup Again: 1984-85

A 17-6 home win over Leicester gave Bath a satisfying start to the 1984-85 season, followed by an away win at Llanelli, 27-5. But by Bath's own standards there was an inconsistent feel to the early games.

Neath's 28-13 win at the end of September — revenge for that hammering at Bath the previous season — merely underlined Bath's indifferent form. So Bristol must have fancied their chance to erase recent indignities when the two teams met at the Memorial Ground for an evening match on 23 October. More, Bath had to field a less experienced back division than usual. The Irishman Roy Palmer was at full-back, and Dean Padfield joined Alun Rees in the centre, with Keith Plummer on the right wing.

It was a night of chill and tension and drama. Much of the drama focussed on the two stand-offs, John Horton, no longer wanted by England, and Bristol's Stuart Barnes, a decade younger and set for his international debut against Australia two weeks later. On the night the canny old king outwitted the young pretender to the delight of the Bath supporters in the 7,500 crowd. And even the Bristol fans could scarce begrudge Horton the title on the night.

Yet a Bristol win seemed the more likely as the game moved into its final quarter with Bath trailing by six points to 16. Then Horton struck. First he punted perfectly into the left corner for the unsuspected Trevaskis to nip in and touch down. Roy Palmer converted and kicked a penalty and Bristol were suddenly only a point ahead. Even a typical Barnes break was stopped by a Horton tackle — "One of my six tackles of the season," he said later.

But Horton's wittiest stroke came in the closing minutes. Spurrell and Simpson led a charge, and won a scrum in the Bristol 22. A clean heel — and there was Horton to drop one of his sweeter goals: 18-16. Yet there was still a late penalty chance for Bristol. Barnes missed. Bath had won. So had Horton.

That winter's tale of two talented fly-halves was far from over. One night's action was simply the first scene in an unfolding drama.

Since breaking his ankle the previous November, Simon Halliday had been out of the game. But he was regaining fitness and form with Bath United. He made it publicly clear that he was looking for first-team football, and there were hints, later denied, that the chairman of the England selectors, Derek Morgan, would like to see him in the Bath side. But his restoration was made more difficult because of the excellent form of the red-headed Alun Rees, previously a useful stand-in, and once of Bristol, now adding rugged tackling and the ability to stay on his feet when stopped, to the Bath midfield.

Indeed, Rees's skills were recognised twice at a higher level that season when he played as a first-choice centre for the South-West against the touring Australians (12-12) at Exeter, and in the win against the Romanians (15-3) at Gloucester.

That was the situation, with Halliday having to content himself with second-team games and Somerset appearances, when at the end of November John Horton announced he would retire at season's end. It was a surprise but at least the club was given plenty of notice of the need to find a successor. But the selectors seem to have thought Horton's news offered a way to solve the Halliday dilemma. A fortnight after his announcement, Horton was dropped for the away game at Harlequins. John Palmer went to fly-half — he was no stranger there — and Halliday partnered Rees in the centre. (Bath won, incidentally, 21-12.)

Horton went off for the weekend to his parents' home in Lancashire to think. But as he departed he fired a volley of first thoughts, alleging Bath had bowed to pressure 'from outside' to restore Halliday. He said: "If I had been playing badly, I would expect to be dropped. At present, Bath are saying I am rested and will be back in the side next week. But that only means one of the other players will be left out. That's no way to establish team spirit. I believe the club have to make a firm decision and pick what is considered the best side. If the team tomorrow is considered the best, I would rather the selectors say that. In discussion at training last night, the club seemed

Place-kick for Palmer, 1984.

to think I wouldn't mind standing down for a week, but they were wrong."

The weekend clearly concentrated other minds beside Horton's. He still wasn't happy. But it would not be a satisfactory way for him to finish with Bath if he left now, he felt. "The time to make changes is when a team loses or plays badly. The change last week was made for the wrong reason and that was the basis of my criticism. Just because someone is playing well in the seconds doesn't give him the automatic right to step up into a first team who have been playing very well." Horton's faith in Bath was badly damaged.

Publicly Jack Rowell attributed it all to a misunderstanding and a rota system was announced by Rowell and Dave Robson, the chairman of selectors, with the approval of the captain, Roger Spurrell. Horton was restored for a game at Pontypool, with Rees omitted. Bath lost 18-10.

Amid the kerfuffle over Horton, it was easy to overlook unusual events at Bristol. Barnes had asked to be omitted, citing 'a knock'. His chairman of selectors, Alan Ramsey, remarked: "A little rest will do him good . . .he's not even been finding touch."

Meanwhile, in an away game at Waterloo on 7 January, a weakened Bath won thanks to an unlikely goalkicker who struck four penalties out of five attempts. He was at centre for the injured Alun Rees, and was, said a local reporter, 'adept at setting up attacking moves.' He was Jeremy Guscott, aged 19.

That month Bath's full-strength side now omitted the unfortunate Alun Rees: Halliday was preferred in the opening cup game against the Gloucestershire side, Berry Hill, which Bath won 24-3 but in doing so lost hooker Rob Cunningham, with a fractured arm, for the rest of the cup run. Ronnie Hakin was another casualty.

Snow and ice that winter froze out many matches including a Bath-Gloucester game. In search of match practice, ahead of their next cup-tie, Bath went to Brixham in Devon. To the Devonians' astonishment and their own, Bath lost their 13-month-old unbeaten record against English clubs. Brixham won 9-6. Only Hall and Simpson (and the injured Cunningham, replaced by Greg Bess) were absent. It was a mighty triumph for Brixham but a story likely to be heard by future generations of Brixham grandchildren rather than Bath's.

A week later in the cup game against Blackheath, order was restored with Trevaskis scoring a hat-trick of tries in the 37-3 win. And by the

Promising youngster: Jeremy Guscott, 1984.

Lock Nigel Gaymond, 1985, who later moved to Canada.

time the side had done in Cornwall what they had failed to do in Devon, by winning 67-0 at Redruth, John Horton was happier. "I am not altogether ruling out the possibility of carrying on," he said.

At Sale in March in the next round of the cup, Bath were always in command against a side which was to win the first so-called national merit table. They won 25-15, with David Trick taking over goal-kicking after Palmer missed three out of four attempts.

The win brought Bath to Kingsholm and Gloucester where they hadn't won in 17 years. Alun Rees was restored in place of an injured Halliday, but Bath's selection problems weren't over. The Irish lock, Ronnie Hakin, now 34, refused to be on the bench for the semi-final. He had been disappointed to miss the Twickenham Final the previous year. Now the younger Nigel Redman, even with a strapped-up broken thumb, was again preferred to him.

It was a sad farewell from Hakin, a player who

contributed much in helping build Bath's success, and was now missing the rewards. He said: "I know Bath will get on fine without me. I can't see anyone pleading with me to come back."

On a soaking day, Bath managed that historic Kingsholm win 12-11. But it was as close-run as the score suggested.

Bath scored only one try to Gloucester's two and after Bath were 9-0 ahead after half an hour, Horton's defensive kicking was an important factor in staying ahead. So was the fine tackling. Three tackles in particular late in the game — by Horton (again!) on Hamlin, Rees on centre Price, and Lee on John Gadd — prevented certain Gloucester scores, and Tim Smith failed with a late penalty attempt.

No wonder, perhaps, that John Horton now had fresh thoughts. A few days before the John Player Cup Final he said he'd changed his mind about retiring. He explained that the pre-season England tour of South Africa and a Bath tour of Canada had been part of the pressure influenc-

Proof that Nigel Starmer-Smith (right) once exchanged pleasantries with Roger Spurrell – after Bath's 1985 cup semi-final win at Gloucester.

ing his original decision, but the cancellation of numerous games in mid-season had helped him to regain his enthusiasm. "I am still happy with my form . . .and with the team playing well there is no reason to retire. Next season will definitely be my last."

The Final was at Twickenham on 27 April against London Welsh, winners on the away side rule after a 10-10 semi-final at Coventry. For the Welsh it was the last fling at top level for a long time. But they had some outstanding individuals in their side, led by the electric Clive Rees on the wing. In the centre was Robert Ackerman, soon to move to Rugby League at Whitehaven, and at scrum-half the lively Mark Douglas. But Bath had done their homework and Douglas was largely shut out of the game by the Bath back row.

Clive Rees had chosen to play against the wind, fearing what Bath might have done in a second half with the wind in their favour. Even so Bath, winning the rucks and mauls, were 18-0 up at half-time. Halliday had fed Trick round Clive Rees's back as Ackerman tackled and the winger

scorched home for the opening try. Then to the delight of more than his unofficial supporters' club, Gareth Chilcott scored a try, fed by Hill who had followed a high kick from Horton, in the left corner.

The Welsh came back with five Colin Price penalty-goals in the second half and Bath disappointed many spectators in failing to win by a bigger margin. In truth they had done enough too soon, as it were.

But the Bath joy was inevitably unbounded as Spurrell again held the John Player Cup aloft — and Chilcott was still signing autographs for young admirers 20 minutes after his teammates had disappeared to the dressing-room. On the bench that day with Alun Rees, hooker Jimmy Deane and scrum-half Chris Stanley, were three future internationals — David Egerton, Jeremy Guscott, and David Sole.

But the season's serial story of the two stand-offs was now to take a new twist, almost stealing the limelight from the post-match celebrations. Chris Ducker broke the story in the *Bristol Evening Post* on the Monday after the Final.

Stuart Barnes had left Bristol, and had joined Bath.

His reason was simple. He wanted the success that playing for Bath now apparently guaranteed. A 25-3 Bath win over Bristol at the Rec three weeks before the Cup Final made up his mind for him. "Their speed in producing ruck ball will be vital to me," he said. And there was the chance to work with Jack Rowell, 'the best coach in England.'

At the time Barnes was sharing a house with the Bristol captain, Peter Polledri, who had put the question of Barnes's future plans directly to him.

Barnes explained to Ducker: "I didn't want this to come out now, I wanted the rugby season to be well and truly over. But rumours were flying around and so I told Peter Polledri of my decision today. The time comes when you have to think about your future. In the end rugby is an amateur sport which you play for enjoyment. I am ambitious and I believe that to achieve my goals the only answer is to join the best club in the country."

Barnes was never afraid to say what he felt, as the England selectors were later to discover. But now the switch of clubs by a man who had scored 481 points for Bristol in 52 appearances in a little over two years was a severe blow to Bristol pride.

Alan Ramsey, who a few months earlier described Barnes as 'the hub of the side,' spoke of his own sadness and aimed a dignified boot down the A4. "There are proper ways of doing things and as far as I'm aware, Bristol have had no approaches from Bath to see whether he can be cleared to join them. That, if nothing else, was a matter of courtesy." His chairman, David Taylor, was blunter, accusing Barnes of showing no loyalty and going 'behind our backs.' He seemed to contradict Ramsey by adding that there was no animosity between the clubs; rather he believed Bath's committee to be 'quite embarrassed about it and not at all happy about the way Barnes behaved.'

The Bristol coach David Tyler, who might have been expected to be even more bitter, was generous, and wished Barnes well. "His loyalty has been put in question. But it should not be forgotten that Stuart did more than most to help Bristol win the John Player Cup for the first time."

But that, of course, was the memory that caused many a Bristol supporter to splutter over a pint.

Much of their hope was based on Barnes's future with the club. By going he seemed to be implying that Bristol would be winning no more trophies in the foreseeable future and worse, that their rivals down the road would. It was an unpalatable prediction which added to the hurt of Barnes's defection.

At the time, the club's officials and supporters were not alone in regarding Bristol as one of the top sides in the land. In terms of prestige and past history they were. In potential, so Barnes was saying, they were not. The events of the next few seasons were to prove him right. But that didn't mean Bristol could easily forgive him.

Nor was it clear what his reception at Bath might be. The Rec's most recent memory of him was also from that recent game when Bristol lost at Bath. He was penalised for throwing the ball at a Bath player in a huff (that cost Bristol three points) and also for trying to poach a few yards (while another player was receiving treatment) when he had a kick at goal himself. The referee and a few thousand spectators put him right. And he missed the kick.

At Bath he was likely to replace Horton, who had served his club loyally for 12 years, many of them seasons when Bath were not as strong as they were now. Nor was Horton best pleased. The first he heard of Barnes's move was when the press rang to tell him.

In short, although it took a certain kind of courage to pack your boots and march ten miles down the road to Bristol's arch rivals because they were more successful, Barnes still had a way to go.

As I wrote at the time in the *Evening Post*, for a largely Bristol readership:

"Next season the brilliant if fickle Mr Barnes will have to convince the Bath crowd that he's done the right thing, never mind the Bristolians."

Meanwhile, as most of the attention was given to the furore concerned Barnes, another prominent actor in Bath's successful season was leaving the club. Alun Rees, realising Halliday was back to stay, decided to leave Bath as he moved jobs from Bristol to Gloucester. But he left with no bitterness. "The club have been very good to me," he said. "But once you've tasted first-team rugby it's hard to accept anything else for too long."

Simon Halliday, speaking of his own situation when Rees kept him out of the side earlier in the season, could not have phrased it better.

Wasps Stung: 1985-86

BEFORE the 1985-86 season began, the problem of the competing stand-offs at Bath was solved. Although the club captain, John Palmer, tried to persuade him to stay, John Horton opted to go along the A4 too — but in the opposite direction from Stuart Barnes. He said he wasn't prepared to 'finish' in Bath's second team 'which is what would have happened for most of the season.'

"It's going to be a terrible wrench, but perhaps it's for the best," he told John Stevens in the *Bath Evening Chronicle.* "I think it would have been impossible having us both vying for the same position on the Rec and could have led to unpleasantness, which I want to avoid. So I feel it would be better to make a clean break . . ."

In Horton's first game for Bristol, in September, they lost 28-0 at Cardiff.

A week later, Bristol were playing (or was it fighting?) Newport at home. Both packs had been battling each other from the start and when a general punch-up broke out the referee, George Crawford, a Metropolitan Police superintendent, walked off — and didn't come back. "I was not here to referee a boxing match," he said later. The game resumed under a local referee, a fireman this time, Paul Drake, and Bristol won 21-14. In all the controversy — Bristol were severely reprimanded by the Rugby Union — the debut of a young Bristol full-back was almost unnoticed: one Jonathan Webb.

On the same day as the Bristol punch-up, Bath spoiled Clive Woodward's farewell at Leicester when almost everything went right for them in a 40-15 victory at Welford Road. Leicester's fly-half Les Cusworth was impressed: "It's a very long time since I've seen any senior club performance like that." And he'd helped launch a few special performances himself in his time.

The Bath pack that day was notable for the arrival of three new names who contributed mightily to the efforts of an octet whose oldest member, at 28, was Gareth Chilcott. David Sole and David Egerton had emerged from the United side with John Morrison who had taken Nigel Gaymond's slot alongside Redman.

Gaymond, by now a Canadian citizen, had returned to that country. Sole had taken the loose-head place with Chilcott moving to tight-head and displacing the doughty Richard Lee. Egerton appeared at no.8 against Leicester, Hall and Simpson being on the flanks with Spurrell injured. But as the season went on it was Simpson, apparently, who most often gave way to the tall, tenacious Egerton — another player living and working in Bristol (at British Aerospace), who had chosen to play his rugby in the neighbouring city.

The start of the season was unreasonably hectic — with seven games for Bath in 21 days in September, and seven in 28 days in October. Bath lost at Aberavon by a point, and drew at Llanelli, winning the rest. If a 26-7 tonking of Bristol (John Horton and all) at the Rec on 19 October was particularly satisfying for the home supporters in an 8,000 crowd, the highlight of their early season came on a chilly Wednesday night the next week when the gates were locked on what was claimed as the largest crowd in Bath's history, an estimated 9,000, many of them from across the Severn Bridge. The teams were:

Bath: Martin; Trick, Halliday, Palmer, Trevaskis, Barnes, Hill, Sole, Roberts, Lee, Redman, Morrison, Hall, Egerton, Spurrell.

Cardiff: Rayer; Cordle, Evans, Griffiths, Hadley, Davies, Holmes, Whitefoot, Phillips, Collins, Stone, Norster, Lakin, Scott, Crothers.

It was a famous game and a famous victory, and one still talked about by those who saw it. Stephen Jones of the *Sunday Times* writing years later recalled the memorable evening when Barnes, Halliday and Palmer 'took Cardiff apart with the greatest display of midfield back-play I have seen.'

Yet it all began — and nearly ended — very differently for Bath.

After an 80-metre dash by Gerald Cordle on the Cardiff left-wing, Terry Holmes was over. Straight from the kick-off Halliday palmed Barnes's up-and-under for Lee to collect and the pack swept him over the Cardiff line. But the finest try came when Halliday, in a scissors move

Team effort: John and Becky Horton, 1985, celebrate with (from left) Palmer, Ralston, Trick and Simon Jones in the grounds of Kingswood School.

in the centre, broke through from his own half. As he was held, Hall was in support and strode powerfully on, taking a clutch of Cardiff defenders with him as he touched down.

Spurrell also scored a try but not for the first time that season Barnes's goal-kicking was wayward, and three tries to one were only a 16-13 lead as the game came to a mighty climax in the closing minutes. Norster was held over the line in the corner and in the ensuing scrum Bath won against the head, only to concede another scrum to Cardiff. It seemed a great chance for Cardiff to take the game as Holmes put the ball in. When he did, referee Laurie Prideaux blew immediately for a crooked feed and to Holmes's chagrin — and Bath's relief — the chance had gone and Bath had won a great game.

Why did Holmes err? Old hands afterwards suggested that the experienced international in sensing the chance to win was fearful of the push that would inevitably come from the Bath pack and couldn't resist 'putting it in crooked' in an attempt to compensate.

Two years later in his autobiography Holmes recalled:

"I swear to this day that my feed was straight as a die. With an all-international front row, why on earth should I want to cheat? . . .Still, if we had scored and won, it would have been an injustice to Bath. They had taken us to the cleaners."

But if the Bath midfield scintillated, the impact of Bath's new young forwards was also manifest to Cardiff's redoubtable England international no.8, John Scott. "That lad's about the best I've played against this season," he said later, and admitted he didn't even know the name of the 'lad' — who had made one tackle in particular that threw Scott yards back. It was David Egerton.

A few weeks later, Terry Holmes had moved, unsuccessfully as it turned out, to Rugby League. The two Cardiff wingers that night were to follow him, but with more success, a few seasons later.

(A few days after the Cardiff game, Bath's coaching trio of Rowell, Robson and Hudson created controversy amid sensitive skins in the Union game's hierarchy by spending a day or two with Hull Kingston Rovers RL club to see how the professionals did things and what Bath might learn from them. The establishment may as well have saved their huffing: in retrospect, given subsequent playing records, Hull KR would have done better, perhaps, to have learned from Bath.)

The Cardiff game I single out from among the many notable encounters with Welsh clubs, not simply because it was a great victory for Bath, packed with skill and drama, but because it epitomised all the best features of the Anglo-Welsh

Halliday goes for the line against Wasps, 1986, Dawe and Simpson supporting.

encounters which are now largely a matter of memory with the advent of the leagues.

Some of the early season zest evaporated in November, with narrow defeats at Gloucester and at home to Neath acting as useful medicine for anyone among Bath fans who fancied their side should win everything. Neath won 13-7 at the Rec with the shaven-headed Lyn Jones out-Spurrelling the absent Spurrell in grabbing most of the 50-50 balls on offer.

Then came the first Divisional Championship and the defeats for the South-West (soon to become commonplace), and other disruptions from international calls, which meant that Bath's early-season squad was seldom able to perform together for a couple of months. This, too, was to become a familiar pattern for any successful side with the encroachment of the extra representative fixtures plus the death-throes of the old County Championship which still claimed a few senior players.

But for Bath, one new talent had emerged to fill a problem position, that of hooker.

Injuries had ended Rob Cunningham's career and now his young successor, Greg Bess, was also close to giving up the game because of injury. Mark Roberts and Jimmy Deane had been among useful stand-ins. But on Christmas Eve, Mrs Liz Dawe persuaded her husband Graham, 26 and

captain of Launceston, to have a go at the big-time with Bath.

The farmer and champion sheep-shearer, occasional bell-ringer and keen cyclist, now turned devoted commuter. He would drive the 60 miles to Exeter on a training evening to catch the 5.15pm arriving at Bath at 6.45pm, then get the 10.15pm train home, arriving in the early hours. He was thrust quickly into the First XV, and not surprisingly had a few problems of adjustment in the set-pieces. But his all-round play was to add the fourth formidable new ingredient of change from the previous season's cup-winning pack.

David Trick, sometimes as unpredictable off the field as he was on it, was missing for two months through injury and holiday, but in a run-out against the Royal Navy displayed all his old speed and skills just a few days before the tough cup-tie at Orrell which opened Bath's defence of the John Player Cup. He got the nod for the cup game ahead of another of the comparatively new recruits, the former Swansea wing (like John Horton, a Lancastrian) Tony Swift, who had also been capped seven times for England.

Orrell were one of the success stories of the 1980s, and coached by Des Seabrook threatened to add Bath's to the notable scalps — as they saw it — from the effete Southern clubs. They almost

Stuart Barnes, lately arrived at Bath, complete with moustache, 1986.

Sometimes he smiles . . .coach Jack Rowell in 1986.

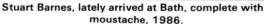

did it. As the decade went on, the Lancashire club became synonymous with powerful forward play. But it was their backs, not the pack, who nearly won the match for them. Teams:

Orrell: Langford; Ainscough, Carleton, Clough, Hook, P.Williams, G.Williams, Fletcher, Hitchem, Southern, Kimmins, C.Cusani, Moss, Cleary, Buckton.

Bath: Martin; Trick, Palmer, Halliday, Trevaskis, Barnes, Hill, Sole, Dawe, Chilcott, Morrison, Redman, Spurrell, Egerton, Hall.

It was a curious game. If Orrell had expected their heavy pack to dominate, they were to be disappointed. The Bath eight outplayed them on the day with Redman again outstanding. If Bath had expected their midfield trio to be too much for Orrell, again they were wrong. Orrell had their

own international midfield of Fran Clough, John Carleton (better known as a wing, of course) and Peter Williams. Their incisive play deserved better reward than the two tries from Ainscough and Clough matching two from Hill and Egerton. Bath were 9-4 ahead at one stage, 13-9 down, and then 16-13 in front before a Langford penalty set up the final frantic drive for the victory Orrell so nearly claimed.

To any neutral observer, the thought may have occurred that on the day the Bath pack with the Orrell backs behind them might have won by 30 points . . .but such fantasies were simply that. As it was Bath came as near defeat as could be, only disciplined defence — they didn't concede a single penalty in the last 20 minutes or so — saving the day, Bath winning on the rule

Barnes, in his first season at Bath, breaks against Newport, one of his former clubs.

favouring the away side in the event of a draw with equal tries scored.

In the circumstances, some of the verbal dismay among Orrell fans when decisions went against them would have startled the Kingsholm faithful. Noting that referee George Cromwell was from Gloucestershire, one Orrell sage decided that explained all. "They're all t'same down there aren't they? It's Bath and ruddy Gloucester old pals' act."

By comparison the fourth-round game at Moseley was a more clear-cut affair for Bath with Hill, Hall and Morrison scoring tries in a 22-4 victory. But the tie cost Bath dear. David Sole was put out of the game after 16 minutes, reeling away from an encounter with Steve Boyle and leaving the field with blood criss-crossing his face. He had a broken nose and cheekbone and that was the end of his season. Fortunately, Bath had the dependable Richard Lee ready to be recalled with Chilcott reverting to his old loose-head role. But a week later, Bath suffered another blow when Hall broke his thumb playing for England at Murrayfield.

If the season had begun with a flurry of games, it was now being frozen out. In common with many clubs Bath were starved of games, and the

fifth-round cup-tie at Old Deer Park against London Welsh on 8 March was their first game since the Moseley match on 8 February. The creaks were audible for both sides. In the Bath team, Simpson was recalled instead of Hall, and Swift was on the wing instead of Trick. Each scored a try, as did Hill in an untidy game dominated by Bath's forward power. They won 18-10. But they didn't need telling that a more convincing performance would be needed in the semi-final in which Bath were again drawn away, against Leicester.

First, though, as Bath went to Bristol for another tilt at their old rivals, the Memorial Ground reckoned it was a great chance to reverse the recent trend with John Horton, back after injury, intent on revenge. Bath, already without Sole and Hall, also lost Redman, Spurrell, and Egerton from the pack — Mark Jones, Kevin Withey and Nick Maslen deputising. Halfway through the first half, Chilcott left injured, Chris Lilley replacing him. Yet still Bristol failed to breach their defences. Tony Swift scored the only try in a 10-3 win in which the makeshift pack acquitted themselves notably.

There was a sell-out at Welford Road for the semi-final on 5 April. Each side fielded 11 players

Happiness is a winger called Trick.

David Sole, 1986.

who had taken part in that 40-15 Bath win at the same ground in September. Leicester had lost Peter Wheeler, but had Dean Richards in their pack this time. Bath fielded five of the same pack. Teams:

Leicester: Hare; Evans, Dodge, Burnhill, Williams, Cusworth, Youngs, Redfern, Tressler, Richardson, Davidson, Foulkes-Arnold, Wells, Richards, Tebbutt.

Bath: Martin; Swift, Palmer, Halliday, Trevaskis, Barnes, Hill, Chilcott, Dawe, Lee, Morrison, Redman, Spurrell, Egerton, Simpson.

Bath's forwards quickly showed their intentions. A penalty was awarded in front of the posts to Bath and they decided to run it. Leicester infringed again and this time Barnes kicked the penalty. But the inference was clear. Redman, Egerton and a thundering Simpson dictated events. Halliday scored the only try of the day, but there was a heart-stopping moment for fans of both sides when a Leicester back momentarily had an overlap late in the game.

Yet few Leicester supporters quarrelled with the result. Indeed, David Hands said in the *Times*: "It was the widest four-point margin I have seen this season."

The crowd would know what he meant. It was the first home defeat for Leicester in the cup and it was an outstanding team that had succeeded. For Leicester, there would be ample revenge only two seasons later.

There was a sad postscript. On the same day,

Paul Simpson in his England jersey, 1986.

Chris Martin in his last season with Bath.

Bristol had dropped John Horton from their team to play Harlequins. By ironic coincidence it was also a Harlequins game he missed when Bath 'rested' him the previous season.

As for Bath, the selection problems for the Final were beginning to emerge. John Hall's broken thumb had mended. But who, if he was recalled, would he displace? Simpson had been outstanding in his stead. Egerton was one of the 'finds' of the season as John Scott knew. Spurrell was, well, Spurrell.

But the pack was not the only headache for Jack Rowell and his colleagues. David Trick, after an ankle injury, was recalled in place of Trevaskis for the rag doll game against Llanelli at the Rec the week before the Final.

He gave a remarkable performance. If he had stood on top of the grandstand with a loud hailer and announced his desire to play in the Twickenham Final he couldn't have made his feelings plainer. Bath won 19-10. Halliday scored one try, and Trick scored two. Two minutes into the second half he had the ball with four defenders in front of him. He was damned if they were going to stop him and they didn't. By dint of speed and, yes, the old trickery he made his point and scored the points. And fed by Spurrell he sped 25 metres for his second try.

Trick was chosen for the Final side — not just for his returned appetite but also for a reason only Jack Rowell and his coaching team, plus a handful of players, knew. The rest of us would find out at Twickenham.

Meanwhile, there was sympathy for Barry

Long-term secretary, for many years synonymous with Bath: the late Jack Simpkins.

David Sole and his Bath bride June, 1986.

Trevaskis, the one uncapped back, who had played in every round but would miss the Final. Twickenham hadn't exactly been his lucky ground. He conceded the fateful penalty which could have given Bristol the cup in 1984; he'd gone off injured in 1985; now he was only on the bench, with Swift, although out of position, preferred to him. Some fans hoped there would be a kind of 'Roy of the Rovers' ending for him with a late call and a winning try. It was not to be. He was joined in his disappointment by Egerton, omitted as the odd man out from the formidable back row quartet at Rowell's disposal. For Sole, still unfit, there could not even be the consolation of a place among the replacements.

Wasps, too, had some notable absentees, including the potential match-winner Huw Davies, and a particular blow fell on the morning of the match when the England prop and keystone of their pack, Paul Rendall, pulled out. But they did include Gareth Rees, the hefty and precocious 18-year-old fly-half who was soon to leave Britain and would return from Canada a few years later in his country's lively World Cup side.

The teams were: **Bath:** Martin; Trick, Palmer, Halliday, Swift, Barnes, Hill, Chilcott, Dawe, Lee, Redman, Morrison, Hall, Spurrell, Simpson.
Wasps: Stringer; Smith, Cardus, Pellow, Bailey, Rees, Bates, Holmes, Simmons, Probyn, Pinnegar, Bonner, Rigby, Pegler, Rose.
Referee: F.Howard

The game began according to the form book with Bath, the favourites, moving the ball and pinning Wasps in their own half for almost the first quarter. Then Wasps were suddenly in front. In a counter-attack at high speed, Pegler and Rose launched Rees with support from Pellow and Bailey and Stringer was over for an unconverted try. Back came Bath, only for Wasps to break away again seizing on another Bath error to send the captain, Cardus, surging through the middle for Pellow to score, with Stringer converting: 10-0 to Wasps. Within minutes it was Cardus and Pegler once more in cahoots, and when Bath in desperation conceded a penalty, Stringer made it 13-0. Wasps' supporters were delirious, the Bath crowd dumbfounded.

I was next to a charming German guest among

Party time for David Sole (left) and Simon Jones.

Bath supporters. "What happens now," she asked me, "Do they have to start again?" "Er, no," I said, feeling chalk-faced, "Not exactly, this is it."

I knew what she meant — and so did most of the rest of the crowd. For Bath it was as if their party was about to be ruined by gate-crashers, moreover they were gate-crashers with style and elegance and adventure. Something had to be done. Bath did it.

Legend has it that Nick Stringer, after kicking his penalty, suggested Spurrell and his team should head for home there and then, or impolite words to that effect. It may have been the extra spur Spurrell's pack needed.

Bath abandoned the open game of their early play. It was up to the forwards to close the game down and give Wasps no chances to pick up on handling errors. First Simpson and Hill made a blindside try for Tony Swift and Trick added a penalty: 13-7. Then Wasps lost their scrum-half Steve Bates with a fracture and his place was taken by the inexperienced Balcombe.

Slowly the pressure told, and after both

Morrison and Simpson had gone close, Simpson put Spurrell over and Trick — the extra reason for his selection was now clear — converted: 13-all. Barnes had a broken toe hidden away in his right boot, John Palmer was only half-fit and said later that he nearly went off at 13-0 down because of his injury. Indeed, Phil Cue was ready in the players' tunnel to come on after only ten minutes. He wasn't needed. And Trick was entrusted with the goal-kicking. Those kicks were just about the only time he had the ball in his hands.

Again the forward pressure told and Hill darted over, Trick again converting: 19-13. Chris Martin made a vital tackle when Simon Smith looked likely to bring Wasps back in the game and then Simpson, one of Bath's heroes on the day, crashed over for another try which Trick converted: 25-13. In injury time the brave Balcombe added a try for Wasps making the final score 25-17.

Wasps had played inventive, adventurous rugby in that first quarter. Bath perforce abjured the same kind of thrilling open play. But only Bath

Simpson and Hall on the burst.

on such an occasion could so determinedly have clawed their way back into the game and by the final whistle have crushed the challenge of their lively opponents. When the Waspish gate-crashers had finally been evicted, everyone was able to relax once again — but somehow the party seemed a little dull.

For Bath, as well as being a quite remarkable transformation from a seemingly lost position, it was also one of the games which their critics, growing in number, pointed to in evidence. These carping folk somehow implied that in crushing the life out of Wasps' challenge, Bath had also spoiled the game. On the contrary, Wasps' initial impudence and Bath's measured, massive response, made it the classic drama it was.

Thus, when John Palmer held the cup aloft to the delight of the Bath supporters, he was acknowledging also the players' achievement in showing once more that Bath could win the big games even when the odds seemed against them. It was a habit Bath were only occasionally to lose in the seasons ahead.

If the season had been notable for the emergence of Sole and Egerton, neither of whom made the Final side, and Dawe who did, it was also a triumph for Redman and Morrison, aged 21 and 22 respectively, who had been revelatory in the second row, offering youth and strength and balance instead of years of experience. Their elders, Simpson and the inspirational Spurrell, had also come back powerfully when it counted.

Meanwhile, the occasional sad counterpoint from the Memorial Ground, Bristol, that had been noted throughout another great Bath season, finally ended. John Horton, plagued by a groin injury and some loss of form, announced his retirement, aged 35. And he meant it this time. "My only regret," he said, "is that I couldn't have achieved more at Bristol." He played 16 games for them in one of their most disappointing seasons.

No matter; at Bath few had done more than John Horton to make the dawn of their glory days possible.

Wasps Stung Again: 1986-87

A S THE 1986-87 season began, the new club captain, Richard Hill, reflected on the pressures of the previous season, with its congested fixture list, emphasised by the coming of the Divisional Championship. "It was a real struggle to regain our edge in time for the John Player Cup," he said, "and to be honest we never really performed consistently well. That mustn't happen this time. This year we haven't gone so mad on training. I'm hoping we can build to a peak more gradually."

Hill was also well aware of the growing criticism of Bath's style of play, particularly as seen by a handful of critics a few times a year. "There's nothing worse than having your centres coming off the field moaning about not seeing the ball. This season we must be more adventurous." Simon Halliday for one was seen to be saying "Amen" to that — or words to that effect — in more than one match when his impatience with being a spectator of yet more back row moves for much of some key games was clear.

Another of Bath's fleet-footed backs had literally done a runner after the Twickenham Final, too. David Trick had decided to abandon rugby, at least for a time, to have one last attempt at his first love — athletics.

But he broke his vow to help out in the third game of the season — a dour and dowdy 6-3 win over Leicester at the Rec in which he stood in the wind and rain for long enough to be sure his pre-season decision had been a wise one, no doubt. The game was marred, incidentally, by what appeared to be a serious neck injury to John Palmer. Two promising centres, Ben Cundy, and — when he could be spared from his shifts as a Badgerline country bus driver — Jeremy Guscott, competed to stand in for Palmer.

There were other new recruits and thrusting youngsters to ensure competition for places.

Bristol barrister Fred Sagoe was hardly a youngster — he had been playing as a full-back for Clifton for some seasons — but he brought strength if not pace to the left wing. Two young locks, Damian Cronin and Mark Jones, were also performing usefully when given their chance —

in an early season win at Pontypool, for example, and Cronin kept John Morrison, one of the previous season's young titans, out of the side for several early games. David Sole, too, was back in contention and in September made his first appearance, as a replacement, since his serious facial injury in February which had cost him a Cup Final place.

But one celebrated career was almost over. Roger Spurrell, Bath's venerated snapper-up of the 50-50 ball and first cup-winning captain, played three games in early season — fittingly, against Welsh opposition — before giving way to a player in the same mould, but more than ten years younger, Andy Robinson. And when Robinson wasn't playing, Nick Maslen, not Spurrell, was called in to deputise.

There were notable victories that autumn, at Newport (33-6), 28-6 at home to Cardiff, whose three-quarter line was Cordle, Ring, Donovan, Hadley, with Rayer behind them, to offset a disappointing home defeat to Llanelli (3-6). Bristol were beaten yet again in a curious game at the Memorial Ground in October when Bath, 21-6 ahead with 52 minutes gone, ended up 21-18 winners, having been punished for thinking the game was beyond Bristol's grasp. The touring Fiji Barbarians were also beaten 35-4.

But the casualties were beginning to mount up. Palmer was back, but Trevaskis had a shoulder joint in plaster and Chris Martin had dislocated his shoulder — an ominous pointer to his future, incidentally. There were defeats, too, in late November that confounded all Richard Hill's pre-season hopes that 'this time it'll be different.' Bath lost 12-9 at home to Gloucester, and Neath with Jonathan Davies inspired, won 26-3 at The Gnoll.

That night at Neath with Davies ("I scarcely laid a hand on him," said Robinson ruefully afterwards of a brilliant Davies try) was also a useful piece of his rugby education for the young flanker whose progress was rewarded with an England squad selection — after 15 games for Bath plus divisional matches for the South-West. But at 5ft 9in tall he was already a realist about his international future. "I'd like to be a couple

Speed of pass: Richard Hill in peak form.

John Morrison in action in his last season with Bath.

of inches taller,'' he admitted, ''but I can get on the floor quicker than guys of six foot five. After all, a flanker's job is a ball-winner.''

Robinson was one of 12 Bath players apparently in contention for England places. For a hastily-arranged England v The Rest game on 3 January, Halliday, Barnes, Hill, Chilcott, Dawe, Lee, Redman, Hall, Simpson and Egerton were all on call (with Sole in the Scotland squad.)

Two months earlier, John Palmer had bowed out of an England squad and any further representative rugby. That decision, rather than mass selection for their country, was to be the controversial pattern for Bath's relations with the England selectors that season and next.

But Bath, two days before that England trial, were playing Cardiff at the Arms Park on New Year's Day in a game sponsored — in innocence of the predatory intentions of the England selectors — by British Gas. In the circumstances, and with only Martin, Swift, and Palmer of the regular side on show, Bath came away with a creditable 32-21 defeat, Swift. Cronin, and the stand-in no.8, Colin Bevan, scoring tries.

On 24 January, Bath's new John Player Cup campaign opened, at home against Plymouth Albion, unbeaten since October. They eventually won comfortably, 32-10, with tries from Morrison (two), Swift, Barnes, and Hall. But Plymouth, with their gangling winger Walklin prominent, and Martin Livesey, later to go to Richmond, useful at fly-half, were in contention for much of the game.

Paul Simpson, chosen for England against Ireland after three seasons in the cold, was at no.8, only to lose his Bath place to John Hall — switched from the flank — for the next game. Worse was to come for Simpson. Embarrassed by the choice for front and back rows, Bath were officially, briefly operating a rota system. Hall, Egerton, and Robinson played in the 30-4 home win in the fourth round John Player Cup-tie against London Welsh in mid-February. David Sole was also on the bench.

This time there were four tries — from Swift, Barnes, Sagoe (deputising for the injured Trevaskis) and Palmer. The latter's try was the kind of highlight which turned on its head much of the criticism of Bath's style of play. The move, about five minutes from the end, began deep in their own half, with Sagoe, Halliday, Palmer, Barnes, Morrison, and Sagoe again all handling before Palmer crossed the line. No wonder he gave a brief pirouette of pleasure as he touched down.

Trick, in his last season for the club, recaptures old excitements for the home crowd.

And what of the rota system? Sole was in for Lee a fortnight later for the home tie in the John Player Cup against Moseley. But Simpson was again omitted and this time he was told the back row had been picked on merit. 'Simmo', as the crowd called him, dropped successively by England and Bath, admitted he was bitterly upset but he wasn't going to do anything hasty. "There's only one way to go now and that is upward, and I plan to do that at Bath."

But England's love affair with Bath was cooling yet further. Stuart Barnes, fed up with sitting it out on the bench and seeing what some agreed were at the time undistinguished performances from the incumbent fly-half (Rob Andrew, formerly of Nottingham but now of Wasps), told the England selectors he preferred to play for his club than watch for his country.

It was a controversial decision (and is dealt with in greater detail in a later chapter). It also added fresh supplies to Bath critics' storehouse of barbs.

Moseley proved a major threat to Bath's cup progress, and if full-back Ian Metcalfe, otherwise outstanding, had kicked his penalties his side could have won. As it was, a dropped-goal, and some notable defensive kicking by Barnes, plus a penalty try, gave Bath a 12-3 win even narrower than it suggested. In an untypical piece of

petulance near the end, Palmer even thumped the unfortunate Metcalfe (who had tackled him when he hadn't got the ball). "I shouldn't have done it," Palmer said afterwards.

Moseley were perhaps unlucky that day. But they were to take sharp revenge quite soon.

Barnes, of course, had excused himself from the England game in Wales on 7 March. But four Bath players were there. Richard Hill was captain. Gareth Chilcott was alongside Graham Dawe in the front row, and John Hall was at no.8. A dull, negative game in poor conditions is now remembered not for the rugby but for the fighting in which Wade Dooley, the Preston Grasshopper and Blackpool policeman, also punched his weight in the England second row. Chilcott, although seen in the role of peacemaker when Dawe got involved in the mayhem, was one of four players dropped because of their conduct by the selectors. Hill, too, was so punished, not because of what he had done, apparently, but because as captain he was held responsible for his players' lack of control. England, not that it mattered much, lost, 19-12.

In all the furore surrounding the match, there were more important events than rugby that weekend which added some sobering perspective: 187 people perished off Zeebrugge in the ferry

John Hall, 1989.

Herald of Free Enterprise.

As for the Cardiff incident and the subsequent suspensions, the fact that three Bath players figured so prominently gave yet further ammu- nition to those who saw their dominance as in some way unhealthy for the English game. That was always a bizarre view, arising out of envy rather than sense. But the Cardiff incident was probably the crucial tiff in the fading, uneasy courtship between Bath and the England selectors.

There were, therefore, thoughts not only of the previous season's 16-all tussle to whet appetites when Orrell were drawn at home to Bath in the semi-final. Wasps were drawn at home to Leicester. This threw up the oddity that England's competing quartet of fly-halves were all involved: Andrew and Cusworth at Sudbury, Peter Williams and Barnes at Edge Hall Lane.

There was pre-match speculation that Cronin might displace Morrison but the latter was retained, and Bath had only two changes from the side which met Orrell the previous year. The Lancashire side had five changes, and were missing their experienced full-back Simon Langford. Williams, Carleton and Clough again made up a potentially dangerous midfield trio. But the game was won up front, where the Orrell front row was in constant disarray against Sole, Dawe, and Chilcott, and Kimmins and Dave Cusani outsmarted at the line-out. The Orrell pack was further humiliated by having four pushover tries scored against them, five of Bath's six tries coming from the back row — two each to Hall and Egerton, and one to Robinson, Hill getting the other.

For the anti-Bath lobby the result was shattering. They had hoped to see Bath limp back down the M6 and M5 in humiliation. Instead, Bath had seen off a redoubtable side. Ah, yes, said the critics, regrouping rapidly, what about all those forward tries? All so dull and slightly unsporting. It was hardly a view shared by Orrell. Or, inevitably, by Bath whose discipline, teamwork motivation, had been first-class. So had their game plan.

In the Final they would again be playing Wasps, 13-6 victors over Leicester.

There was time before that for a notable game against old friends Bristol, at the Rec. Bath, without five first-choice forwards, and held by Bristol until late in the game — Bristol coach Mike Rafter thought his side would win — eventually won by 30 points to eight, their 16th successive victory since a depleted side lost 28-26 at Waterloo on the day of the England trial.

Bath had found the previous year's Final against Wasps tough enough and although Bath had beaten them 22-6 in early November, Wasps at Twickenham in 1987 were evidently likely to be more formidable than in 1986.

There were five changes compared with the earlier XV — Huw Davies at full-back, Simms and Lozowski at centre, Andrew at fly-half, and Paul Rendall returning at prop — and all were internationals. Teams:

Bath: Martin; Swift, Palmer, Halliday, Trevaskis, Barnes, Hill (capt), Sole, Dawe, Chilcott, Morrison, Redman, Robinson, Egerton, Hall.
Wasps: H.Davies, Smith, Simms, Lozowski, Bailey, Andrew, Bates, Rendall, Simmons, Probyn, Pinnegar, Bonner, Rigby, Rose, Pegler (capt).
Referee: F.Howard

Bath had Lee, Guscott, Simpson, Bess, Cue and Knight on the bench; Wasps' replacements included Pellow, centre in the previous year's Final, and the young lock O'Leary.

Wasps' captain David Pegler had been frank enough in advance about both sides. "Bath test your defensive capabilities to the limit. There's 12 stones of Hill coming at you one second and an instant later it can be 16 stones of John Hall — two different tackling propositions." Wasps would seek to tease and tire Bath by running at them at different angles from deep positions.

But if Bath were forewarned, they still appeared surprised by Wasps' vigour. And whatever Wasps' stated game-plan had suggested, it was from the forwards that they drew their strength. For the spectators, committed and uncommitted alike, it was a curiously unappealing Final, with neither side breaking the stranglehold imposed by the shambling setpieces on the flow of the game.

Increasingly, the battle between the front-rows, and between Jeff Probyn and David Sole in particular, overshadowed the game. Both men — and their captains — were spoken to by the referee Fred Howard. Years later, in his rugby autobiography, David Sole said he remembered little of the game because of a kick on the head — he even wondered what Gregg Bess was doing on the pitch: Sole was apparently unaware that his partner Graham Dawe had left the field, injured, and replaced by Bess.

Wasps, with a penalty and a dropped-goal, had taken an early lead, and although Redman went over for an unconverted try from a tapped penalty to reduce the score, Wasps foraged and spoiled and effectively killed Bath's rhythm, so effective at Orrell, just before half-time, Huw Davies scored a converted try (soon after Bess replaced Dawe) to make the score 12-4.

After half-time, Tony Swift also went off, replaced by Guscott, and when Barnes missed successive penalties the nail-biting among the Bath players and their supporters intensified. It was that sort of game. Wasps seemed unable to capitalise on their advantage, Bath unable to make an impression.

Then, the source of much of the apparent problems — the front row — gave Bath their chance. Probyn was penalised for collapsing, and Barnes, with about 12 minutes of normal time remaining, kicked a penalty: 7-12.

At last Bath lifted their game, Egerton and

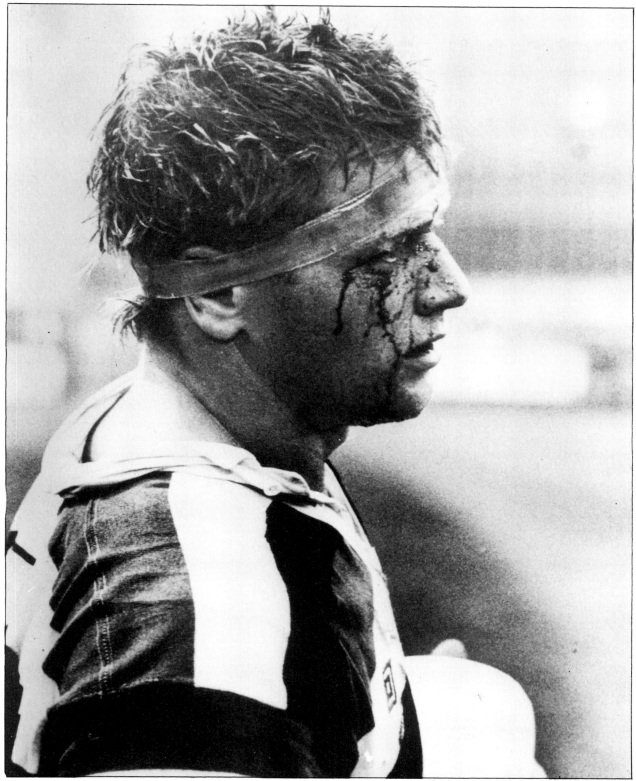

Graham Dawe unbowed, 1987.

Robinson in particular imposing themselves in the loose, Bath won an attacking opportunity close to the Wasps' line. Hill employed one of the season's party pieces. He made quick extra space, running flat from the base of the scrum, before hurling out a long pass for Halliday, bursting on to it, to storm over the line for a vital touch-down near the posts with Wasps clinging to his every limb. Barnes converted, and the cheers from Bath were of relief and disbelief in almost equal measure, as Bath led for the first time, 13-12.

Wasps, too, seeing the cup slipping from them, began at last to seek to raise their game and threatened to score again. But another try came instead from Bath. Barnes kicked into the corner, Sole won the line-out and Redman made it to the line. Now surely Bath had won, seven minutes into injury-time. The delight for Bath was expressed unexpectedly as hundreds of young followers rushed on to the pitch. By the time it was cleared for Barnes to attempt the conversion, it was also inevitable that when he succeeded — as he did — the lads would pour back. They did.

This time, although referee Fred Howard was apparently prepared to play on for yet more injury or stoppage time, the Twickenham authorities prevailed on him to forget it. Bath had won 19-12, and it was nearly ten minutes before captain Richard Hill could reach the trophy his side had won.

It had been an uninspiring game. Wasps thought they had done enough to win. Many a fair-minded Bath supporter had become resigned to the end of the great years of cup runs feeling that Bath could scarcely complain. Then came the Hill-and-Halliday try which deserved to swing any match — and the win, against much of the play, was suddenly in Bath's sights. Even Jack Rowell admitted afterwards: "Wasps won 60 per cent of the game and were so much better than we expected."

But the fury that followed the remarkable win, and directed against Bath and their supporters, was as if a thousand Disgusteds of Tunbridge Wells were venting their anger in one great shout. They were asking how these people, some of them (surely not?) even thought to be wearing Bristol Rovers scarves (who also played in blue and white . . .) could so have invaded the — how does the cliché put it? — 'the hallowed turf' of Twickenham?

John Reason was particularly robust in his unreasonableness in the *Sunday Telegraph* speaking of Bath's 'rabble they call their supporters' swarming all over the pitch and refusing to go off.

The invaders' real crime in such eyes, I suspect, was to support a team that had won the cup for a fourth successive time. And those same fans — not to mention people like Gareth Chilcott and John Hall — hadn't gone to the right school. They weren't even Londoners, or Harlequins, or, dammit, Wasps.

A few critics noted that Twickenham itself was scarcely blameless in this curious drinks policy. I went to the ground carrying a can of Pepsi for my teenage son, Barnaby, who I was meeting inside (and who, a few years later, was himself helping organise the Twickenham Universities

Athletic Union Finals). "You can't take that in, sir. Drink it or dump it," I was told, and the attendant indicated a large skip for such items. Inside the crowds were swigging pints in cardboard cartons, courtesy of the countless bars of Twickenham.

Neil Macfarlane, former Minister of Sport, said afterwards: "It is nonsense for the RFU to stop people bringing alcohol into Twickenham and then make it freely available." Or even Pepsi.

So some of the pitch invaders had supped a jug or two of Twickenham's best. But that was not a hanging offence. And the invasion was of good-tempered relief rather anything nastier. One or two wiser voices, though, rather like the sage old grandfather in Prokofiev's musical tale of Peter and the Wolf, wondered what would have happened if Bath had been only a point ahead after the Redman try and conversion. Would added time have been played?

Yet, according to one of Bath's critics on this occasion, even more was at stake than mere rugby. Thus Alan Watkins, the excellent political columnist who relaxed with rugby, another love, in *The Independent* once a week, pontificated in especially patronising prose:

"The Bath children might have thought the match was ended. But invading the pitch before the conversion demonstrated an ignorance of the laws of the game, to say nothing of the law of the land."

There, we were lucky not to be up before the Twickenham beak on the Monday morning . . .

But Mr Justice Watkins hadn't finished. Indeed, the pain of being right was evident as he sighed:

"I took no pleasure in this spectacle. But I felt vindicated. Several months ago I wrote in *The Independent* that Bath's supporters were badly behaved . . ."

But if the critics were out in force, so were the defenders.

David Hands in *The Times*, scenting the more absurd notions about Bath's success — should they be barred from the John Player Cup because they would keep winning it? — remarked:

"Rather there should be disappointment that other clubs have not matched the standards Bath have set. Their consistency . . .every now and then produces marvellous rugby. That Bath have been unable to give of their best in Cup Finals is a pity, but they should be judged on their achievement over the season as a whole, not by the occasional visit (*by Judge Watkins perhaps?*) three or four times a year."

Stephen Jones in the *Sunday Times* was another emphatic defender, making a similar point about the need to see Bath regularly. Do so, he asserted, and: "You will see enough attacking rugby to

Caterer Cronin, 1987.

tide you over very nicely indeed. Don't talk to Cardiff and Newport about Bath being forward-dominated. Both these clubs have been cut to pieces by dazzling attacking play."

And, as if he might have had his colleagues Reason and Watkins, on that occasion officers'

mess lawyers both, particularly in mind, Jones added gently:

"The last word goes to Bath followers. They are a marvellous bunch, even more so when they are behind fences."

Point (and cup) taken.

Leagues Begin, Bath Slip: 1987-88

BATH'S critics — and Moseley — were about to have a better campaign, for once. The 1987-88 seasons saw the start, or rather stutter, of the Courage Clubs' Championship whose leagues were to transform the game in England. At the time, the way in which the leagues began seemed peculiarly amateur even in an amateur game. With the benefit of the perspective of several seasons on, the initial year appears yet more eccentric in its mishmash of conflicting aims and interests.

For junior clubs, the complications of eventual relegation and promotion were complex enough. For the senior clubs, it was hard to gauge whether this was a serious competition or merely a variant on the earlier, unsatisfactory merit tables which had lately provided the nearest equivalent to establishing national and regional placings over a season. They were daft enough — Bristol, Gloucester, and Bath all having missed qualifying in the past for the John Player Cup because of their alleged failings in regional tables, such as perhaps not meeting Exeter or Camborne.

But the first Courage season for the top clubs provided no fixed dates for the league games, clashed with Home International squad demands, league fixtures coinciding with Divisional Championship days, with four points awarded for a win, two for a draw, and one merely for fulfilling the fixture. All this was largely the result of the need to reconcile the league's needs with existing fixture arrangements. But it hardly made for a coherent, gripping start to the new regime.

None the less, Bath coach Jack Rowell was well aware of what lay ahead. He said as the season began: "We've been the best side in England for over five years. The players are young in years but old in terms of experience and success. A number of them have only recently returned from the World Cup, so I know my major problem this year (will) be one of motivation."

It may have been a problem that was never solved. Bath were to have their worst start to a season for years, and it was indicative of what lay ahead. The team was looking ill-prepared and occasionally ill-tempered in early season games against Pontypool, David Bishop and all (a 14-12 home defeat) and Bath then lost their opening league fixture at Leicester, 24-13.

Absences of key players emphasised the amateur status of the game. But it probably did nothing to help cohesion on the field. David Trick had returned, but David Sole had gone to Scotland and Edinburgh Academicals. John Palmer missed several games so as to concentrate on his teaching career in the first term of the school year. Stuart Barnes had a holiday. Injuries robbed the side of Halliday for part of the season and of Trevaskis and Hall for most of it. Then Chris Martin, having played only two league games, went off two minutes into a 27-14 away defeat at Llanelli with — yet again — a dislocated shoulder. It was his fourth such dislocation and effectively ended the career of a powerful attacking full-back who, conscious of his injury problem, began the season saying he wanted to become a back-row forward.

After the Leicester setback, Bath struggled to overcome Moseley 14-0 in the second league match, and the first to be played at the Rec. That was followed by the Llanelli defeat and an away failure at Aberavon, where Bath went down 16-13. For the third league match, Bath went to Nottingham minus Barnes and other regulars and lost 25-15. It was not surprising, therefore, that Bristol were confident of ending Bath's record of ten successive victories when the two met at the Rec on 17 October, a week after the Nottingham defeat.

For this game Bath made two selections, involving players in their 30s, which were to be a familiar feature of much of the season. John Palmer was at fly-half — his position early in his career — and Phil Cue, 274 appearances for Bristol behind him, replaced Martin at full-back, in preference to the Bath University student, Audley Lumsden. Halliday returned from injury

Kevin Withey, a season before his glorious moment at Twickenham, 1990.

Back row stand-in and stalwart, Nick Maslen.

and starred in a re-run of his party piece with Hill, scoring from his scrum-half's long flat pass on the burst, to help Bath to a 15-point lead after only 15 minutes. Thereafter Bath held on without adding to their score to win their second league game, 15-9, and their 11th consecutive victory over Bristol.

But, as if to confirm that this was not to be their season, Bath lost their next league match — three defeats out of five — as many as they were to lose in any one of the next five league seasons. The victors this time, 19-15, were Wasps playing at home. Martin, Palmer, Trevaskis, Sole, and Hall were missing from the Cup Final side of six months or so earlier. Worse was to come.

A week later, as Bath struggled to draw 9-9 at home to Coventry, they lost Barnes with a crushed cheekbone. It was to put him out of the game for three months and when he returned Bath's season was already effectively over.

A week after Barnes's injury, however, in a Courage League night match before a typically noisy Kingsholm crowd, Bath showed some of the ability to come back about which even the players had begun to wonder. "Tonight restored my faith in the side," declared Simon Halliday after he had played an outstanding part in Bath's 16-9 victory. The centre himself had scored, again from his speciality with Hill, but Bath were behind until the 73rd minute when Egerton scored the second try, and Palmer at fly-half dropped a late goal. Only a touch-judge's controversial decision about a foot in touch denied Halliday a brilliant second try.

Two weeks later, there was another Courage League defeat. This time there was a good excuse: it hit Bath when they were depleted by the calls of the Divisional Championship. But although, under the league rules, they could have called off the game, they chose to play.

A recruit from Bristol, Barry Whitehead, was at full-back. The team was: Whitehead; Stevens, Lumsden, Guscott, Blackett, Cue, Hill, Lilley, Deane, Lee, Jones, Miles, Withey, Simpson, Maslen. The reserves came close to holding a strong Waterloo side, before going down 17-10. (It was the first game of senior rugby where I heard racial jibes from spectators. It came from a couple of middle-aged Waterloo supporters. Perhaps Bath's contingent of black players — a feature of later Rowell teams — made an easy target for people expecting an easier Waterloo win. It remains a rare occurrence and Bath supporters have been quick to protest wherever it has happened.)

Bath had now lost four and drawn one of their eight league matches. The motivation Jack Rowell had been worried about was still suspect. Richard Hill, who himself had an indifferent season so soon after being England's captain, was later to admit that the team was out of sorts in preparation for the season. Drastic remedies were sought: "We treated the two months from January as pre-season training." In this way they hoped to be at full pitch for the John Player Cup once more.

The opening third-round tie for Bath was due at Lichfield on 23 January, but it was snowed off. Gallantly, Streatham-Croydon filled in by coming to the Rec for a friendly — and lost 84-0. Whatever it did for the visitors it was a timely practice match bringing together the Bath first team for their first game together for several weeks, given the competition from Divisional Championship calls and injuries.

Even so, such was the competition for places, there was no room for Bath's latest international cap when the Lichfield game took place a week later. John Morrison was still preferred in the second row to Damian Cronin, who had played his first game for Scotland in Dublin that month.

Cronin's selection, by the way, was something of a coup for David Sole during his time at Bath. Perhaps the surname alerted him. Sole discovered that the Bath-schooled, Guildford-raised Damian, who would scarcely have known Sauchiehall Street from Princes Street, had an Irish father and was born in Germany . . .but had grandparents

from Lothian on his mother's side. That was good enough for Sole and for the International Board regulations, and Cronin was now good enough for Scotland — if not, always, for Bath apparently.

Bath swamped Lichfield with nine tries in a 43-3 win, including two each from Swift and Guscott. Ominously, however, only two of the tries were converted.

Two weeks later, Bath were away in the fourth round, this time at Leicester, winners at Welford Road in that first league game. Now Cronin was in the side which had Cue and Palmer at full-back and fly-half respectively. Bath's pack on a squally wet day was tremendous, with Cronin fully justifying his selection in harness with Redman, and Egerton and Hall having outstanding games. Behind them Palmer was inspired at fly-half with his kicking from hand and made some of the 12,000 crowd realise that the Horton-Cusworth era of English stand-offs could have been graced by John Palmer, too, if he had not moved to centre in recognition of Horton's skills all those seasons ago.

Bath's lead of 13-0 which included a try from Egerton and a Palmer dropped-goal seemed inadequate reward for their dominance, particularly when Hare led a breakaway for a try to reduce the arrears, and both Guscott and Swift seemed to have scored tries, only to be brought back for five-metre scrums.

But Dusty Hare had an off-day with his kicking, and when the Leicester right flank had a sudden opportunity to make a break late in the second half, Bath must have been glad that the speedy Barry Evans was off injured by that time and his replacement was overhauled. Nevertheless, the Leicester coach, Peter Wheeler, was generous in acknowledging the play of Palmer and his pack. Indeed it was — with the Gloucester game — Bath's best performance of the season so far in bad conditions. *The Times* noted that Bath had won 29 line-outs to Leicester's eight, and that there were 43 passes from Hill to Palmer at fly-half, compared with 12 from Leicester scrum-half Nick Youngs to Cusworth.

There was time for a friendly against Gloucester — if that's possible — at the Rec the next week before the fifth-round tie away at Moseley. Gloucester were leading Bath by 19-9 early in the second half only for Bath to surge into a 26-22 lead which Gloucester levelled at 26-all in the closing moments.

Then to The Reddings. Ninety seconds after the kick-off, Phil Cue scored with a penalty and, thought the crowd, Bath were on their way. But, no. Peter Shillingford went over for a try after 13 minutes and that — in spite of constant Bath pressure — was the end of the scoring. Bath

David Egerton, 1988.

Winger Fred Sagoe, 1988.

succeeded with only the first of 13 kicks at goal, including six dropped-goal attempts by fly-half Palmer. His dream day at Leicester seemed far away.

Perhaps Bath changed their kickers too soon after Cue failed to emulate his first success. Both Guscott and Trick failed, the winger hitting a post with a penalty attempt in one of the final kicks of the match. Perhaps they had missed the tactical skills of Barnes, although John Palmer was himself a considerable playmaker. Perhaps they missed John Hall, injured and off midway through the second half. Perhaps they had given too much at Leicester. Perhaps, some said, they were paying a price for not giving rein to the talents of the backs.

Perhaps the Bath side of 1987-88 was missing not just a Sole, a Martin, a Barnes, but the incentive and desire to keep on winning. Whatever the reasons or the excuses, even Moseley in gaining revenge for their cup defeat at Bath the previous season, knew that Bath had helped to beat themselves.

Jack Rowell, like Peter Wheeler before him, was generous in congratulating the winners, and sensible in defeat. The run of 22 successive cup victories was remarkable, and it had to end sometime. But for Bath, the opening league programme already in tatters, it was the end of February and there was nothing at stake for the first time in five seasons. Except perhaps to recover their good habits out of the limelight.

Meanwhile, three days after the cup exit, Stuart Barnes, returned from injury with a boot of irony, kicking three penalties, converting two tries, and dropping a goal in a night match against Exeter.

In March there was an exciting 28-23 win at Swansea with two tries from the blossoming young Guscott and two dropped-goals from Barnes, and a home league win over Orrell, 23-18.

But if Moseley and Wasps had each enjoyed a moment of reckoning, another was to come for Bath on 2 April, in a friendly against Bristol. David Trick was on holiday after the Hong Kong Sevens, and Bristol arrived at the Rec fresh from beating Moseley in the John Player semi-final by 34-6, thanks not least to five conversions and a try by their full-back, Jonathan Webb.

Bath had made one change by choice. Significantly another bright full-back prospect, Audley Lumsden, was preferred to Phil Cue, and Fred Sagoe was on the left wing. And in spite of Sagoe's try for Bath, they at last fell to Bristol after 11 wins, by 16-15. Stuart Barnes congratulated the winners: "Bristol are still my second-favourite club." If it may also have been the first time since his departure from Bristol that he had pondered again on that decision, he can scarcely have mused for long — even though Bristol, not Bath, were at Twickenham.

For Bath there was a home league win against Harlequins, 21-9, a week later, and the confident West Country prediction that Bristol could win against the London side in the Final at Twickenham on 30 April.

On that day, Harlequins hit Bristol while the West Country lads were still enjoying the sense of being back at Twickenham and ran up an 18-0 interval lead. It was to Bristol's great credit that they hit back to be only 19-21 behind by the 65th minute in another fine Twickenham fightback. Simon Hogg was, controversially, denied the verdict with a dropped-goal attempt, and Bristol lost 22-28. But it had been a brave day out in Bath's stead.

South of Manchester on the same day, Bath made sure of fourth place in the inaugural Courage League season by winning 46-17 at Sale, with tries from Kevin Withey (2), Bamsey, Kipling, Guscott, Lee, Hill, and Sagoe, with Guscott converting five, and Palmer two. Sale, who failed to win a match all season, were relegated along with Coventry: two distinguished clubs failing the Courage League test at the first attempt.

In the first Courage League season (when not every club played the same number of games) Bath had finished with six wins from 11 games, one draw, and four defeats. Leicester won the title and

deservedly, with Bath having at least the consolation of that notable win in the cup at Welford Road to offset the home league defeat.

But Bath's season was probably their worst for five years, The loss of key players through injury had been a considerable blow, even though stand-ins had made shift bravely, but the side's play had too often been stodgy in the absence of the playmaker Barnes who played in only four of the 11 league games. It was the season which came nearest to justifying critics' allegations of the team's tendency to seek safety in adversity by relying unduly on a forward-dominately strategy.

There was further evidence of this in the try-scoring records of some key backs or rather the lack of them. Trick, who played in nine league games, scored no tries. Halliday and Palmer (who played seven each) also failed to score any tries, and Guscott in his ten league games scored only one and that in the last match. Tony Swift's three tries in eight league games made him top try scorer of Bath's first Courage League season. But the poverty of the chances given to the backs, as indicated in the score-sheets, seems now laughably incredible given what was to follow in later seasons.

During the season a few of the players who had figured in Bath's first team as stand-ins for more famous names had moved on to retirement, like prop Chris Lilley, or to work elsewhere, as had utility back Andy Janes, or to look for an opportunity with other clubs, like Mark Jones who had gone to Wales.

A week before Bath's and Bristol's seasons ended, a former Bath player made both his comeback and his farewell. In a public display of unashamed and popularly acclaimed sentiment by the club, a fly-half named John Horton was invited to play against Bedford at the Rec. Bath won 35-7. Inevitably, the guest dropped a goal, and, although he didn't score a try, he did convert someone else's, to great applause, at the very close. But memories were perhaps particularly stirred by seeing again those ground-gaining, perfectly-placed, touch-finding kicks from the old master.

Afterwards, Jack Rowell presented an inscribed tankard to John Horton. Any rancour from the manner of his departure three seasons earlier was formally forgotten. At last, too, the crowd cheered its informal farewell to a former skipper who helped keep Bath afloat in queasy times, and steered the team towards its first successes. It was a handsome moment of rugby, Bath-style.

The First 'Double': 1988-89

IF THE previous season had seen Bath falter in the first, unsatisfactorily organised, Courage League, the opening of the 1988-89 season could hardly have been different.

Stung by this reverse — as the old-time soccer writers used to say ("Which side kicked-off with a rush?" asked one of that famous breed, as he arranged his notebook and pencils, having arrived a minute or two after the start) — Bath came hammering back to show their rivals that the lapse was essentially temporary.

The season opened, after a club tour of the Far East with old heroes such as Chris Martin and David Trick in the United side, alongside one of the newer stars, Scotland's adopted son, Damian Cronin, while the first team was astonishing the Welsh with a 50-9 win at Pontypool. Audley Lumsden, now first choice at full-back, scored two tries and so did Barnes, now captain instead of Richard Hill.

A week later, Bath opened the league season — all games were now on fixed Saturdays and no longer clashed with the Divisional Championship — at Harlequins. It is worth noting the Bath team that day. It was perhaps a sign of their coming consistency that there would be only two changes from that team and the one which would once again play in the Twickenham Final at season's end. And only one of those changes would be for preference.

The team that played Harlequins on 12 September 1988, was: Lumsden; Swift, Halliday, Guscott, Sagoe, Barnes, Hill, Chilcott, Dawe, Lee, Morrison, Redman, Hall, Egerton, Robinson.

There were four tries, by Swift, Guscott, Hall and Dawe, in Bath's 26-9 win. But it was marred by the sending-off of Richard Hill. The Harlequins' scrum-half elbowed Hill out of the way to retrieve the ball for a quick penalty, only for Hill to swing a punch which knocked Richard

A stern-faced Tom Hudson keeps the players at it, summer 1988.

Hall and Harlequin Mickey Skinner compete.

Flanker Withey hands off a Swansea tackler.

Moon to the ground. It was no time for jokes about a Moon seeing stars . . .the Welsh referee Gareth Simmonds dismissed Hill (his first such sending off).

A fortnight later, with Steve Knight a capable replacement for Hill, Bath ran in three tries to none in a 19-9 league win over Gloucester at the Rec. It included a pushover try for no.8 Egerton. "I hate to admit it, but they're just better than anyone else," said Keith Richardson, the Gloucester coach, afterwards.

But whatever glory lay in store for Bath in 1988-89, there would be none for their full-back in four successive Twickenham Finals. Chris Martin, attempting a comeback yet again, this time on the wing in a home game against Aberavon, once more dislocated his shoulder in making a try-saving tackle.

In the first away league game of the season on 10 October, Bath again scored three tries to none in a 19-6 win at Rosslyn Park, where Cronin was a late replacement at no.8 for an injured David Egerton.

The previous season when Cronin won his first Scotland cap, Kevin Coughlan, who covered Bath for the *Bristol Evening Post*, mentioned the recent death of a great Bath supporter, Reg Monks, who had started a picture gallery in the clubhouse when Mike Beese was capped (while with Liverpool) in 1972 and had added others as they were capped.

Coughlan noted that with Cronin's selection for Scotland, Bath could in theory field a team of players capped in the 1980s while at the club with only one or two playing out of their normal position — and he named the side.

His article caught the imagination of the club and they asked the RFU if they would care to send a representative side to play Bath in a charity game. The RFU, rather churlishly, declined offering as a reason the danger of setting a precedent . . .The Welsh Union also said no. Finally the press again came up with a suggestion and Ralph James, secretary of Public School Wanderers agreed to provide a team including 14 internationals. Proceeds from the game went to the Great Ormond Street Children's Hospital.

The Wanderers promised to bring to celebrate that special piece of Bath history the Australian winger Ian Williams, an Irish contingent including hooker Steve Smith and Willie Duggan, and such Welsh luminaries as Malcolm Dacey, Mark Jones, Mark Wyatt, and Richie Collins. The score, which hardly mattered, was a remarkable 54-55 to Bath. Clive Norling was the referee. The date was 12 October 1988.

In the Bath team, Barnes was at full-back where he had played as a replacement for England to allow John Horton to play at stand-off, and Chris Martin was fit to play on the wing. The team as selected was: Barnes; Martin, Halliday, Palmer, Trick, Horton, Hill, Sole, Dawe, Chilcott,

Don't look now, but . . .Chilcott sells a safe pint, 1989.

Redman, Cronin, Hall, Egerton, Simpson or Robinson.

In the event, the Wanderers team was not quite as strong as billed and David Egerton was still injured, but at least that solved Bath's back row problem, Simpson playing at no.8. But David Sole, no longer with the club, was unable to make the journey from Scotland because his wife was in hospital, and Richard Lee (an England 'B' player) made up the front row. Bath were able to omit Tony Swift (whose caps for England came when he was at Swansea). A little more than four years later, five further Bath players had been capped for England (no prizes for naming them) and another for Scotland.

But ten days after that remarkable celebration it was back to stern league rugby with a home game against Bristol. It also marked the return to league games of Richard Hill, apparently much chastened after his suspension. He said he had drastically changed his outlook on the game since being sent off against Harlequins.

"I realise I felt too tense, too aggressive," he admitted. "But the incident with Richard Moon was a real shock for me as well as for him. We had a chat the other week and I apologised again. I'd like to think we are friends once more. Not being captain any more helps. The pressure's off.

My form did suffer and now I can concentrate on my own performance there has been a marked improvement."

Hill indeed scored the only try in the Bristol game, Barnes dropping a goal in Bath's 16-9 win. But Bristol played outstandingly and only some crucial errors which led to Bath points marred their game. It was though, significantly, a comparatively bad day for their England full-back Jonathan Webb, who happily was in excellent form at Bristol the following Wednesday when, in a rousing performance the South-West beat the visiting Australians 26-10, scoring three tries.

As the South-West tended to do better against touring sides than against the other English divisions, it may be worth recalling those who played so well that night, all bar one players from the three main clubs in the area. Team: Webb; Carr (both Bristol), Halliday, Guscott (both Bath), Knibbs (Bristol); Barnes (Bath), Harding (Bristol), Preedy, Dunn, Pascall (all Gloucester), Morrison, Redman, Hall, Egerton, Robinson (all Bath), Alan Buzza (Cambridge University, and later Wasps) replaced Halliday, injured in the second half.

Bath again played overseas opposition on 24 October, this time Pierre Villepreux's Toulouse side, who had just been narrowly defeated by

Egerton and Cronin – happy winners in a 1989 league game over Nottingham.

Neath on a short tour. In the absence of Swift, Halliday, and either Trevaskis or Sagoe, it was a chance for stand-ins Hobbs, Bamsey, and Blackett to sample a big-game atmosphere. Toulouse, too, were without Charvet and Bonneval. But in a game which saw first Toulouse and then Bath apparently holding a winning lead, the final score was 24-all with the excellent referee Colin High muttering to Barnes as he tried a final shot at goal — "Go on, don't spoil the night — miss it." Barnes missed. But he probably tried.

The next league action brought crushing revenge for Bath's narrow defeat at Moseley in the cup game the previous season. This time, and with Cue standing in for Barnes, Bath scored eight tries including three for Guscott and two for Hall,

with three conversions, all by Guscott, in a 38-0 victory.

The following Saturday, Bath made it six league wins out of six, scoring five tries to none, including two more for Guscott, in a 36-12 win over Orrell. The three-quarter line that day was unusual, Palmer and Guscott being flanked by Sagoe and Trevaskis on the wings — one of the rare occasions when those two wingers played in the same side. Swift and Sagoe were the wings when Bath won their third league game in successive Saturdays, this time at home to Wasps, 16-6.

By year's end, therefore, the players were unbeaten in the league, looking forward to a New Year break in Lanzarote, and the start of another cup campaign. Indeed, by the time they had beaten

Meet the sponsors: in January 1989, SWEB deputy chairman John Seed and club captain Stuart Barnes clinch the deal with a symbolic gesture.

Cardiff, 35-4 at the Rec, with both sides below strength (and Barnes was trampled on and needed stitches) the side was still unbeaten all season, having drawn with Newport as well as Toulouse.

In January the league programme resumed with Egerton and Guscott each scoring two tries in a 21-7 win at Liverpool St Helens. It was not the best of games, with the coming decline of the home side already sadly in evidence, and Bath not at their best but with the referee one of the more prominent performers on the day. Given the geography and the lure of the emerging Guscott, it was not surprising to see numerous Rugby League scouts in a crowd in which Bath supporters also seemed to outnumber the loyal local fans.

The third round of the Pilkington Cup was on 28 January, with Bath playing Oxford at the Rec. The South-West Division One club were not having the happiest of seasons. Bath, 34-6 up at half-time, scored 16 tries, including four each for Lumsden and Swift, and three for Sagoe, with nine conversions, in an 82-9 victory.

Next, in the fourth round on 11 February it was the turn of Hereford, from the Midland Division One. They fared much better, provoking Bath into an edgy, irritable first-half performance with brave tackling keeping the score to only 4-0 at the halfway stage. Then Bath burst loose, and ran in a total of ten tries, with four for Fred Sagoe.

But just in case Bath thought this season was only about winning, their unbeaten record was finally taken from them when, without Barnes, Halliday, Chilcott, and Robinson, they lost in a 'friendly' at Kingsholm, 12-18. Until then, Bath had been unbeaten in the first 30 games of the season. The defeat was also on the eve of the next big match — a Pilkington Cup fifth-round home tie against Bristol, the previous season's beaten Finalists.

Seven weeks earlier, Bath had made commercial history by sealing a sponsorship deal, worth £155,000 over three years, with the South-Western Electricity Board. It was hailed as a mutually useful piece of business. SWEB and their guests were out in force for the first major match during their sponsorship — the cup game against Bristol.

It was a day of steadily pouring rain, and as the sponsors entertained their guests the talk was increasingly of 'how can they play in this?' Indeed, parts of the pitch were under water and there was a strong hint that Bath didn't want to play. Later both sides talked down possible motives for wanting or not wanting to play. No, said Bristol, it's insulting to suggest we wanted to play only because the rain would be a great leveller.

But although the protected peerers through the clubhouse window speculated on what might not be, the view from the soaking open side crowd was rather different. Having borne the opening heavens for an hour or so waiting for the kick-off, the faithful paying public might well have turned nasty if the game had been called off. Eventually, all argument was ended and the crowd — if not the players — were delighted when the London referee, Andrew Mason, decided the tie should go ahead.

The preamble is essential in order to appreciate the game that followed, described by more than one experienced commentator as the greatest cup-tie the game had seen. Five years on that assessment might still be valid.

Any running rugby was only possible, and that barely so, in the early stages. After a Webb penalty, Bristol went further ahead, when Collings, Harding and Hogg fashioned a chance for the full-back to run in for a try behind the posts, which he also converted: 9-0 to Bristol. Bath replied when a Bristol error in the scrum gave Hall and Hill the chance to break, with Barnes and Halliday combining to send Guscott slithering and splashing over the line. Indeed, it was as well that the centre had already shaken off his pursuers by the time he splashed down. The pool in which he landed was such that a heavy tackler could, conceivably, have run the risk of drowning Guscott if his head had been face down in the water. Nor is that an exaggeration. The thought occurred in several later moments, too.

There was no conversion from Barnes, and Webb with a penalty increased Bristol's lead to 12-4 at half-time. At that stage both sides changed their shirts — a point worth recalling in looking at pictures of that remarkable occasion. The jerseys are virtually obscured under the mud and rain, but they are the 'clean' strip.

Two Barnes penalties early in the second half set up the rest of the game with Bristol still 12-10 in the lead, with both teams squelching and sliding about with immense commitment. Bath pressed consistently in the final quarter with Barnes and his boot persistently putting his side close to the Bristol line with accurate touch-finding. But there would be no spectacular tries on such a day, particularly not in the drenched second half.

In truth, if Bristol made a tactical mistake it was that they often tried to play their way out of trouble. The fly-kick down the pitch was a likelier weapon, forcing the defence to turn awkwardly and splash uncertainly after the ball. Choreographing the water ballet in such a way also seemed to be Bristol's best chance of adding to their score.

Finally, with Bristol's defence seemingly

And the rains came . . .the Bath-Bristol cup encounter in February, 1989, when the referee finally decided the game should go ahead.

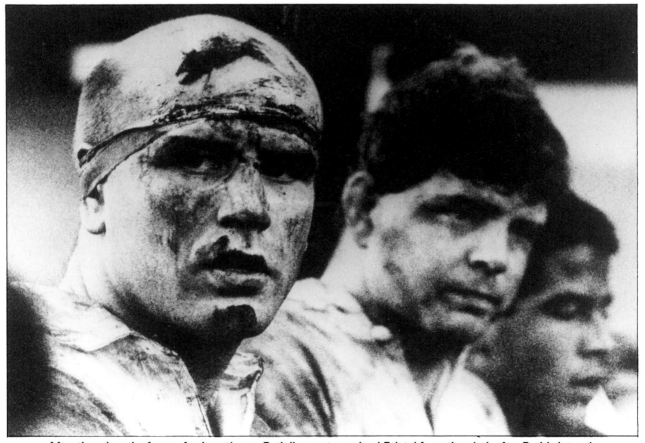

After the rains, the faces of exhaustion as Bath line up to applaud Bristol from the pitch after Bath's late win.

impregnable, even when Bath forced eight scrums near the Bristol line, the game was suddenly turned around. The ball squirted untidily from the Bristol scrum and before Harding could kill it, Richard Hill had darted through the mud to score. There were about eight minutes to go and Barnes missed with the conversion. Bath, behind the whole game until then, were 14-12 in the lead.

There were still some tense moments, and the inevitable hopes of a penalty opportunity for either side. Wisely, the excellent referee, Mr Mason, eschewed any such easy options in a game which must have been an ordeal for him as well as for the two teams.

When his final whistle was sounded, the spectators, unlike the pitch, were drained of excitement. For the soaking Bristol team, shaking with a mixture of chill and emotion back in their dressing-room, the defeat must have been hard to bear, so great had been their second-half defensive commitment. For Bath, the relief at snatching a late win in conditions when all conventional ploys were impractical, must have been immense. But there was little elation on the faces of either team as they left to the crowd's applause, so punishing had been the 80 minutes.

And, as Bristol left to ponder yet again on the what-might-have-beens, Bath waited to know who their semi-final opponents might be. Harlequins were drawn at home to Leicester. Bath must travel to Kingsholm — and Gloucester. Ouch!

Before then there was some unfinished business in the Courage League, with a home game against Nottingham. Bath had only to win to take the trophy, even though there were two further league games to play. But when Stuart Barnes happened to see the cup — the RFU had it all ready and waiting — he said "Take it away." And he admitted afterwards that he couldn't bear to touch it when the game was still to be won. It was, by 22-16, with Barnes having an outstanding game. But Bath were pushed hard, Nottingham becoming the first side to score two tries in the league season against Bath (one a beauty from winger Hackney after Sutton's break and chip) and to record so many points in one game against Bath. A Barnes dropped-goal was perhaps the crucial difference on the day.

But before returning to the cup once more, Bath found themselves in another sour wrangle with Bristol.

Three days after the Nottingham game and 11 days before the semi-final, the two clubs were due to meet in a friendly at the Memorial Ground. Bath cried off, claiming they could not field a strong enough XV, with injuries and five players absent on international duty. Bristol were angry,

claiming that £10,000 in sponsorship was lost and guessing correctly that Bath's coaching staff simply didn't want to risk injuries to players. "Are sponsors more important than players?" one Bath official pondered publicly, with no prize for guessing his answer.

For a time the bickering awoke memories of the Barnes bust-up. Bristol's feathers were only finally smoothed when Bath accepted blame for the mix-up and offered to forfeit their home advantage in the corresponding fixture the next season.

The semi-final at Kingsholm was as grim and unforgiving a spectacle as the two sides could produce. It was decided on penalties, for Bath, 6-3. Curiously, and in spite of much early Gloucester pressure, it was a game Bath won more comfortably than the score suggested — as even neutral observers remarked. Like John Horton before him in similar circumstances a few seasons earlier, Barnes pushed Gloucester back time and again with his touch-kicking, and Gloucester proved tactically inept when it came to using attacking options. It was almost as if they were playing in the wrong code — hoping for a penalty shoot-out perhaps?

The poverty of Gloucester's ambition on the day was bizarrely demonstrated in the dying moments of the match, when Gloucester's fly-half Mike Hamlin insisted on putting the ball into touch yet again even from a penalty awarded inside the Bath half in injury time. It seemed not to occur to him that a tap move might at least have produced the threat of a try. As it was the referee Roger Quittenton almost at once blew the final whistle: there was no time for the line-out. Even the Kingsholm faithful were in despair at their team's timidity — or poverty.

Perhaps the reports of this dour encounter, however, confirmed the fears of those who thought like Harlequins' coach Dick Best who remarked when the semi-final draw was announced, with Leicester his visitors: "At least it ensures there will be one good footballing side in the Final." And if he didn't mean Bath or Gloucester, his team missed the chance to prove his debatable point, losing 7-16 to Leicester.

But if the Best man was missing the big event, for many of the uncommitted the Final pitted two of the best sides in the country against each other, with Bath believing it was to be their chance to show some their best form at Twickenham at last. Four days after the semi-final they received a nasty shock. If it was bad for Bath and their supporters, it was much worse for Audley Lumsden.

The Bath University student had been one of the stars of the season at full-back with his

Hill breaks with Simpson on the right, 1989.

attacking play adding a new and exciting dimension as his 20 tries and selection for England 'B' had already demonstrated. Twickenham would have been an ideal setting for his talents to be seen by the wider public.

Lumsden was one of only three of the semi-final side to play in a midweek game, which Bath won 32-19 at Plymouth. Late in the game, making a head-on tackle to avert a try, he was injured, leaving the field 'dazed' as the first reports said. In fact it was a serious injury. He had damaged the main vertebrae in his neck and was in hospital in Plymouth, his head immobilised in a surgical collar.

A few days later he returned to Bath, but to Royal United Hospital. He would have to wear a steel 'halo' round his head for two months or more. Bath's worries — remember the cancellation of the Bristol match — about pre-Final injuries had been sadly justified.

There was inevitable speculation about who would take Lumsden's place in a position he had lately made his own. Bring in Phil Cue from the United side? Fly Chris Martin (dicey shoulder and all) back from New Zealand where he was now living? Move Barnes to full-back and bring in John Palmer, now only an occasional player (and on a skiing holiday at the time) to his old berth

at fly-half? None of these seemed sensible options.

While the pondering continued, a below-strength Bath side lost 17-13 in a midweek home game. A Bath debutant that night was a young student centre, Philip de Ganville. But the star was Newport's lively young full-back Jonathan Callard, who scored an impudent try and kicked three penalties. Callard, who had been at St Paul's College, Cheltenham, was to be Bath's full-back in the coming season.

Leicester's secretary murmured mutinously when he heard Callard had asked to join Bath, amid wide speculation that he might be eligible for the Final. "It is up to Bath to square it with their consciences," he said. "We won't be protesting but I wonder how their second-team full-back feels?" But there wasn't such a player.

Bath had lost Lumsden, and the promising young reserve Andy Hobbs, through injury. Chris Martin, finally defeated by successive injuries, had emigrated. Phil Cue was playing at fly-half, as in the game against Newport (and Callard), with the reserve centre Keith Hoskin at full-back.

Against Waterloo in a league game a few days later, the full-back was again Hoskin, who scored a try in a 38-9 demolition of the Lancashire side. Cronin, in particular, staked his claim for a Final place (Redman and Morrison played in the

Who's a lucky boy then? Gareth Chilcott and bride Ann.

Nigel and Lorrinda Redman, 1989.

Gloucester tie) with a fine display including two tries, for one of which, in apparent defiance of the coaching manuals, he ran almost half the length of the field as Waterloo tired in the face of defeat and relegation. (It was a bad season for Merseyside, Liverpool St Helens being the other relegated side from Division One.)

Bath's injury problems were compounded when another great servant of the club, the uncapped wing Barry Trevaskis, who had missed much of the season with injury, was injured yet again on his comeback in a midweek game. It was effectively the end of his Bath career, and guaranteed a Final place for a son of Ghana, the flamboyant Bristol barrister, Fred Sagoe.

With the league title long since won, and Leicester not involved in relegation issues, the two teams nevertheless had another appointment a week before the Twickenham Final: a league match at Welford Road. There was a half-hearted and futile attempt to persuade the authorities to regard the Pilkington Cup Final as a league game as well.

In the event, and in spite of irrelevant protests from the Senior Clubs' Association ("It goes against the spirit of the thing") both inevitably fielded Second XVs. Although Bath scored three tries (Bamsey, Deane and Maslen) to one, Phil Cue's kicking on the day was second-best to John Liley's and Bath lost their only league game of the season, 12-15.

And the full-back for the Final? Instead of changing two positions by moving Barnes (and he wouldn't hear of it anyway) Lumsden's place was given to John Palmer, not unfamiliar with the position and a beautifully balanced player. But his lack of match practice would inevitably mean that it would be a pressure game for him too. And, like his opposite number for the Tigers on the day, Dusty Hare, Palmer announced that it would be his last appearance for the club. At 32 he was to concentrate on his teaching career.

Look back to the team for the first Courage League game against Harlequins in September and a reason for Bath's excellent season was evident: Lumsden was the only enforced change, and Redman the only player omitted on form (for Cronin) from seven months earlier.

The Twickenham teams were: **Bath:** Palmer; Swift, Halliday, Guscott, Sagoe, Barnes, Hill, Chilcott, Dawe, Lee, Morrison, Cronin, Hall, Egerton, Robinson.
Leicester: Hare; Evans, Dodge, Bates, R.Underwood, Cusworth, Kardooni, Redfern, Thacker, Richardson, Foukes-Arnold, Tom Smith, Ian Smith, Richards, Wells.

For Bath, there was a familiar start to a Twickenham Final, going behind early on, and 6-0 down at half-time, to Dusty Hare's boot. "Easily the best start we've had on this ground," joked John Palmer after the game. It could have been worse. Sagoe was fooled by a wicked bounce from Kardooni's kick ahead just before half-time, and the scrum-half only just failed to score.

It was a mighty struggle, before what was a world record crowd for a club game. Bath had taken the field to Leicester (and neutral?) boos, and with Robinson and Hall going into the game nursing injuries, and there were times around the halfway mark when for Bath supporters the unthinkable was happening — their pack was not exercising its expected control, and the tactical kicking of Hare, Dodge and Cusworth constantly forced Bath back.

Even with two second-half penalties from Barnes to bring Bath level, the outcome was uncertain. It seemed, too, that Bath's cause would not be helped when David Egerton limped off with a knee injury after 53 minutes. Oddly, that setback revived Bath, with the replacement Paul Simpson, having watched what was going amiss,

intent on putting matters right. His was a vital extra ingredient, and with Damian Cronin — thoroughly justifying his selection — having one of his finest games for Bath, the forwards slowly took charge.

Once, Cronin erupted from a line-out to allow Simpson to put in Sagoe with a rare chance of a try, frustrated by great Leicester defence. In turn only a fine tackle by Sagoe stopped Barry Evans scoring a try for Leicester. Bath with Cronin outstanding, won seven successive line-outs in the final quarter, and Palmer made one typically clever break.

But the try that won the game was a characteristic piece of Barnes's determination. Hill went close and from the five-yard scrum, Leicester defended valiantly against Simpson's surge only for Hall to take the move on. Hill fed Barnes and the fly-half, with the hint of a dummy, careered over on the blindside to score.

Barnes missed the conversion, but what John Hall called 'the toughest Final we've played' was effectively over. Fred Howard blew for time a minute later and Bath had won the first Pilkington Cup and their fifth trophy at Twickenham.

For Dusty Hare it was not the ideal way to make a farewell. But the crowd had applauded him generously. For Audley Lumsden, watching in his surgical 'frame' it must have been a strangely sad but glad occasion. For John Palmer it had been an unexpected way in which to bow out from the game. Speaking like a drowning man who had survived he said: "In the last two minutes I could see my 15-year rugby career going through my mind. There's no need to play on now."

For the uncommitted — and many partisan supporters too — the tension of the occasion had been impressive. But once again Bath had been unable to show their southern critics the fund of inventive rugby of which they were capable. Leicester, celebrated for their open play, had been similarly reined in on the day, as neither side was able to impose itself on the other.

It was a good Final for all that. Michael Austin, writing later in *Rothmans Rugby Union Yearbook* said:

"As an expression of rugby's hard, competitive though pure elements, there has been no better Final."

It also drew from the experienced Chris Ducker, then chief rugby writer of the *Bristol Evening Post*, this comment:

"One day Bath will relax just a fraction at Twickenham and give opponents, even of Leicester's quality, an almighty thumping."

It was a prophecy that was soon to prove remarkably prescient.

Audley Lumsden, complete with medical 'halo' after his serious neck injury, joined the celebrations in Bath after the 1989 Cup Final win over Leicester.

Gloucester Routed: 1989-90

WHAT do you win after you have won everything? It sounded arrogant but that was the question for Bath as, after a pre-season tour to France, they faced the challenge of the 1989-90 season.

For Audley Lumsden there was a welcome return to light training after his serious injury. The rest of the players had Jack Rowell's words to sober them: "We've got to work harder on the basics . . .The real work begins when you have to maintain success."

But for two stars of the Bath success there was controversy as they announced they were quitting divisional and international rugby for the immediate future. Barnes said that by playing in divisional games he would be blocking the way for other fly-halves in the South-West. Nor could he spare the time from work and his duties as Bath captain. Hall insisted there were too many demands on players. It was the most public revelation of the Bath disenchantment with England duties which had run on for some seasons (and is discussed at greater length in a later chapter).

For the club, after an initial win at home against Pontypool, it was immediately down to the new Courage Clubs' Championship campaign, with last season's late recruit, Jonathan Callard, in the full-back vacancy, scoring a try on his league debut in the 32-12 beating of Harlequins at the Rec on 9 September.

It was an odd game, with Harlequins, 12-6 in the lead, falling victim to some comical errors. Barnes, having misdirected his kick-offs, handed over to Guscott whose kick-off bounced towards Gavin Thompson under the Quins' posts. He seemed nonplussed by the danger and allowed another Bath league debutant, the former Plymouth Albion winger, Steve Walklin (it was to be his only league game for Bath), to wrestle the ball away. From the ensuing surge, Guscott made ground and Callard scored by the posts.

Next, the visitors' full-back Ray Dudman kicked for touch from deep in goal. Bath won the line-out and Dudman, behind his own line, dropped Guscott's high kick. Hoskin, playing

centre for Bath, was there to score. For Barnes who scored two tries and converted four of his side's six, it was a useful day to outshine the Cumbrian David Pears, fly-half for Harlequins and fancied as an England contender. It also rather cruelly underlined Barnes's strength of mind in waiving aside England chances.

A week later Bath's expansive ambitions were again appeased when they beat the Romanian army side, Steaua Bucharest, 32-12. The fixture had echoes of the rumpus the previous season over the cancellation of the game with Bristol: this time Moseley, although given fair notice, were displaced. They were not pleased, claiming they had lost around £6,000 on the cancellation. In the event, the Romanians were so depleted that David Trick was on the bench for them. Bath also included another debutant, Nigerian Steve Ojomoh, an England Colts no.8.

(Only three months or more later, of course, the Romanians were to have a more important battle on their hands with the downfall of Ceausescu. The captain of the Steaua side that met Bath, Florica Murariu, was to die in the fighting during the overthrow of the hated regime. There were, indeed, far worse things than cancelled rugby fixtures.)

For Bath, there was now another date to remember at Kingsholm in the league. Stephen Jones in the *Sunday Times* described it as 'the most awesome match in the history of league rugby . . .(of) . . .an intensity scarcely believable.'

It was a game which Gloucester dominated from the start with Bath striving to stem their forward pressure. There were numerous confrontations between players and after Fred Howard had warned both teams, Gareth Chilcott could have no complaint when he was sent off soon after the start of the second half for kicking a Gloucester forward.

Curiously Chilcott's dismissal, with Morrison going to prop and Egerton into the second row, brought Bath storming back into contention. To quote Stephen Jones again:

"Thereafter the game erupted, not with savagery, but with brilliance as Bath finally stirred

Martin Haag, 1989.

Adedayo Adebayo, 1989.

themselves and proved that they could play better with 14 . . .''

Egerton scored a try for Bath, and Blackett on the wing just failed to hold a Guscott pass with the line before him. For Gloucester, a Derek Morgan 'try' was disallowed for offside. But the decisive score came when John Morrison tried to hoof a loose ball over the deadball line, only to miskick miserably to give Kevin Dunn a chance to touch down. Gloucester had won 13-6.

With Barnes nursing an injured hand, Guscott went to fly-half in a 17-14 win at Neath — the last of six games the side had played in September.

But by mid-October and their third league match, players continued to make their own problems. In a comfortable win against Rosslyn Park, Swift scored two of his side's six tries. But towards the end, John Hall, who had also scored a try, was sent off for a silly, blatant late body-check on Park flanker Tony Brooks (a former Bath

player), having already been warned. The off-the-ball incident and Fred Howard's prompt reaction happened so quickly that some of the crowd thought Hall was merely running off to have attention.

It didn't need a Lady Bracknell to observe that successive sendings off in league games of key forwards looked like carelessness. But others had stronger words for it. More, it drew the attention of the RFU, Bath having also had Walklin sent off for dissent on the pre-season French tour, and a youth-team player had also been dismissed. Nor, incidentally, were the club's sponsors, SWEB, in their first full season, particularly pleased at such behaviour.

The next rebuff for Bath came from Toulon, whose counter-attacking from deep outwitted Bath at the Rec 26-16 in spite of three tries for Tony Swift. The game was notable for the microphone worn by referee Clive Norling. Later,

Vital tackle by winger Peter Blackett for Bath against Bristol in the 14-13 league win at the Memorial Ground in 1989.

some choice, but too-brief excerpts in referee's "Franglais" were heard on BBC-2's *Rugby Special*. Jack Rowell, incidentally, was appalled — not by Norling or his microphone but by more bread-and-butter matters. "We were short of desire, which isn't Bath," he said.

It didn't seem the best of preparation for the following week's away Courage League game at Bristol, in which the prop Victor Ubogu, carefully nursed by the club so far, would be playing his first full league game in Chilcott's place. Again, Bristol were fancying their chances of at last laying the bogey in their recent games with Bath.

Two Webb penalties and a Collings try for Bristol against a penalty by Barnes had put Bristol 10-3 ahead at half-time and the home side's control did indeed seem complete. The game had started in reasonable weather but before half-time the heavens had unleashed a constant downpour. I was but one of many hundreds of spectators, ill-prepared for such sudden bad weather, standing wet and steadily chilling in the open, who decided to opt for a hot bath instead. I confess, too, that I left because Bristol's stranglehold was such that it seemed Bath would find it even beyond their powers to plot their way back. So, probably, did many more spectators. Oh we of little faith . . .

Soaking in a hot bath and listening to BBC

Radio Bristol's commentary as the teams played on in the cold rain, I heard the miracle unfold and cursed my faint-heartedness even as I cheered on the players vicariously.

Early in the second half, a Barnes penalty had been matched by a third from Webb for Bristol, leaving Bath 13-6 down. But then Barnes made a darting blindside break and Swift was over in the corner: Bath 10, Bristol 13. With seven minutes left, Barnes pounced athletically to collect a difficult pass from Hill, enabling Guscott to throw a long pass to Blackett and the left-winger was over for a winning try in the corner: 14-13.

Not only had the unlikely happened, but both tries had come from the wings. They later made instructive viewing in HTV's highlights of a game which was yet another example of Barnes's tactical sense making a vital difference to Bath's fortunes.

The last word goes to the Bristol crowd — and the many Bath supporters there too. They gave a great ovation as the players left the pitch — and they probably deserved one for themselves as well.

The Bristol game was the first of four successive Courage League games. It was followed by a home win over Moseley, 27-9 in which Simon Halliday scored two tries, and the Moseley centre Chris Spowart was sent off for punching Robinson. The win sent Bath to the top of the league with 17 tries in their five games. But their next game, away to Orrell (and with Hall back from suspension) produced no tries and a much tougher task. Orrell missed their chances to topple the leaders, and a Barnes penalty with almost the last kick of the game gave Bath a win they scarcely deserved.

Chilcott, back from his suspension, returned for the away game with Wasps but Egerton, injured at Orrell, was missing. Adedayo Adebayo, the latest of Bath's African contingent, came in at centre for the unfit Guscott, and had a decisive impact on the game — and more particularly on Rob Andrew — when his mighty tackle on the England fly-half set Barnes hacking on the loose ball and picking up for Hill to send Swift in for a converted try. Even though Barnes had to go off with an injury, Bath maintained their domination and with further tries by Swift and Blackett won 18-9.

Indeed, all these tries by backs in league games provided an effective counter-blast to a quoted remark by the Harlequins centre Will Carling that Bath had talented backs 'who are under-achieving.'

This was, of course, an echo of earlier complaints about Bath's tactics (and discussed in a later chapter). But Wasps and Bristol, for example, could testify to the effectiveness of Bath's try-scoring wingers. And Carling's words seemed even odder when his own (under-achieving?) club had conceded five tries to Bath in the opening league game of the season — all of them to backs. But it wasn't Carling's year at club level. Asked, as England's captain, to make the Pilkington Cup draw his first 'take' from the bag was a home tie for Bath — against Harlequins. He joked at what his teammates would do to him as a result.

But that was for the New Year. In the annual lull between league and cup with the inevitable Divisional Championship filling the gap, more interesting events were taking place at Bristol, where Jon Webb, already dropped by England and the South-West Division, was about to be dropped by Bristol, too. He talked with Chris Ducker about the frustration caused by the Bristol backs' lack of confidence. "I wouldn't dream of playing for any other team than Bristol, who gave me the opportunity to be an international. But, without wanting to sound bitter, I have become frustrated this season."

The league season resumed on 13 January at home against Bedford, everybody's favourite fall guy in their only season in the top division, and — as Robert Armstrong in *The Guardian* shrewdly observed — old-style amateurs whose temporary status was 'a bizarre accident.' He added:

"Here we had a bunch of well-meaning players, who did not lack for courage or tenacity, yet their levels of fitness, organisation and basic technique were so far removed from the modern first-class game that it was obvious the two clubs inhabited different worlds."

Bedford conceded 14 tries, with four each for Swift and Guscott and three for Callard, with Barnes converting ten. It was the kind of useful day out under match conditions when a side like Bath could, begging Carling's pardon, run through their repertoire of party tricks. It was also a day when, with the Romanian events very much in people's minds, the crowd contributed more than £1,700 in aid of providing kit and equipment for Romanian rugby in memory of Murariu and his fellow international Radu Durbac, also slain in the fighting.

The Bedford game was the last easy win (76-0) of the season for Bath. In another wet day's mauling, Bath beat Harlequins 9-0 in the Pilkington Cup, Cronin scoring the only try in conditions bad enough for both sides to change shirts at half-time. It was also a day of duels between England players and contenders for their jobs — Winterbottom and Robinson, Skinner and Hall, Pears and Barnes, Ackford and Redman. On the day the Bath contenders could reasonably consider that their side's victory had proved a point to the England selectors.

In the fourth round of the Pilkington Cup Bath were at home to a once famous Yorkshire club Headingley, where Peter Winterbottom first came to prominence. (Now, the club's name is no more: it has merged with Roundhay, to become the distinctly duller-sounding Leeds.) Headingley's cause was not helped by the departure to Rugby League before the tie of their centre, Simon Irvine, and the absence, injured, of their former England prop, Paul Huntsman.

But on the day they gave a sturdy performance, leading by a penalty-goal before Bath took control with two tries from Hall and one from Egerton. When, five minutes into the second half, Redman scored a fourth try, making the score 25-3, memories of the Bedford tally came to mind. But that was the final score, Headingley's outstanding defence frustrating Bath's fans as well as their team. The Yorkshiremen earned their applause: for seven sublime and satisfying minutes they had led the cup-holders on their own patch.

There was time for a bad-tempered 12-9 home win in a so-called friendly over Gloucester before the next cup game. The Gloucester match was only memorable because referee Roger Quittenton was at home, thinking the game was on Saturday: it was on Friday night. Ashley Reay, a Bristol

Front five: (from left), Redman and Cronin prepare to pack down with Lee, Dawe, and Chilcott against Welsh opponents in 1990.

Andy Robinson, 1989.

Steve Ojomoh, 1989.

Society referee, came from Frome to take charge and the kick-off was delayed for 40 minutes.

Bath next beat Richmond in the fifth round of the cup, away, by 35-9. The Second Division side, coached by Bath's former hooker, Rob Cunningham, were not flattered by six tries for Bath, two of them from Guscott — the last a remarkable solo run close on time. A Richmond wing was Jim Fallon, a South-West divisional player, soon to return to the region — and Bath.

But a rather bigger name now confounded the rugby world. Jon Webb, by Bristol, was joining Bath. He explained that he had no longer been enjoying his rugby. "I could not really see anything changing at Bristol in the foreseeable future. The potential at the club is enormous but is not being fulfilled."

Stuart Barnes, so conscious of having made a similar move five years earlier, said Webb would obviously strenghten the squad at Bath, but would

have to work 'very hard' to earn a first-team place at Bath, especially as Jon Callard was performing so well.

Bristol's coach, Bob Hesford, was gracious enough to admit: "Perhaps he suffered in the past for the way we played." Indeed, anyone who had seen Webb's last games for Bristol could testify to his loss of form and flair in a Bristol side notably lacking confidence. For the moment, Callard's place was secure, as Webb started with Bath third team, the Spartans.

But speculation about Webb's future was almost overshadowed by yet another gratuitous incident against Plymouth Albion — scene of the serious injury to Lumsden. This time, John Hall, not long back from suspension, was sent off for kicking an opponent in a ruck. Swift scored three tries in a 38-14 victory against a Plymouth side which again included winger Walklin, home after his brief spell with Bath. But inevitably, Hall's

Stand-in scrum-half Steve Knight.

dismissal took the headlines. A 90-day suspension followed and that was the end of his season.

It was not the best of curtain-raisers to the resumption of the league programme against Nottingham at Beeston, who were in mid-table.

Perhaps Bath became complacent with the home side lacking four internationals — Brian Moore, Simon Hodgkinson (who had taken Jon Webb's England place), Chris Gray and Gary Rees. Whatever the reason, Bath never got to grips with the task and lost almost at the last when, having stopped Gary Hartley short of the line, Bath saw prop Dave Hindmarsh pick up and score a winning try.

Two weeks later, for the Pilkington Cup semi-final at Moseley, Bath produced a shock for those who had not been watching Bath closely. Jeremy Guscott was dropped. Jack Rowell explained the decision by referring to the pressure Guscott had been under: "We felt he just needed a rest. Suddenly the lad was playing for England, the British Lions, and had become a world figure in the game. He was trying to build a new career outside rugby as well." In what was briefly to become a familiar pattern, a Second Division Rugby League side, Huddersfield, were bandying

figures of £300,000 in reported attempts to attract Guscott.

Guscott's place for the semi-final at Moseley went to Adebayo. But Guscott opted to 'rest' by playing in the Bath United side (together with Jon Webb) against Richmond Vikings. Another key choice, reflecting the trend of future preference, was the choice of Ubogu at prop instead of Richard Lee. A slimmed-down Simpson was Hall's replacement.

This time there was no cup slip-up at Moseley (winners over Bristol in a previous round). Bath won 21-7 with three tries (Callard, Swift, and Chilcott) to none. In the other semi-final Gloucester had won at Northampton 17-12.

But before thinking about the Final both Bath and Gloucester had eyes on the league title. The week after the semi-final Bath, without Barnes, Halliday, Guscott, Chilcott, and Hall, slipped up even more badly than at Nottingham, with a clumsy, unimaginative performance against a sharp Saracens side, new to the division that season. An Egerton try for Bath was not converted, and when Ben Clarke, the Saracens' impressive no.8, made the burst for a try by fly-half Lee, it was Sean Robinson, brother of Bath's Andy

Robinson who was captaining his side for the first time, who converted to win the game for the Londoners and effectively end Bath's title hopes.

Tony Russ, Saracens' elated coach, was tempted into a prediction about the forthcoming Pilkington Cup Final. He probably spoke for much of the rest of the London-based rugby fraternity when he predicted: "It's going to be the most boring final of all time . . .Both are so predictable these days — as Bath clearly demonstrated here. Their tactics weren't working but they didn't try anything different. Neither is flexible — they can't change their tactics, so it's just going to be thud and blunder on 5 May. The Cup Final will be decided on penalties."

His baleful prediction, which briefly stung the joint pride of the West Country, was to be as hugely inaccurate as Chris Ducker's — mentioned at the end of the previous chapter — was to prove accurate.

Gloucester, while Bath were giving best to Saracens, had overcome Orrell 16-10 at Kingsholm and seemed on course for the league at least. It was understandable that there was less notice taken of a bizarre but, as it was soon to appear, significant result at Bristol where the home side lost their lock Adams, sent off after 90 seconds, and the game to the visiting Wasps by 21-22.

Bath put on some of their party tricks in the run-up to Twickenham. Against Llanelli in the 'rag doll' match at the Rec, they fell behind to a try by Andrew Morgan within 35 seconds of the start — only to hit back with eight of their own in a 42-14 win. Halliday and Egerton each scored two, but perhaps the finest moments came with two tries from the recalled David Trick whose display brought back memories for many supporters of his starring part in what they were already inclined to regard as a golden age of Bath three-quarter play. They were never quite sure when it was: but they remembered it well. The truth was that it had never really gone away — it had merely been overlain on occasion by the demands of league and cup rugby.

A spectacular celebration of the backs' renaissance, indeed, was only a few weeks away.

Meanwhile, yet again Bristol fancied their chances in the promised encounter (making up for the previous season's controversial cancellation) at the Memorial Ground in a friendly. Hill, Guscott, and Egerton were all playing in the sunny fields of Bermuda. No matter. Adebayo turned in a hat-trick of tries in a 23-15 Bath win. And Jon Webb was in for the injured Callard in another win over Llanelli, 31-19, this time at Stradey Park, with two tries each for Adebayo and Bamsey. But for Paul Simpson who had replaced

the suspended John Hall on the open side, a knee injury ended his game at half-time — and cost him his place in the Cup Final side.

Then came the last Saturday of Courage League games, with Bath having lost their chance of repeating the double, and Gloucester clear favourites to win the league and eyeing the prospect of emulating Bath's feat. But they had reckoned without the Nottingham factor. The Midland side, having effectively spiked Bath's hopes, now did the same to Gloucester who lost 12-3 at Beeston. Perhaps Bath hadn't warned them.

Wasps, who won against Saracens the same day, had also won the title — never having led the table at any time in what had seemed one of their less notable seasons. It was a remarkable and unexpected climax which also took the game's rulers by surprise. The trophy — tsk, tsk — was in waiting at Beeston (so was BBC-2 *Rugby Special*) for Gloucester to collect. Wasps had to make do with a replica.

Bath met Leicester at the Rec, with the free-scoring Adebayo again running in two tries in a 26-15 win which included five tries (Callard, Barnes, and the replacement flanker, Kevin Withey) to one by John Liley. It was Les Cusworth's last game for his club and he was applauded on to the pitch by the Bath crowd. As at Dusty Hare's farewell Bath provided fitting opponents but also a defeat for the departing hero.

All told it was a result that, coupled with Gloucester's defeat and Wasps' surprise snatching of the Courage title, emphasised the importance of the one-point win for Wasps at Bristol and Bath's woeful day at Saracens.

Bath had scored more and conceded fewer points than any other side. But they had lost three games. That was one too many. Swift had scored ten tries in the 11 league games, and Callard six in 11, Barnes scoring five tries in ten games, and Guscott four in nine.

Barnes was as frank as ever: "We should be celebrating the league title. We aren't because on occasions — particularly at Saracens — we played badly. I hoped that if we lost the league it would be won by a team showing the style we showed in winning the double. But we felt we've thrown it away rather than it being taken away." But he conceded that Wasps had been the most consistent side. Like tortoises in the table they had overtaken Bath's confident hares. And if there was again a hint of arrogance in Bath's comments about showing style — well, the team would soon be justifying it to even the most sceptical of critics.

But Bath's disappointment was mild compared with Gloucester's. From a confident vision of two titles, they had seen one such hope dashed against

Egerton breaks from a scrum, 1990.

all expectation so adding apprehension to their reduced ambition as Twickenham beckoned. Their apprehension was well justified.

Stephen Jones, after the Pilkington Cup Final, summed up the day thus in the *Sunday Times:*

"Any doubts that Bath are the leading club team of the era in world rugby can be quietly laid to rest. For Gloucester, there can never have been a bigger disaster . . .for the neutral, it was an agonising sight to see a proud club so mercilessly thrashed."

But that is perhaps to anticipate the event. The game was to mark the farewell in the Bath side of centre Simon Halliday, whose legacy of ankle injuries were thought to need a long rest, and of the greyhaired yeoman in the Gloucester centre,

Balloon boys . . .Andy Robinson and his father Ray.

Friendly rematch as Chilcott and Mike Teague (then with Gloucester) help sell posters for charity, 1990.

Richard Mogg. Kevin Withey, a Bath solicitor, was called to the open side of the Bath pack in the absence of Hall and Simpson. Callard, Adebayo, and Ubogu were new to Twickenham Finals.

The teams were: **Bath:** Callard; Swift, Halliday, Guscott, Adebayo, Barnes, Hill, Ubogu, Dawe, Chilcott, Redman, Cronin, Robinson, Egerton, Withey.

Gloucester: T.Smith; Morgan, Caskie, Mogg, Breeze, Hamlin, Hannaford, Preddy, Dunn, Pascall, Scrivens, Brain, Gadd, Teague, I.Smith.

Referee: F.Howard

It was a hot, steaming May day about as far away in atmosphere from the murk and rain of a growling Kingsholm day in January as could be imagined. Bath had known many a dour endurance battle in such conditions. Of late seasons they had often won there, nevertheless, but with narrow margins, including two semi-final by 12-11 and 6-3. On this Twickenham summer's afternoon, Bath were fleeter of foot and a league away in speed of vision and imagination than their floundering opponents.

The opening score came in a fashion which surprised the crowd — but had surprised Gloucester, and perhaps Bath, even more. Kevin Withey, having poached the ball from a line-out, burst past Morgan and the Gloucester halves and thereby claimed his place in rugby history by running 60 metres or more down the touchline for the first try.

After 39 minutes, Bath were 28-0 ahead, and by the time John Gadd was dismissed in the third quarter for stamping on Egerton were leading 28-6. But perhaps the humiliation of Gloucester on the day was best illustrated when in one of their rare attacks, the unfortunate Tim Smith gave the remarkable Tony Swift a chance to intercept. Swift sped 90 metres to touch down in the heat — the lack of credible chasers emphasising Gloucester's lack of pace.

Bath scored eight tries in all — the others coming from Guscott, Callard, Dawe, Robinson, and — to great applause — Ubogu, who relished the chance to run at the bemused Gloucester defence late in the game. Barnes converted four and Halliday, surprisingly not a scorer, was given the chance to convert the last try. He took it. Dunn scored Gloucester's try. Bath had won 48-6. Chris Ducker's prediction, not Tony Russ's, had been made glorious reality.

Jack Rowell called it the best performance he had seen from Bath in his time with them, and singled out Nigel Redman for his outstanding all-round play. He called it Bath's 'best team ever'.

Summer wedding for Jeremy and Jayne Guscott, 1990.

He added: "We've always striven to get a balance between forwards and backs and I think this time we succeeded."

But already he was looking ahead: "Keeping things fresh from now on is the challenge we must meet." His captain Stuart Barnes was looking forward and back: "I'm still annoyed at throwing away the league title, but everybody must realise

now that we are not easing up. We want to get better and better."

And in Gloucester? Steve Fraser, rugby reporter in its evening paper, *The Citizen*, faced the Kingsholm tribes honestly. He wrote:

"The Bath team took club rugby to new heights."

Barnes in typical action, at Twickenham 1990.

Guscott breaks against Gloucester in the 1990 Pilkington Cup Final.

Victor Ubogu checks on his fingers as the players celebrate the 1990 Twickenham win.

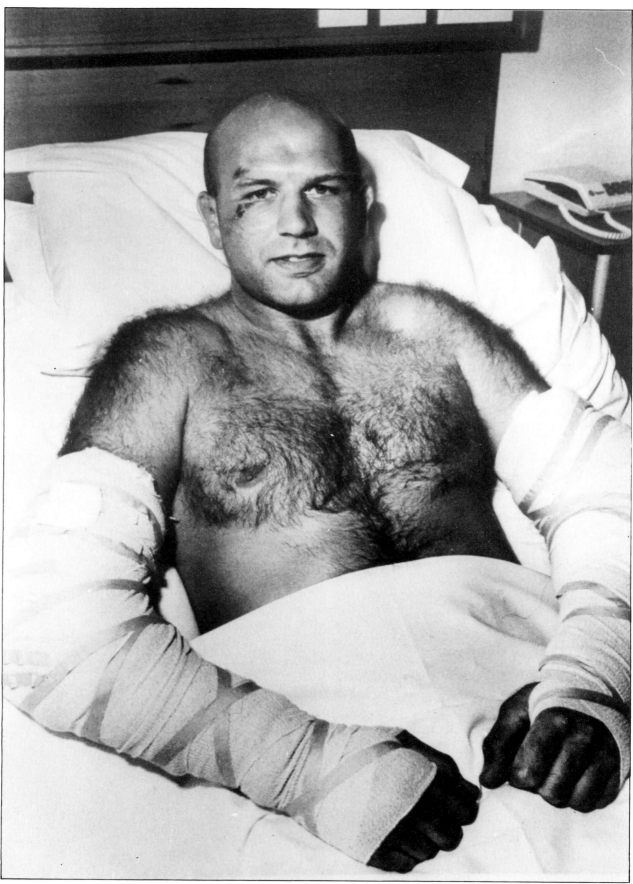

Arms and the (Red)man: the Bath and England lock recovering after operations on his arms, 1990.

Champions Again: 1990-91

THE man who had started the great try-rush against Gloucester in the Twickenham Final in May provided the first of the surprises for Bath even before the 1990-91 season had started. Like the others, soon to follow, it was hardly the best of overtures to the new campaign.

Kevin Withey, and another earlier Cup Final participant, Fred Sagoe, announced they were joining Newport in time for the start of the first season of league rugby in Wales. Three reserve backs, Westcott, Sparkes, and Plummer — were going with them.

Withey, a former Bath schoolboy now a solicitor in the city, said his reasons for moving had nothing to do with job opportunities. They were simply concerned with his playing ambitions, understandably fuelled by his share in the glory of the recent triumph at Twickenham.

"I have had six years playing second fiddle to players like Roger Spurrell and Andy Robinson. When it came to the crunch last season I would still only have played the big league or cup games in the event of injury. Last season's Twickenham Final was a marvellous experience. But I was only selected because John Hall was suspended. And possibly if Paul Simpson had been fit I still wouldn't have made the side. At 28 I need to try something new."

(Withey's sweet-and-sour taste of the big time had its repeat in the *Official Yearbook of the Rugby Football Union* a few months later. It honoured Withey with a full-page colour action picture of him from the Final — and managed to spell his name wrongly in the caption, thus perhaps emphasising the point he was making.)

The better-known John Morrison, dropped for the May Final, was another who took his boots elsewhere. Reversing the usual trend, he went to Bristol. Like Withey, he still wanted the best. "I am still ambitious to reach the very top. But the only way I will be noticed is by playing first-team rugby."

Three other players left Bath for Clifton, one the reserve centre Ben Cundy. But the others — Barry Trevaskis, for many years a good servant to the club, and Phil Cue, who had helped fill gaps at full-back and stand-off in recent seasons — were at the close of their careers.

The players' moves came amid widespread allegations of 'inducements' being offered by clubs throughout the land to attract new talent — inferences that were to continue with the increasingly fierce competition — and threat of relegation — arising from the new league structures. In Bath's case there was some muttering about Newport, although any resentment was officially denied. (Nevertheless the home game against the Welsh club due on a Wednesday night in early September was called off — Bath, conveniently, being able to point out that they had lost eight players to a South-West game against Leinster, and had seven others injured.)

Further, when the club's handbook to mark its 125 years was published soon afterwards, captain Stuart Barnes contributed a light piece about the pre-season Australian tour and recounted some of the players' adventures. Then he ended:

"It is that feeling of fun and togetherness that has sustained Bath over the years and makes the club special. That is what made the departure of several tourists to clubs not so distant so sad. To many it has felt as if the club had been used; and without doubt the element of poaching and avarice represents the gravest threat to the game we all love."

But all such debates, including that involving the departure of Withey and Morrison, were dwarfed by the resignation of the two other members of Jack Rowell's coaching triumvirate, Dave Robson and Tom Hudson.

The row that led to their departure was perhaps inevitable given the way rugby clubs were organised and the ambitions of some of those concerned with how the players performed, regardless of the mutual courtesies normally due between one club and another.

The break when it came had been foreshadowed in the earlier dust-up after the cancellation by Bath of a 'friendly' at Bristol in the 1988-89 season. On this later occasion Bath were due to open their season with a traditional fixture at Pontypool on 1 September. But Bath's coaching team, given the OK from Twickenham, had also arranged to play Romania that weekend (the visitors were due at Leicester four days later.) Concerned at the effect on relations with Pontypool if there was a late cancellation, the Bath committeemen said 'no' to

Romania. Mud dramatically, messily, hit the fan.

Jack Rowell, away on business when the committee decision was taken, was concerned about it on his return and — as will be seen — both games were played. By then Hudson and Robson had already resigned. Hudson explained: "We have taken Bath as far as we can with the present management structure. We want to make the club world class, but I don't think that is possible . . ."

There was more. Hudson argued that the fixture arrangement exploited young players and was 'not conducive to peak performance'. He claimed that up to 30 hours a week were devoted by the coaching team to 'performance' even though they were all amateurs. "We have revolutionised training philosophy and taken on player welfare, career structure, apprenticeships etc — and all we have had from the committee for the last six years is confrontation, not co-operation."

The implication was clear. Bath, the departing pair suggested, were worrying too much about domestic fixtures when the world beckoned.

As for Jack Rowell, he talked with the committee and their decision was changed. Far from cancelling either game the club decided to go ahead with both — in successive days. But Rowell did not seek to hide that the departure of his two lieutenants in so public a fashion was a blow to morale.

In a public comment at the time which suggested he could have had a distinguished career as a diplomat, he said: "Tom and Dave were doing their usual stint with a great deal of zeal and suddenly something like that blows up. As far as the Romanian visit was concerned, I got what I was after. It was all sorted out by playing two games in one weekend. It was too far down the line to cancel a scheduled fixture against Pontypool but for me the Romanian game was a big opportunity. They've just emerged from an horrific period — some of their players were killed — so it's a privilege to be able to do a bit to help them."

Privately, he thought Hudson and Robson had been wrong to go as they did.

But the team had two games to play in two days. On Saturday, 1 September, this Bath side lost 34-17 at Pontypool. It was largely a United XV (Webb still playing second string to Callard): Webb; Trick, I.Palmer, Saverimutto, Fallon, Book, Knight, Chilcott, Deane, Crane, Reed, Adams, Olds, Ojomoh, Maslen.

The following day Bath beat the Romanians 38-9 with this team: Callard; Blackett, Bamsey, de Glanville, Adebayo, Barnes, Hill, Ubogu, Dawe, Lee, Haag, Cronin, Hall, Egerton, Robinson.

Perhaps the biggest cheer of the afternoon came when Audley Lumsden came on (as a replacement for an injured Adebayo) for his first major appearance since breaking his neck. But the irony of the day was the presence at the Rec of Tom Hudson and Dave Robson, in a coincidental new role as advisers to the Romanian rugby authorities . . .

Three days later Bath had a home game against Toulouse, scoring ten tries in a 44-6 win and drawing from the celebrated French coach Pierrre Villepreux, the comment: "Bath's linking between forwards and backs is done at such speed . . .most unusual for an English side." Another three days — and it was Llanelli away and a 12-28 defeat.

As hectic starts to the season 1990-91 just about set the record given the close-season defections and the departure of Hudson and Robson. But it was the players who had borne the burden of the pre-season tour to Australia including games against the club side Randwick, and Queensland, and on their return four games in seven September days. In the next four weeks they were also due to meet Cardiff, Neath, and Ulster, among others.

Stuart Barnes, in suggesting there might be too many tough games, put matters — and perhaps the frustrated ambition of the departed coaching staff — in frank perspective. He pointed out that Bath were due to play the comparatively unglamorous (my words not his) Liverpool St Helens in the opening Courage League match on 22 September. That, he insisted, was the most important game of all those they were playing at the start of the season. Bath warmed up for that by scoring eight tries in a 45-23 home win over Cardiff, each side fielding eight internationals.

This year, for the first time, the Courage League Division One had been increased to 13 clubs. Bedford had been relegated but had been replaced by two clubs — Northampton, new to the top flight, and Liverpool St Helens, coached by the distinguished former England wing, Mike Slemen. The Merseysiders had also won promotion to the top division in the leagues' first season, but failed to survive one campaign.

For Bath's league opener against Liverpool St Helens, Callard was at full-back, Swift and Adebayo on the wings, and Guscott and Bamsey (Halliday had, indeed, left after the May Cup Final) in the centre, with Barnes and Hill at half-back. In the pack, Redman was still missing, absent since the summer after operations on his elbows; Chilcott and Egerton were injured; and Paul Simpson's departure in the previous season's cup semi-final was, it turned out, his last appearance for Bath. Ubogu was in the front row

Audley Lumsden.

Tom Hudson.

with Dawe and Lee, Haag partnered Cronin, and Nick Maslen joined Hall and Robinson in the back row. There were seven tries in Bath's 46-3 win.

Before the next league game, at Northampton, on 13 October, Bath lost Adebayo, injured in a 25-6 home win over Ulster, and Egerton, who damaged his shoulder in a 27-13 win over Neath at the end of September and was to be absent for five months. Blackett and Ojomoh replaced them at Northampton, and Redman, fit again, returned for Haag at lock. Webb replaced Callard at full-back.

On the day, Redman's return was brief. He had broken ribs in the first half-hour. Hall moved to the second row and the replacement hooker, Jimmy Deane went into the back row. Webb and Hall scored tries, but Bath came perilously close to defeat before the hugely partisan home crowd. Once a catch in defence by Cronin at a line-out

proved crucial, and a fine saving tackle from behind by Peter Blackett stopped Tim Rodber, when the Northampton no.8 seemed sure to score. A late dropped-goal from Barnes eased the tension.

The following week there was another nail-biter in the league against Orrell.

Bath had started with two brisk tries, from Guscott and Swift. But as Orrell pushed back into the game, and landed a penalty, Barnes broke only for his pass to be intercepted ("I should have dummied him") by the Orrell fly-half, Martin Strett, who ran 50 metres to score by the posts and convert his try. Bath were 8-9 behind. Orrell only faltered after losing their lock Chris Brierley, dismissed by referee Ed Morrison for kicking Hall. Thereafter Barnes made the game Bath's with a penalty, and a conversion of a Robinson try.

Bath had now won narrowly against two sides who fancied their prospects of taking the league title. On the third Saturday of successive games,

Guscott battles to catch Harriman of Harlequins, 1990.

Bath's double success was shown in a curious perspective when Orrell beat Northampton by 60 points to nil.

Bristol meanwhile, with John Morrison in their pack, were making their annual challenge to turn the tide against Bath, who were without Cronin as well as Redman, Egerton and Chilcott from the pack — the Cornish recruit Andy Reed made his league debut at lock alongside Martin Haag. Again, Bristol showed a lack of confidence in their backs, and a medley of errors, one involving James Johnston, a reserve wing who had joined Bristol from Bath, gave Webb two penalty goals.

But the decisive moment came late in the second half when Ojomoh, who made a notable impact at no.8 for Bath, won a line-out to set up Ubogu on the charge. From the laid-back ball Guscott quickly chipped through as the cover defence sought to smother him and with a remarkable piece of skill Jon Webb was able to bend on the run to scoop the loose ball into the hands of Adebayo for the left wing to score in the corner and complete Bath's 10-3 win.

Wasps came to Bath a week later, for a game to raise funds for the family of their promising young winger, Raph Tsagane, who had been

Athleticism from Redman, proving Bath do sometimes win a line-out ball.

killed in a car crash near Bath on the previous season's Easter tour, and for Stephen Roberts, a Bath colt, paralysed in a game at Nottingham.

The game ended, fittingly, in a draw, 26-26. David Trick, given a conversion attempt with virtually the last kick of the game, hoofed it high on to the roof of the stand to final applause. More than £18,000 was raised, with Nottingham handsomely contributing £2,000.

Harlequins, top of the table with a game more played, were the next visitors in a Courage League game, and Redman was back in the second row in place of Reed. But Harlequins lacked Paul Ackford from their pack, where Neil Edwards and Troy Coker made up the second row. Bath played as if they wanted to win: Harlequins were surprisingly short of confidence in ideas and confidence behind the scrum, with Pears's judgement notably second-best to that of his opposite number, Barnes.

As before in a game between these sides, crucial errors (two of them again at full-back) gave Bath the chance to take charge. After Barnes had put Bath ahead with a penalty after 21 minutes Harlequins were given an equalising opportunity — only for a touch-judge's intervention which brought a ticking-off for Quins' flanker Mickey Skinner and reversal of the referee's decision. Almost immediately the floodgates opened. After

a Barnes break, Hill passed to Webb who chipped to the corner for Adebayo to touch down, Barnes converting. Then mistakes by full-back Thresher led to Haag taking Barnes's pass to score. A Barnes penalty meant Bath had scored 16 points in almost as many minutes to lead 16-nil at half-time.

The following week Bath had another major challenge, this team at Leicester who had moved into second place in the table. Dean Richards was missing from the Leicester side. It was a fascinating struggle. Bath provided one thrilling move from deep in their own 22 with Webb, Guscott, and Adebayo combining superbly, a forward pass spoiling the scoring chance. The game was decided on penalty-goals, with Bath winning 9-3. The victory meant Bath had a game in hand over their rivals and the cushion of a two-point lead and home advantage in their next important league game, in March against Wasps.

But Bath's confidence was doubly high. In the third round of the Pilkington Cup the next Saturday Leicester were again their formidable opponents. But Bath would be at home, and, although Richards would be back for Leicester, the Midlands side lacked wingers Rory Underwood and Evans, plus the lively Neil Back from the back row, from the team Bath had defeated at Welford Road.

Bath, by contrast, although still with Ojomoh

Career building . . .bricklayer Jeremy Guscott.   The gasman cometh: Guscott takes up the pen for British Gas.

Bandaged for charity: cheerful Chilcott, 1990.

Joining the tug-of-war: Chilcott is the anchor.

Big moment for small boy: captain Andy Robinson face-to-face with Bath mini-rugby player Andrew Mead, 1991.

Cuddly Coochie, 1990.

Prop Richard Lee, near the end of his career, 1991.

Steve Ojomoh bursts past a tackler.

deputising at no.8, had only one absentee from the earlier game. Centre Jon Bamsey had been injured in that match, and Adebayo was moved into the centre, with Blackett coming in on the wing. As it happened Adebayo had an unhappy time in his change of position but blame for the shock that came to Bath could not be laid at his door. Leicester simply had Bath on the back foot throughout the game, and seemed to have a greater desire on the day. They had also learned tactical lessons from the previous game.

The only try came from the Australian/Irish fly-half Brian Smith (later to move to Australian Rugby League). He won the chase to touch down from his winger Sandford's kick ahead. Barnes was nursing what proved to be a pelvic injury, and Bath had only one penalty shot at goal. But there could be no excuses. At no time did Bath look as if they could win. Against the home fans' expectation, Leicester, 12-nil victors on the day, had also given Bath their first home cup defeat since 1982, ending also Bath's cup record of 22 unbeaten games since losing at Moseley 3-4 in 1987-88.

For the Tigers, it was a wonderful revenge for their 1989 disappointment. For the Bath faithful, that dark November afternoon was in every sense a far cry from the euphoria of a summery May and a shocked Gloucester earlier in the year. Crowds totalling around 21,000 had seen successive, tremendous tussles between the two clubs.

Barnes was to be out of rugby for three months; Adebayo, for reasons of injury, and commitments in the Universities Athletic Union competition (he was studying at Swansea) played only one more game that season for the club. But the Nigerian's absence paved the way for the impact of a left winger who had slowly been serving his Bath apprenticeship, in spite of injury, since joining from Richmond at the start of the season: Jim Fallon.

But before returning to the chase to regain the league title now they were out of the Pilkington Cup, Bath's players were dispersed into divisional matches, international calls, and — for the club — an international tournament (shades of Robson and Hudson?) in France to mark the centenary of the Toulouse club.

Bath teams shorn of most of their better-known players nevertheless did honourable duty across the Channel in November and December, beating the Soviet Union (it still existed) 13-7, losing to Toulouse 23-6 in front of a 12,000 crowd, and

A surgical strike in the snow: a try for Jon Webb.

losing 60-19 to Fiji. Remarkably they were only 22-15 down at half-time to the Fijians.

The side that represented Bath that day is worth listing, because although far from full-strength it mixed one or two comparatively established players with young thrusters — and in the centre a young New Zealander, Laurie Heatherley, who was to make curious rugby history the following season:

Webb; Fallon, Heatherley, Bamsey, Lumsden, Redman, Sanders, Chilcott, Dawe, Lee, Haag, Crane, Maslen, Ojomoh, Adams.

Webb, Lumsden, and Adams had the temerity to score tries against the Fijians.

Elsewhere, Bristol had recruited the former Bath hooker Rob Cunningham as coach to assist Colin McFadyean; Simon Halliday was returning to the game after an operation on his ankle, with Harlequins Second XV; Barry Trevaskis played in the Courage League for Clifton; and John Hall, having yet again won back his place in the England side, lost it again after injuring himself in squad training, consequently missing Bath's games, too, until February. Jon Callard, meanwhile, was the first-choice replacement at stand-off for the injured Stuart Barnes.

Callard, indeed, was one of several replacements including Knight, Maslen and Ojomoh — there was no Barnes, Hill, Hall or Egerton — when the league season resumed in mid-January. Bath struggled to beat the unfancied Moseley 11-6, Swift and Adebayo scoring tries.

In February games were snowed off, including the league game at Gloucester, but Bath managed to fit in a scoring spree against Barnstaple (68-0) and Ebbw Vale (58-0) to stay in practice, as well as revenging themselves on Llanelli 34-14 before the serious business called them again. More, the four absentees from the Moseley game were fit to meet Wasps in the Courage League clash in early March. Redman was omitted in favour of Haag and Cronin in the second row, and Fallon made his League debut on the left wing.

It was an uneasy game, with Wasps clearly limiting their ambitions to containing Bath in a tight game.

At half-time the sides were level at 6-6, in an exchange of penalties. Barnes was injured in tackling Rigby soon after the interval but continued in a somewhat dazed way to play on. Wasps at one stage were leading 12-9; Rob Andrew kicking a penalty almost every time Wasps had made it into the Bath territory. But at last Hill, with five minutes to go, wriggled in for a try converted by Webb. It seemed Bath at 15-12 had won the day.

Not so. As they set up an attack in their own half, Bath lost the ball and the Wasps' lively flanker Rigby broke through. He fed Fran Clough with an inside pass, and the former Orrell and England centre angled his run cleverly to wrong-foot the Bath defence and make it into the right

Training talk – Jack Rowell and Chilcott, 1991.

Confidence: de Glanville, scorer of four tries in a friendly against Barnstaple, who lost 68-0, 1991.

corner in spite of Fallon's despairing chase. Wasps had won 16-15.

With eight Courage League games played and four to go Bath were still in front of the pack on 14 points, two ahead of Orrell, Leicester, and Wasps. Bristol did them a favour, beating Leicester 10-6 at the Memorial Ground.

A few fainthearts feared Bath were about to falter in league as well as cup. They had noticed the next test was at Nottingham, where ambitions had been undone the previous season. And there was still a re-scheduled league encounter at Kingsholm . . .

The fears were groundless. Barnes scored two tries and Webb kicked four penalties in a 22-9 win at Nottingham (where the young prop Mark Crane made a rare league appearance in place of Richard Lee). Results in other games combined to suit Bath. Wasps could only draw 21-21 at home against Northampton, Leicester lost 12-5 to Harlequins, and Orrell won 15-9 at Gloucester.

At Gloucester, where Crane was preferred to Ubogu in the front row alongside Chilcott and

Dawe, and Redman to Cronin, Bath conceded 26 penalties in the wind and the rain — and five successful penalty goals. But three tries — one of Webb's two after a powerful blindside break by Barnes; another coming from Chilcott in a happy return to Kingsholm — were enough to claim the game 17-15 for Bath, who also survived the second-half loss of an injured Hall.

The league title now firmly beckoned with a home game the next week against Rosslyn Park. Guscott scored the first try after only 90 seconds, and there were seven in all including two for the scampering Tony Swift on the right wing. Again Bath lost a back-row forward, Egerton this time, and Ubogu came on as replacement, Mark Crane moving to the back row for the second successive week. Crane's brother, Geoff, incidentally, came on after seven minutes as a replacement forward for Park — another occasion when brothers have played on opposite sides in a League match (Andy Robinson and his brother Sean at Saracens had already played in the same matches.)

Fittingly, although Park staged a revival late

Stuart Barnes receives the Courage trophy from RFU president Mike Pearey in April 1991, the second time Bath had won it.

More beer goes to waste: Courage champions, 1991, in an impromptu celebration. Back row (left to right): Webb, Fallon, Robinson, Guscott, Ojomoh, Redman, Ubogu, Barnes, Haag, Hall, Dawe. Front row: Swift, Chilcott, de Glanville, Hill.

in the game to enhance their contribution to a flowing game, the last try of the day went to Stuart Barnes, so essential to the side's success. There was not even the presentation of a replica trophy on this occasion — perhaps the rugby authorities couldn't believe that Bath were to make sure of the title before the final Saturday in spite of the evidence of that two-point cushion.

While Bath were beating Gloucester in a friendly by 32-19 the following Saturday, the

The 1991 National Sevens winners also avoid drinking the ale: Simon Jones (coach) with Fallon, de Glanville, Lumsden, Ojomoh, Lewis, Haag, Adams, Callard (captain) and Sanders.

Pilkington Cup semi-finals were played. Orrell, in spite of their huge win over Northampton in the league, were tactically numbed by Wayne Shelford's men and lost 18-10 away. Harlequins beat Nottingham 22-18 in the other tie, and were also to win the Final.

The Courage League trophy presentation took place at Bath's final home game on 27 April when Saracens, useful spoilsports in the previous season, were outplayed on this occasion. Bath scored eight tries, including a first league try for Fallon, and two for a brilliant Guscott, in a 49-6 win.

Bath had finished three points ahead of their nearest challengers Wasps and that one-point home defeat by the London club no longer seemed so important.

Next day the first National Sevens Tournament was held at Bath. And by way of a surprise bonus, Bath won that too. They beat London Irish 28-6, Rosslyn Park 18-6, Harlequins 10-0, and Leicester in the Final, 24-10. Best of all from the club's point of view it was the work of the younger

players at the club, including one or two who had not had the best of luck in injury or selection for a season or two.

Those in the winning Bath squad were Jim Fallon, Phil de Glanville, Audley Lumsden, Steve Ojomoh, Iestyn Lewis, Martin Haag, Gareth Adams, and Jon Callard. As captain, Callard had a simple explanation for their unexpected success: "We picked those who really wanted to take part."

It was also a useful reminder, as another successful season came to its end, of the young talent knocking on the first-team door.

For two of Bath's outstanding international forwards, however, the season had not ended so happily. Indeed in each case there was inevitable speculation that they might not play again. David Egerton, the no.8, was injured against Rosslyn Park. His damaged shoulder would keep him out of the game until February 1992. John Hall, hurt at Gloucester in the preceding match, would miss the whole of the next season — a season which was to be remarkable even by Bath's recent standards.

Deduction: 1991-92

THIS was the season of the impudent match-winning drop goal at Twickenham which sealed another cup triumph for Bath. It was the season, too, of the conversion kick which over the months proved so vital in keeping Bath in the race for the league title.

And it was also the season in which Bath found themselves hobbled in that race by a knot they had tied for themselves. How the players overcame the handicaps unexpectedly placed upon them and claimed a double reward is the story of the dramatic season of 1991-92.

In a wider world of rugby, it was the season of the World Cup in the home countries and in France, which claimed Webb, Guscott, Hill, Cronin and Redman from Bath.

The absence of Guscott in particular and a collarbone injury for Jon Bamsey who had played in eight league games the previous season, meant that the promising Phil de Glanville had another younger partner for the opening game at home to Pontypool. He was Iestyn Lewis, nephew of a former Bath scrum-half, Steve Lewis, and another from the useful local nursery of Bath University. His opportunist try, plus 16 points from the reserve fly-half Duncan Willett in kicks at goal, gave a Bath side shorn of nine or ten regulars a 28-12 win.

There was encouragement too in the form of Audley Lumsden who struck up a lively link with Fallon, each scoring a try. And in the inevitable absence of Egerton and Hall there was a welcome first appearance of Bath's best-known close-season acquisition, Ben Clarke, the Saracens no.8, who like Callard, had studied agriculture at neighbouring Cirencester. That was Bath's claim on him as 'almost a local'.

After another home win in the rag doll game against Llanelli, 25-9, Bath, although still around half-strength, fielded their strongest side of the season so far against Cardiff at the Arms Park on 21 September 1991, in what proved to be their first win there since fixtures began in 1924. Such an historic victory deserves the names of the team that day:

Callard; Swift, de Glanville, Lewis, Fallon, Barnes, Sanders, Chilcott, Dawe, Crane, Haag, Redman, Robinson, Clarke, Ojomoh.

The only try of the game from de Glanville,

seizing on a perfect grubber kick into the corner from Barnes.

But there was also a comic note to an incidental blow for Bath that day. In spite of the win, Gareth Chilcott, back in the dressing-room after the game was grumbling about the fall-off in scrummaging power in the last 20 minutes. Nigel Redman broke in to say he hadn't thought they'd done badly considering they were by then down to seven men in the pack.

"What're you talkin' about, seven?" snorted Gareth. Then, as Kevin Coughlan reported in the *Bristol Evening Post*, it dawned on Chilcott's teammates that he hadn't been aware of the dismissal of the eighth forward. "And him a World Cup TV commentator!" added an unnamed colleague.

But if the joke was briefly on the doughty Chilcott, it was no joke for Bath. The missing forward was Ben Clarke, dismissed for stamping which brought him a 60-day suspension.

There was, though, the first of a handful of rare first-team games for David Trick against welcome visitors, Cork Constitution. The weather, wet and gusting, was against good rugby. Lewis and Ojomoh scored tries in a 13-3 Bath win. But yet again injury marred the day. Adedayo Adebayo went off with a serious knee injury, so ending his season after only 44 minutes of his first appearance of 1991-92.

But Callard had also taken a knock, Lumsden had gone to Oxford University, and as the divisional games were again being played, Bath used the little-known Laurie Heatherley at full-back in wins over Richmond, London Scottish, Plymouth Albion, and Neath (a second successive victory for Bath at The Gnoll, incidentally.) The New Zealander also played full-back at Kingsholm in a friendly which ended Bath's unbeaten start of eight games. The 14-12 win probably gave Gloucester as much — or more — satisfaction than their victory over Ireland in a World Cup warm-up game.

But back to Heatherley. In the circumstances, and with Callard still unfit, it was hardly surprising that when Jon Webb, back from World Cup duty, but unfit with flu, withdrew belatedly from the opening Courage League game the following week at Sunbury against newly-

Vintage Richard Hill . . .hurling a brisk pass to his stand-off in a 1991 league win over Rosslyn Park.

promoted London Irish, Jack Rowell didn't hesitate to persevere with Heatherley.

Another absentee that day was Jeremy Guscott (Iestyn Lewis deputising) still not back from World Cup duties. But he was not out of the headlines. On the contrary he was happily making them in an agreement with the *Sunday Mirror*. Would he or wouldn't he be switching to Rugby League? If we wanted to know we'd have to buy the *Sunday Mirror* on 10 November, we were told. (Some of us presumed — nay, hoped — that at least Jack Rowell, if not Geoff Cooke, knew the answer in advance. He did.)

In retrospect, it's probably true that a lot of people thought Guscott would go — otherwise why have the big production number? — and in the best traditions of national paper tactics, one or two rival papers went in for 'spoilers' suggesting Guscott might be on his way to Leeds (who had taken the All-Black John Gallagher none too successfully) or to Widnes (new home of Jonathan Davies) or an Australian club, North Sydney. There was even a report that he would stay with Union but move to Harlequins — an idea Guscott dismissed without benefit of the *Sunday Mirror*.

But Bath — and England — could relax. Guscott wasn't upping sticks. "My wife Jayne and

I are happy staying where we were born and bred and where we have our friends, and I have known in my heart this would be my decision for some time," said the man who first played for Bath at mini-rugby as a child.

And he explained that he had rejected offers from three Rugby League clubs in England and one in Australia, offers which could have made him a millionaire.

Nor was the *Sunday Mirror* the end of the razzmatazz.

Next day he met local press and television in his new role with British Gas as public relations man — or was he a sales executive? With him was his manager Maria Pedro. She was properly positive about the player she, rather than another professional game, had snapped up: "He's gorgeous, articulate, self-possessed without being arrogant and passionately interested in what he does. He can bring the female population into rugby."

And as well as British Gas South-Western he had also signed up with Storm, a London model agency. The local boy had indeed made good — and it made good reading and viewing, even if there were a few cynics who wondered why exclusive stories and glitzy media sessions were necessary to say nothing had changed. But the

The pack in charge as Robinson prepares to release the ball.

'Carry on Jerry' show did offer some clearly heartfelt thoughts from the man himself about the game he played and which millions, including a few thousand Bath supporters, now knew he wasn't abandoning.

"What it boiled down to was the game of Rugby Union against the game of Rugby League. I rightly felt that Union is a far better game than League. Rugby Union gives me what blood in your veins gives you, it gives me life. I am staying in union to play the game I love . . .until I decide to retire. I've been attached to Bath since I was seven and I've enjoyed every second of it. I didn't see myself playing for another Union club . . .I have another four or five years in me and I don't intend to waste them."

Guscott also made the point that it had taken Jonathan Davies two years to come to terms with his new code — "And it would probably have taken the same for me." And he admitted a sense of anticlimax after the World Cup. "Having played on a world stage, playing in front of a few thousand people just doesn't feel the same." But he was back in training for Bath.

And Bath? Brian Ashton, the backs' coach, was delighted with the news (and, yes, Jack Rowell had let him in on the *Sunday Mirror's* 'secret').

For the wider local public, who might still be a trifle baffled, the *Bath Evening Chronicle* offered some help in an editorial. Admitting some puzzlement at the apparent potency of the player's 'marketing worth' it stressed that the simple point for any Bath supporter was that Guscott 'has not been lured away to that strange northern game with not enough players on the pitch'.

As for the true fans, Glen Leat, one of the club fanzine's founders, probably summed it up: "I'm pleased but surprised because I thought Jerry had done everything he could possibly do in Rugby Union . . .but if Jerry ever does go it won't be the end of the world because Bath have great strength in depth."

Coincidentally, that particular Bath 'strength' was to be unexpectedly punished after the opening Courage League game the following Saturday.

In advance, special attention that day was focussed on the London Irish winger Simon Geoghegan, Ireland's exciting World Cup winger, and Jim Fallon, whose early-season performances for Bath had confirmed the high hopes entertained after his five league games in the second half of the previous season. At Sunbury, too, Fallon, himself the son of a former London Irish centre and Oxford Blue, Terry Fallon, made his mark. His burst in a switch move gave Heatherley the chance to score and put Bath 7-6 in front midway

Catch! Andy Reed in one of his early games for Bath, against Plymouth Albion, one of his former clubs, in 1991.

through the first half. Even so, the Irish were ahead at half-time 18-13, including a try by the international centre David Curtis, and Bath knew they were in a scrap.

In the second half, a Barnes break let Fallon in to put Swift over for a try by the posts. The Irish hit back with another penalty to stay within a point before Barnes, de Glanville and Swift sent Fallon in for another try.

But in spite of Bath's four tries to one, the Irish fought to the end in hope of a converted try that would have given them a famous First Division victory. But the 5,000 crowd had great entertainment — and Bath a fright.

Bath also had two vital points — or so they thought. But next day highlights from the game — including Heatherley's try — were shown on BBC2's *Rugby Special* . . .

But before consequential sparks flew so unexpectedly from the Sunbury encounter, Bath had another date — two weeks before the University match — at home to Oxford with the students pushing a Bath side with four internationals hard in a 19-3 Bath victory, Ben Clarke scoring a try on his return from suspension. But Bath, intent on the following week's Pilkington Cup opener against Nottingham, also kept their

attacking ploys under wraps in case of spies from Beeston. It was also, as it happened, the last game another World Cup man, Scotland's Damian Cronin, was to play for Bath: he was bound for London Scottish.

A name missing from the Oxford side at the Varsity Match, incidentally, was Audley Lumsden. As if one serious injury hadn't been enough, he broke his right ankle in what — for him and his Oxford teammates — was a gratuitous November sevens tournament in Dubai.

There was also a brief flare-up of the cat-fight between Bath and Bristol officials — now almost an annual event — with Bath saying they would be playing the Italian side Treviso at the Rec rather than Bristol in the scheduled end-of-season game at the Memorial Ground. Bath secretary Clive Howard, recalling that Bristol had called off their visit to Bath for a friendly last season because of a rearranged league match, said: "It's Bristol's turn to come to us."

But in truth it was simply recognition that the wider game and its attractions were changing — for Bath, if not yet for Bristol. (As it turned out, Bristol couldn't have fulfilled the fixture anyway — a rearranged league game was played that day instead.)

Something rather more serious, however, now broke over Bath's heads. There had been a reference on BBC *Rugby Special's* TV highlights of the London Irish match of Heatherley being 'on holiday' from New Zealand. And some upright citizen (or rather, armchair viewer) had a question. Who was this Heatherley Bath had sneaked in among their try-scorers?

The RFU Senior Clubs executive announced through its secretary, Peter Jackson, that it had received a complaint from an individual 'not from the West Country' which led it to inquire about the registration of Heatherley. Bath had admitted an administrative error in not registering him as required under the rules of the Courage League and had been duly docked a point.

Club secretary Clive Howard, complaining that the club had been given no advance notice or the opportunity of a hearing, and saying Bath would appeal, pointed out: "It's not as if we tried to sneak David Campese into our side without anyone knowing."

But Peter Jackson was firm and, up to a point, revealing. "Someone noticed this while watching the game on TV and informed us," he said. "The feeling was that we somehow had to make clubs responsible for registration and that this would smarten them up. I suppose it is unfortunate that this should happen to a club like Bath. There is a distinction between an unregistered player and an ineligible one. Had we been dealing with ineligibility, the situation would have been much more serious."

There were red faces among Bath committee men over the simple clerical cock-up and team secretary Richard Seaman owned up to the error: "If we had realised he wasn't registered, we wouldn't have played him against London Irish."

But although the innocent Heatherley had been a genuine playing member of the club since the start of the previous season rather than someone imported at short notice, and wasn't a first-team regular, Bath's appeal was inevitably rejected. It was clear that in future clubs would do well to register everyone on their playing staffs for the Courage League — in case of emergency.

As for the players Andy Robinson, club captain, who attended the appeal hearing, was bold in his determination whatever he may have said in private: "We will just have to win the league title with 23 points instead of 24."

Other clubs, including Harlequins, pleaded for Bath. And Sammy Southern, captain of Orrell, rivals for the league title and, like Harlequins, major actors in the season's events, spoke for most senior clubs perhaps when he remarked: "If we or anybody else win the league by one point and

Bath have a better points difference then we will not feel true champions."

The docking of a point at so early a stage of the season seemed, as indeed it was, a severe handicap to Bath, and it was to colour the rest of the season for all the Courage Division One title contenders.

Perhaps the most pertinent comment on the circumstances of the complaint came later in the *Rothmans Rugby Union Yearbook 1992-3*. Noting Bath's secretarial error in not registering 'a fourth-choice full-back' the writer (presumably editor Stephen Jones) remarked that the informer 'lacked the backbone to reveal his identity'.

Bath's players had other things on their mind beside League points, won or docked: the Pilkington Cup third-round tie against Nottingham took place at the Rec 48 hours after the deduction of the point.

Whether it was the nursing of the ploys against Oxford University now paying off, or simply the players showing their morale was undented by the Heatherley affair, they turned on one of their more classic performances against unfortunate Nottingham.

The Midlanders, without international forwards Chris Gray and Gary Rees, and with Jon Webb's rival Simon Hodgkinson switched to fly-half, had another late withdrawal — the flanker Danny Bourne, topically enough, being ruled ineligible.

But even a full-strength Nottingham would have had difficulty in containing Bath on that day, as they ran in ten tries, two each to Fallon and Guscott (like Webb, making his first appearance since the World Cup), and one each to Barnes, Swift, Ojomoh, Webb, Ubogu, and de Glanville. Webb converted six.

At least four of the six tries came from planned and rehearsed moves carried out to perfection in a cup-tie.

Nevertheless there was also an incident to check the enthusiasm when, with Bath 40-0 ahead, play was halted for nearly quarter-of-an-hour for what appeared to be a serious injury to the Nottingham prop Tony Shephard, who was left immobile after a maul which followed a high kick from Hodgkinson.

The referee, Steve Griffiths, sent the teams to the dressing-rooms to keep warm and Dr Jonathan Webb and another doctor ensured Shephard was kept immobile until an ambulance arrived on the pitch to take him to hospital.

Shephard had ignored medical advice the previous year after surgery on his neck not to play again. Now it seemed his career was over. But happily he was able to travel home with his teammates after the game. Soon after the game

Adebayo in full cry against Gloucester's Derek Morgan.

resumed Hodgkinson too left the field with back trouble.

Watching the game had been the new England coach, Harlequins' Dick Best who could hardly complain about the running talents of the Bath XV. (His England 'B' colleague, one Jack Rowell, presumably knew something about them already, but even he, often taciturn, was expansive enough afterwards to talk of 'breathtaking' passages of attacking play.)

It emerged later that one inspiration for some of Bath's new back moves had been Stuart Barnes's Barbarians trip in Scotland where he and the South African full-back Andre Joubert had worked out various moves whose key seemed to be to strike the sparks on the gain line rather than ten yards behind it. Barnes was even bold enough to say he rated the current three-quarter line as the most effective in his seven years with Bath.

But if the Nottingham display had been something of a Lord Mayor's Show, the Courage League game at home to Northampton the following week, the first Saturday in December, was the inevitable dustcart.

Early problems in the front row, with Baldwin, Olver and Pearce joining the Bath trio of Chilcott, Dawe, and Ubogu in an irritating contest of wills,

were never satisfactorily resolved by referee Chris Rees. Pulling down, wheeling and other misdemeanours may have entertained the sextet involved: they were mightily boring for the spectator. Nor were the line-outs much happier, although Bath largely nullified the height of Martin Bayfield.

Fittingly, penalties decided a messy game. Jon Webb kicked five goals from six attempts, John Steele, by contrast, kicking only one from five shots at goal, but adding a dropped-goal in Bath's 15-6 win. Bath had taken vital league points but Northampton, if not the spectators, must have been satisfied at the prospect of meeting Bath at Franklins Gardens in the next round of the Pilkington Cup.

But the Saturday after the tetchy league win over Northampton, Bath were at Orrell, scene of some tough games in recent seasons, in one of the few league fixtures which survived freezing weather. From a tap penalty in his own 22, Jon Webb gave Swift the chance of a break, and when Ojomoh won the ensuing line-out, good work by Clarke and Robinson enabled Barnes and Dawe (acting as centre) to send Swift over on the right for a try, Webb converting to give Bath an early 6-0 lead.

Kimmins slowly controlled the line-out, and

A hitch in time for Chilcott.

Victor Ubogu as the Rec crowd loves him – breaking against Llanelli.

Bath's pack which had been the stronger in the scrummaging, lost its hold when Chilcott had to leave the field after the first half-hour, with a damaged shoulder, after Orrell collapsed a scrum. He was replaced by Mark Crane with Ubogu switching to loose head. But Bath never again held forward supremacy and were increasingly pinned in their own patch. Heslop eluded Webb to score a try, adding to Strett's first-half penalty.

But despite the Orrell pressure, it still looked as if Bath might steal the game, when Barnes's hoisted kick and the subsequent ruck gave the stand-off a neat dropped-goal. At last, as the spectators froze with cold and anticipation of another Orrell disappointment, Strett warmed to his responsibilities and popped over a winning dropped-goal with five minutes left. Neither a Guscott break nor a long-range penalty attempt by Barnes could save Bath. They had been beaten by a better side on the day and had conceded both points, adding to the famous deduction.

For Orrell, it was also a famous victory which consolidated them as contenders for the Courage title and consolation, no doubt, for Sammy (expletives undeleted) Southern whose colourful encouragement of his team in the build-up to the game was later to be seen by an enthralled — or appalled — public in a BBC TV documentary.

Meanwhile, back at the Rec, Bristol were the visitors in the third successive week of league fixtures. Yet again Bristol believed they had a good chance of succeeding with a weaker Bath pack and the Orrell defeat provided psychological benefits to add to Bristol's so far unbeaten league season.

Alas for Bristol optimism. One of their wisest supporters, John Mason, wrote in the *Daily Telegraph*:

"What is this magic formula that Bath possess? How is it that in the absence of four first-choice forwards they could still reduce a capable Bristol pack to the edge of frustrating impotence? In short, a ferret would be envious of Robinson."

But, as Mason acknowledged, Barnes, too, and Webb, were the other members of a Bath trio whose tactical nous (to use a good North country word) was in a different league from Bristol's in muddy conditions which didn't encourage open play. In particular the tactical kicking of the two Bath backs was in cruel contrast to that of Bristol's fly-half David Thomas and his young partner Kitchen.

Unlike Bath's experienced tacticians, Bristol invariably chose the wrong option and were punished, the 9-4 final score scarcely reflecting the hold Bath had on the game, Bristol's late consolation try for skipper Derek Eves being too

Yet another try for Swift, this time against Pontypool.

late to offset Webb's two penalties and a Guscott dropped-goal. Bath's front five that day deserve a mention — Mallett, Atkins, Lee, Haag, and McCoy who, like Atkins, made a league debut.

Two of the missing Bath forwards, Dawe and Redman, had been on holiday, skiing in the French Alps, and were properly thrust in as the only first-teamers (more shades of the diminishing importance of such fixtures) in a game at Swansea three days after Christmas. Having survived the icy slopes, Dawe was taken off in the first half at St Helen's, with ligament trouble. Bath, with Heatherley again at full-back, managed tries from Bamsey, Book, and McCoy in their 48-19 defeat by the Welshmen. Dawe would be fit again for the following Saturday's vital league game.

Bath's supporters, never mind the players, drew a deep, deep breath as their side entered 1992 with three points already lost, only four league games played, plus Leicester, Wasps, Gloucester yet to come — and first, Harlequins.

League Title: 1991-92

OF ALL the kicks at goal Jon Webb attempted for Bath and England that season, there were few rivals for the vital pot at Harlequins' posts in injury-time during the dramatic, rugged, bitter game at The Stoop on 4 January 1992.

The old morgue-like ground was jammed with around 7,000 spectators for the clash — the press box alone had seen nothing like it before — between teams coached by Dick Best, of England, and Jack Rowell, of England 'B', and including around a score of international players past, present, and future.

One World Cup star was missing — Jeremy Guscott, modelling in the United States. "What can you say?" mused Rowell. "There's a lot of money involved and it's part of his income. In an amateur game you can't tell people how to make a living. If the World Cup makes stars of these players . . ." His place was taken by Jon Bamsey. Only eight of the Harlequins team that day would be in the second tense meeting between the two later that season. Bath, by contrast, fielded 14 players who would also feature in the second game. Teams:

Harlequins: Pears; Wedderburn, Carling, Halliday, Thompson, Bray, Glenister, Leonard, Moore, Mullins, Russell, Coker, Skinner, Langhorn, Winterbottom.

Bath: Webb; Swift, de Glanville, Bamsey, Fallon, Barnes, Hill, Chilcott, Dawe, Ubogu, Haag, Redman, Robinson, Clarke, Ojomoh.

Harlequins caught Bath cold at the start and virtually froze them out of the first half. From a scrum in the opening minutes, Mickey Skinner bounced his way past Robinson to send Will Carling in for a try, converted by Pears. Soon afterwards Dawe, still intent on his seasonal battle with Brian Moore, was penalised for elbowing the England hooker, and Pears made it 9-0.

Three times Harlequins went over the line in a battering 15 minutes of the Bath 22. Each time referee David Leslie said they had not touched down. But he did award a try when they didn't — a penalty-try when a scrum collapsed on the Bath line. Again Pears converted, and then added another penalty. Bath were 18-0 down, and were being thoroughly outplayed.

But just before Pears's penalty late in the first half, Harlequins had their momentum disrupted for the first time by an injury to the former Bath favourite, Simon Halliday. He was hit in the face by a flying boot (from a Harlequins foot, as TV pictures would show, and not from a vengeful Bath player as some mischievous souls first suggested), and had to be replaced.

Almost on half-time Bath, too, were awarded a penalty try, converted by Webb, on one of their rare excursions upfield, and suddenly there was the glimmer of hope for the bruised Bath bodies at the interval.

So it proved, with Harlequins in turn beginning to lose their earlier confidence as Webb added first one and then a second penalty. With the score at 18-12 and half an hour to go, Harlequins did themselves a second bad turn. This time the Australian lock Troy Coker was sent off for punching or kicking — it wasn't clear — and the Bath pack clawed their way back into contention against the seven men.

Then in the closing moments with only injury-time left, Bath opted to run a penalty near the home line. Haag and Ubogu were stopped but the ball came back to Barnes who sent de Glanville over in the inches of space that were available. (For his effort, the Bath centre was gratuitously punched — it was that sort of game.)

Thus it was that Jon Webb, operating at Southmead Hospital, Bristol, that morning, and not having had the happiest of days on the pitch, had a touchline conversion to seal the great fight-back. "I certainly couldn't look," admitted Philip de Glanville later. Webb looked, and kicked, and levelled the scores.

Bath had saved the day and Harlequins, the likely winners for the first time in a league game with Bath when they led 18-0, had somehow ended up sharing the points. It had hardly been a game of flow and elegance, rather of bad temper, skulduggery, and two penalty-tries. But the lifeline provided by Dr Webb with his match-saving stitch-in-time was crucial to Bath.

Without it, they would have been five points adrift. With it they were four points down — and titles could be won with that record.

But the next Saturday they had another big task on their hands — against the current league leaders, Leicester, at the Rec, who had so shocked Bath by dumping them from the cup there a year earlier. Guscott was back from his catwalk; Iestyn Lewis partnered him in de Glanville's absence through injury.

On the day it was one of Bath's more breathtaking performances, as different from the grim game and circumstances at The Stoop as might be imagined. As Steve Bale reported in *The Independent* it was 'a breathtaking riposte' to recent misfortunes.

"Bath at bay can be a magnificent spectacle."

The pack overwhelmed a Leicester eight lacking lock Martin Johnson and flanker Neil Back, and when Andy Robinson went off injured 20 minutes into the game, John Mallett came on with Ubogu switching to the back row as a free spirit.

In the first quarter Swift (two) and Fallon scored tries but there were still a few in the crowd who wondered if Leicester might mount the kind of comeback Bath had managed the previous week. But tries by Fallon and Mallett soon after half-time meant Leicester were 27-3 down after 47 minutes. Guscott did not score, but had one of his best games for the club. ("One of the finest Bath performances I can remember," he said later.) Perhaps he was celebrating his freedom from the shadow of Rugby League.

In all Bath scored seven tries, five to the wingmen including a hat-trick for Swift, and one to Lewis. It was a day of sweeping Bath moves too when Fallon's body strength and his ability to break tackles (ask Steve Hackney) was never more evident in contrast to the more elusive skills of Swift on the other wing. By contrast with the Bath master of ceremonies, Stuart Barnes, Gerry Ainscough at stand-off for Leicester had an unhappy time (perhaps he was yearning for the Orrell pack) for his new club, and Rory Underwood had nary a chance.

Fallon forces his way over to score against Leicester in a 37-6 home league win in 1992.

Chilcott (he's somewhere there) joins the women of the club, 1992.

Another contributor to a game which showed that league rugby need not be a tale from Grimm was the referee Fred Howard, who had so often figured in major Bath matches. On this day he kept the game moving with his usual good sense and spirit which made his demotion in the international lists all the more perplexing to players and spectators.

Bath then had given notice that they were back in the title hunt, even though they were in fourth slot, now above Leicester and Wasps on points scored, but still behind Northampton, Gloucester, and new leaders Orrell. (A few eyebrows had been raised, incidentally, at the less than full-strength side Harlequins had fielded in their defeat at Northampton the same day. It almost looked as if they had given up hope of the league title themselves.)

But now it was back to cup action, a fortnight later, at Northampton who had run them close at the Rec in the league, and had Wayne Shelford back in their pack to boost the hopes of the home crowd. And again it was a game full of drama and tension.

This time referee Fred Howard made two vital decisions, either side of half-time, which probably affected the outcome. First, with Northampton 6-3 ahead on penalties just on half-time he awarded a further penalty to the home side on Bath's 22 only to reverse the decision on the intervention of the touch judge because of foul play.

Early in the second half Bath were awarded a long-distance penalty. As Webb looked as if he was going to aim for touch, Barnes took the ball, placed it quickly and put it over from nearly 50 metres out: 6-6. Foolishly, Northampton skipper and hooker John Olver argued that the kick had been taken from the wrong spot. Fred Howard thus awarded Bath another penalty from the halfway line. Barnes kicked the goal again: 6-9.

At last Bath began to exert some control, as Northampton for all the line-out skills of Bayfield and power in the loose of Shelford, made little of their possession. Steele equalised with another penalty, and only a fine recovering tackle by Fallon on the home centre MacNaughton after a Barnes pass had been intercepted saved a winning score.

Then came extra-time — and the game's only try. Bath had lost Ubogu late in the second half, and Richard Hill in the first spell of extra-time.

But almost immediately Barnes fed Guscott whose long pass sent Fallon on a 40-metre dash to the corner in all his considerable power. He scored, the conversion was missed. But although Steele missed a kickable penalty the try was enough to give Bath the tie, 13-9, in a game in which they finished the stronger — and none stronger than Jim Fallon.

Two weeks later and it was the fifth round of the cup, again away, this time to Bristol (the draw had made up for the cancelled friendly, no doubt). Bath lacked Hill, for whom Steve Knight deputised. It was a dull shapeless affair by comparison with previous rounds with the two packs in constant disarray.

Bath led 12-6 at half-time. Webb kicked a penalty and converted an opportunist score from de Glanville after a Bath attack seemed to have fizzled out. But it was another of Barnes's here's-the-ball-and-there's-the-posts I'll-have-a-go penalty kicks that caught the imagination. He kicked it from far out on the left to emphasise Bath's lead. In the second half, for all Bristol's attempts (with different half-backs from the league meeting between the clubs) at running, Bath's defence, with Clarke again emerging as a force in Bath's back row, was solid. Another Barnes penalty sealed the win at 15-6.

At least, thanks to the World Cup, there was no pause in the excitement for the fans in this busy season. For Bath, the following Saturday saw league action, at home to Gloucester, who were also to be their opponents in the semi-final of the Pilkington Cup. Bath brought David Egerton back to big-game action on the flank in place of Steve Ojomoh. The Kingsholm side, second in the table, unbeaten, and with a game in hand on Bath, Northampton, and Orrell, lacked their skipper, the Scottish flanker Ian Smith.

Before the game the big crowd held a minute's silence to mark the recent deaths of two great servants at Kingsholm — Terry Tandy, secretary, and Ray Long, former team secretary — and of Bertie Buse, the old Somerset cricketer ("He could make unentertaining play hugely entertaining," wrote David Foot) and popular son of the city, who played full-back for Bath in the 1930s.

It was another remarkable match. Gloucester did little wrong. It was just that Bath outpaced them to score four tries to one. Fly-half Neil Matthews had dropped an early goal for the visitors and for much of the first half they had Bath under constant pressure. But it was Bath who scored the first try with Hill and Webb enabling Swift to score with quick ball from a five-metre scrum. Then five players handled before a quick flick pass from Guscott sent Fallon hurtling almost to the line — when he was brought down de Glanville was on hand to pick up and score. Bath, no doubt to Gloucester's surprise, were 11-3 ahead with Gloucester having had most of the play.

Again, in the second half, when Gloucester attacked and Guscott put in a relieving kick, Hannaford's counter-clearance was charged down by Barnes who scored under the posts, and converted, giving Bath a 17-3 lead early in the half. Then Swift broke brilliantly after another clearance kick and fed Guscott for another converted try. Barnes added two penalties to one he had kicked in the first half, giving him 17 points in the game, while England's soon-to-be record-breaking goal-kicker Webb had a rest.

Hannaford scored a deserved late try for Gloucester which was converted, and Bath had won 29-9, ending their visitors' unbeaten league record. Gloucester had missed Ian Smith (in his absence Andy Robinson scavenged comprehensively), but they hadn't played badly. They were simply victims of Bath's brilliantly ruthless finishing. Robert Armstrong wrote in *The Guardian*:

"Poor Gloucester were rather like a solid pillar of the community meeting with a nasty accident on a day outing."

But could Bath win the league, never mind the cup semi-final? They were still two points behind Orrell and one behind Northampton and all had played seven games. The cynics meanwhile noticed an unexpected winning margin, 16-0, by Bristol at home to Harlequins.

The old cliché had soccer managers consoling themselves on being knocked out of the cup by saying they could now concentrate on the league. Harlequins had turned the old cliché on its head: they were simply concentrating on the cup.

Meanwhile in the sadly devalued, but still enjoyable, encounters between clubs from either side of the Severn Bridge, Bath had a Friday game against Newbridge. Bath fielded many of their youngsters in the 50-7 win of 11 tries. But the game is chiefly to be remembered, perhaps, as the last appearance for Bath of the sturdy reserve, Laurie Heatherley, who was returning to New Zealand. That night he played in the centre but didn't score. But he will live on in Bath's rugby history as the player who, through no fault of his own, became best-known for his only league appearance for the club.

Oddly, with Callard injured as well as Webb, Bath again had to improvise at full-back for the important league game (but weren't they all?) at Wasps, centre Jon Bamsey taking over.

Bath led 17-3 at half-time in a comparatively run-of-the-mill encounter, with Wasps failing to fire even in the line-outs where Haag and Redman

Fallon surges through Wasps' tackles.

had the edge over O'Leary and White, and Robinson held the best cards in the loose. Bath's first try, from quick thinking by Richard Hill, was his first in the league since the home defeat by Wasps the previous year. Fallon, Clarke, and Swift were the other try-scorers, Graham Childs replying for Wasps. Again in their contrasting ways, Fallon and Swift had proved as effective a pair of finishers as any in the top division.

Meanwhile, Gloucester had lost their title chance, beaten 10-17 at home by Northampton, but Orrell were still two points clear of Bath, with games against Harlequins and Wasps to come.

The next Saturday Bath won 32-0 at Rugby, going 12 points up in as many minutes, after two Barnes penalties and a grateful de Glanville had collected Richard Pell's attempted dropped-goal in his arms and run 85 metres for a converted try. (But de Glanville was injured in scoring and was replaced by Steve Knight.) Redman, Swift, Fallon, and Robinson also scored tries.

The win put Bath back on top of the division, but Orrell who had a blank day, and Northampton only a point behind, each had a game in hand. Bath's points differential was healthily ahead of their rivals — 123.

Now, in the last of this further clutch of three successive league Saturdays came Nottingham to the Rec, fielding only six of the side whacked 52-0 in the third round of the cup and bravely fighting against relegation. Watching was Bath MP and Tory party chairman Chris Patten, just days before the General Election in which he was to lose his seat. (Trivia-hunters should note that this may have been the only time a future governor of Hong Kong has watched a Courage League game at the Rec. But I suppose historians would point out that he didn't know he was to be governor at the time . . .)

Bath were without Guscott and de Glanville in the centre, Bamsey and Lewis deputising, and although Bath scored three tries (Hill, Egerton and Robinson) to none, penalty-goals from fly-half Guy Gregory twice cut the deficit to only four points in the last quarter. Robinson's converted try in injury-time gave Bath their 25-15 win, which flattered them and was bleak reward for Nottingham, unrecognisable as the club thrashed by Bath in the cup.

The result added to any apprehensions Bath supporters had about the Pilkington cup semi-final at Kingsholm, and cheered the folk of Gloucester. Importantly for Bath, though, their first-choice centres were back. Teams:

And sometimes they stopped him: Fallon is tackled in the cup win against Gloucester, 1992.

Gloucester: T.Smith; Perrins, Cummins, Caskie, Morris, Matthews, Hannaford, Jones, Dunn, Phillips, Scrivens, Sims, Ashmead, Masters, I.Smith.
Bath: Webb; Swift, de Glanville, Guscott, Fallon, Barnes, Hill, Chilcott, Dawe, Ubogu, Haag, Redman, Robinson, Clarke, Egerton.

The final score, 27-18 to Bath, gives little idea for posterity of the closeness of the contest. Gloucester's pack sucked their opposite numbers into a constant match of ruck and maul, drawing reward from the too-frequent penalties conceded by the Bath eight. When Bath did give their backs a chance in the first half, Barnes, Webb, and de Glanville combined beautifully with Swift coming round outside to enable Guscott to send Fallon striding in for a fine try converted by Barnes, levelling the scores 9-9. By full-time the score was 15-all. For Gloucester Tim Smith had kicked three penalties and he and Neil Matthews each dropped a goal; Barnes also added three penalties.

In extra-time another Tim Smith penalty had given Gloucester the lead and even though they had lost key players in Cummins and Sims through injury (the latter after a saving tackle by Barnes) the Kingsholm courtiers were prepar-

ing to crown their team as conquerors. It was not to be.

With barely four minutes of extra-time remaining, and Bath three points down good work by the Bath pack, with Egerton and Robinson to the fore, gave Hill the chance to feed Barnes. His pass to Guscott saw the centre throw a long pass immediately to Fallon. And outside Fallon was the remarkable Swift, far from his own wing, to hurtle home in what Stephen Jones in the *Sunday Times* next day called 'one of the movements of the season.'

But there was more to come. No sooner had Barnes converted, 21-18, and Neil Matthews in hope of quick reprisal had chipped ahead, than Guscott fielded his kick, soared down the left touchline to put Fallon in once more for another superb try, with Barnes again converting handsomely: 27-18.

No wonder that even before the final whistle ended extra-time, taking Bath to Twickenham, Gloucester's players looked as shattered as their supporters were shocked: they must think there is no justice in the world, sighed the *Gloucester Citizen* on the Monday. The outstanding Dave Sims admitted: "I feel thoroughly depressed. We all desperately wanted to get to Twickenham."

Determination from Graham Dawe.

Afterwards, the critics in crowd and press box wondered why Bath had turned on such brilliance so sparingly and so late, albeit devastatingly. But that gave small credit to Gloucester whose limited tactic had all but succeeded against a Bath pack no longer so dominant as some of its predecessors. Yet Bath's brilliance behind the pack on occasion this season had recalled the heyday of an earlier back line. Now, though, the sheer glorious gall of some of the inventiveness was almost impossible to defend against — ask Nottingham in cup, and Leicester in league, who had encountered similar ploys scything through their defences.

Stephen Jones again: "Bath have the ability, when they need to, to rise to a different planet."

No wonder he hailed them as the best club team British rugby has seen. And he's a Welshman.

One other point from the game was the impact, evident all season but now seen by a wider audience, of the men outside Bath's inventive midfield: in particular Fallon's strength as a foil to the lighter, fleeter Swift.

Together they were as telling a pair of club wingmen as any in the country: by contrast the Underwoods were starved of the ball in their semifinal at Harlequins, where the talented Gerry Ainscough had another unhappy game for Leicester at fly-half. Harlequins failed to add to their 15-3 half-time lead, and Liley's converted try kept the result uncertain for much of the second half with Harlequins short of their best form.

But the Final many in the game had hoped for — with each set of supporters wanting the other club at last to get their comeuppance — was in sight.

Still, Bath had now to resume the league chase, this time at Rosslyn Park. And, as against Nottingham, Bath found that threat of relegation put heart into their opponents and a scare into the travelling Bath supporters.

Again, too, Bath raced into an early lead, with a Barnes dropped-goal after 90 seconds, followed by a brilliant move with Hill and Barnes feeding Lewis (in for Guscott) whose clever inside pass to Fallon deceived the defence for the winger to score and Barnes to convert. Two penalties meant that Bath were 15-0 ahead. Then they seemed to lose interest or thought the game was won, and even though Barnes struck another penalty, Park hit back with two tries to close 13-18 before Barnes kicked his last penalty after marshalling his forces for another attack. Bath, outscored by two tries to one, had been fortunate to escape more punishment for their comparative nonchalance and their 21-13 win doomed brave Park, president Andy Ripley and all, to relegation.

How careless Bath had nearly been was at once emphasised by the other results that afternoon.

The biggest cheer of the day came in the Bath dressing-room when they were told the other results. Wasps, who had lost four successive league games, had beaten Orrell with the last kick of the match; Nottingham had thwarted Northampton 18-9.

Poor Orrell. They had only to keep on winning to take the title.

They were leading 9-0 at Sudbury, and in spite of a Wasps' fight-back that gave them a 10-9 advantage, Martin Strett kicked a penalty three minutes from time to give Orrell a 12-10 lead and a hand on the trophy. Then he missed an even easier one, and Orrell's tactical nous deserted them in the final minute as Fran Clough, once an Orrell player, sent Wasps downfield once more.

Although Orrell cleared the ball, not without a tangle or two, and won the ensuing line-out, poor Dewi Morris failed to find touch with his clearance kick. There, one of rugby's forgotten former stars, Huw Davies, in for the French-domiciled Rob Andrew at stand-off, took aim and dropped a winning goal from 45 metres: 13-12. The lads from Lancashire fell to their knees in dismay.

Now Orrell were two points behind Bath, who topped the table, but Orrell had a game in hand, against Harlequins. But if Bath beat Saracens a fortnight hence at the Rec their great differential of points scored would be decisive, regardless of the deducted point.

Steve Bale in *The Independent* assessed the situation acurately: "The head gives Orrell a residual chance of the Courage Clubs' Championship but the heart says it has gone, shattered by their fallibility whenever a prize stands glittering before them."

There was one other shock result that same Saturday. Nottingham, elated by beating title hopefuls Northampton, were dismayed that Harlequins had gone under 29-20 at Rugby, Nottingham's main competitors for relegation.

But at least the Londoners put up a proper fight — and fielded a full side — in the key Easter weekend league game at home to Orrell. Martin Strett's fallible kicking did his side few favours in a game they largely dominated but won only 10-7, with Halliday's late try giving Orrell a brief scare.

(Sandwiched amid all the league excitement a Bath second string lost 23-31 at the Rec to Benetton Treviso, from Italy, in an enterprising fixture shorn of one of its other attractions: the hoped-for appearance of Michael Lynagh for the Italian side didn't materialise.)

Now all depended on the final league Saturday, with Orrell at home to Nottingham, hoping that Saracens, who had once before scuppered a title

Martin Haag making the catch against Benetton Treviso, one of Bath's many foreign opponents, in April 1992.

for Bath, might repeat the feat. Orrell, for their part, would need a massive win otherwise to overtake the Bath scoring advantage. It was not to be. They won 20-6, (Martin Strett missing seven out of nine shots at goal) and that was enough to make Nottingham the unluckiest relegated side in the First Division's short history.

As for Bath, was there for some perhaps a sense of anticlimax with Saracens not at their best and the home side therefore finding a win comfortably within their grasp, as they led 17-0 at half-time? That seemed a somewhat churlish view: and how much greater would have been the anticlimax for the Bath faithful if it had only needed Orrell to win to deny Bath the title?

On the day the former Saracens man Ben Clarke scored a try, and Jim Fallon, another of the successes of the season, added a try in what, the crowd was soon to discover, was his last appearance in Bath colours on the Rec. But that Barnes, playmaker for much of Bath's outstanding back moves throughout the season, should score two tries seemed especially fitting.

As for Saracens, their day was marred with the sending-off of flanker Justin Cassell for kicking at Andy Robinson. The Bath skipper claimed that it was partly his fault. "I was hanging on to him after the tackle and he tried to shake me off. It

was just a shame he caught me on the head," said Robinson.

(There was some applause as Cassell was dismissed by referee George Seddon. Criticism that this was unsporting was answered by a claim that some were showing support for referees imposing needed discipline. Robinson's appeal on Cassell's behalf helped save the Saracen's place on the England 'B' tour of New Zealand, to be coached by Jack Rowell, captained by Barnes, and for which Fallon, de Glanville, Dawe, Haag, Clarke, and Ojomoh had been selected.)

But back to the game itself. John Buckton, one of Saracens' outstanding players for some seasons, fittingly went over for a late try, to add to Ben Rudling's earlier penalties. Bath had won 32-12. The crowd stayed on at the end and Andy Robinson led his men on a lap of honour after the Courage trophy was presented in front of the main stand. This time the trophy was in the right place.

It was the club's third Courage title in four years, and in many ways the most remarkable. There had been the 'lost' point from the Heatherley registration which had dogged the players like some ancient incubus the season through. Then there was the one-point defeat at Orrell, and the draw at Harlequins. But that, given

Dewi Morris vainly attempts to prevent John Hall's try against Orrell in a 1992 league game, with Ben Clarke joining.

Physiotherapist Julie Bardner takes charge of an injured captain, Andy Robinson.

Ubogu leads the triumphant lap after Bath's 1992 Courage Championship win.

the one-time 18-0 Harlequins' lead was more a point claimed than another lost, thanks not least to Jon Webb's boot.

Even so, Orrell — the only victors over Bath in the league — had the title in their sights until that sad late lapse at Wasps which suddenly threw open the championship once more. If Orrell had won by virtue of that deducted point then Sammy Southern's early season reaction to that decision would have had extra bite. Perhaps the RFU, not to mention Courage, were spared embarrassment when the title was finally won and lost on the field.

There was, though, from many within the game, and from those who paid to watch, genuine

sympathy that Orrell's remarkable contribution to the top-class game had not been rewarded.

Elsewhere on that final league Saturday, two other sendings-off caught more attention than Cassell's dismissal. Mickey Skinner and lock Richard Langhorn were sent off for stamping in the same incident just before half-time at Kingsholm, where their side managed, nevertheless, what they had failed to do against lowly Rugby and win, beating Gloucester 21-18.

It was a severe blow to Harlequins, and a reminder to Bath, if one was needed, that although the league was won the Pilkington Cup Final was only seven days away.

'Double' and Quins: 1991-92

IT WAS the Final for which both sides had been hoping for years — a contest between clubs whose playing philosophies were about as far apart as could be. Yet each emphasised different strands of the game's famous amateur tradition, still surviving in spite of the money swilling around its great occasions.

For Bath, the club was all-important, and every league game, like every cup game, was there to be won and fought for — attractively if need be, doggedly if that was a way to win. Even the friendlies were games to be won not lost.

This was not a win-at-all-costs philosophy, merely a recognition that the supporters and the city and above all Jack Rowell and the tradition he had built deserved only the best efforts from the team that represented Bath. If that meant that playing for Bath, and all it represented, was more important than playing for something called the South and South-West in a Divisional Championship then so be it. And more than one player, to their own and probably their country's cost, had publicly suggested at one time or another that he considered playing for Bath a greater priority than selection for England (Palmer, Barnes and Hall, for example).

Yet none of this prevented the side from playing rugby as exciting as might be seen anywhere in the land — ask Leicester after Bath's performance against them in January: it was a myth to think that Harlequins were the contrasting and exclusive academy of running skills. Bath had them in plenty.

Rather, the difference in the two sides was their approach in the season. Harlequins, as I have suggested, seemed too soon and too often to have abandoned the trudge through the league once a point or two had slipped. Peter Winterbottom, their captain who never gave less than his best himself, insisted when the season began that the team's aim was to win league and cup double. By the time absenteeism had gnawed at such ambition, he admitted: "Unfortunately not all the boys seem to agree with me about the league."

The glamour of the cup Harlequins had won the previous season was all, topped only by representative calls. So it was possible for centre Will Carling, say, to play more games for England and the London Division a season than for his club, other than in cup games.

It was scarcely a policy the 'soft Southerners' could have got away with at Orrell, never mind Bath or Gloucester. (Orrell, indeed, would never forget Harlequins' now distant reference to them as 'a lay-by on the M6'.) Yet the extra irony was that most of the so-called southern softies were northerners as near as dammit — Brian Moore, Mickey Skinner, Peter Winterbottom, David Pears and even Carling, for all that he was born in Bradford-on-Avon in Wiltshire (his soldier father played briefly for Bath). No matter. They were all Harlequins now, running the ball from behind their lines, taking quick throws, quick tap penalties, winning excitingly. But sometimes not.

Too often in the past season in particular Harlequins had apparently allowed opponents off the hook in league games that might not have been vital for themselves but mattered much to rivals for the title or relegation. The circumstances of the defeats at Northampton and Bristol, and particularly at Rugby, won them no friends in the game — and certainly none at Brian Moore's old club, Nottingham.

So it was that the Bath-Harlequins Final brought together sides one of which believed all trophies were there to be striven for, and the other which cared only for the cup when the London Division (coached by their coach) or England didn't beckon their stars.

Even those supporters up and down the land who yearned for Bath's defeat on the big occasion may have found it hard to contemplate the fancy dans from The Stoop proving their point that playing for only half a season could reap another reward at Twickenham.

But there were players, as well as philosophies, in rivalry that day.

David Pears, once of Aspatria, preferred by the England selectors to Barnes as reserve fly-half for the World Cup and in that slot in the semi-final, was now switched to full-back instead of the unlucky Stuart Thresher, with Paul Challinor coming in at stand-off. Each had a fresh point to prove, perhaps, against Webb and Barnes.

Bath's back row, even without the long-absent John Hall, had Clarke and Robinson with similar extra motivation. And once their heads went down, only heaven (or hell?) or occasionally the referee knew what Moore and Dawe would be about.

In the centre, Simon Halliday — making a second farewell appearance on Cup Final day — with Carling offered a direct contrast to the subtleties of Guscott and the emerging skills of Philip de Glanville. On the wings Jim Fallon would be seen at Twickenham for the first time, Tony Swift perhaps for the last, in opposition to the free-running Everton Davis and Mike Wedderburn (Andrew Harriman was unfit).

Team selection at Harlequins had inevitably been complicated by the suspensions of Skinner and Langhorn (and the absence in Australia of Troy Coker as a candidate for the second row). But Neil Edwards, newly capped by Scotland, was fit. And coach Dick Best managed a master-stroke in persuading Paul Ackford, officially retired since the World Cup, and whose last competitive game was four months earlier for the Barbarians at Leicester. Mark Russell, Skinner's replacement, hadn't played for three months.

Bath had one or two selection problems, and some flu symptoms, but Guscott was fit after the shoulder injury which kept him out of the win over Saracens. David Egerton, with rib damage, conceded the role of blindside flanker to the burgeoning Steve Ojomoh. Like Harriman, Egerton was on the bench.

Teams: **Bath:** Webb; Swift, de Glanville, Guscott, Fallon, Barnes, Hill, Chilcott, Dawe, Ubogu, Haag, Redman, Robinson (captain), Clarke, Ojomoh.

Harlequins: Pears; Wedderburn, Halliday, Carling, Davis, Challinor, Luxton, Hobley, Moore, Mullins, Edwards, Ackford, Russell, Sheasby, Winterbottom (captain).

There were 17 capped players in the game and two more on the bench. (Bath's other replacements were Knight, Mallett, Lewis, Bamsey, and Atkins, Harlequins had Killick, Glenister, Thompson, Thresher, and Pratley.)

A capacity crowd of 62,000, the largest for the Pilkington Cup Final, saw Harlequins explode into the game, with only a superb tackle on Carling by Guscott preventing an early try. But Pears kicked a penalty, with only two minutes gone. Half an hour into the game when Bath might have thought they had withstood the brunt of the Harlequins' pressure, Pears kicked to the corner where Moore and Edwards combined at the line-out to set up a maul which put Winterbottom over for Pears to convert.

Although a Webb penalty kept Bath hopes alive, Pears kicked another just on half-time to give his side a 12-3 lead. Ackford, in harness with Edwards, was controlling the line-outs in magnificent fashion and Bath, crippled by lack of possession, also faced fierce Harlequins' tackling when they had the ball. The tension and the thrill of the combat was all that the pre-match anticipation had suggested. Free-flowing movements there were not; instead, great commitment and skill and tackling as each side pressed to find a gap in the other's defences.

Soon after the second half began, Webb kicked another penalty: 12-6, and the tension increased a notch or two. Fallon had gone near being thwarted by Halliday and Davis almost at the last, and as Bath came more into the game it was first Carling and then Wedderburn who put in saving tackles.

But from the subsequent play after Wedderburn's effort, Bath at last drew in the Quins' defence with a burst from Ojomoh. When the ball went wide de Glanville was there, as so often that season, to make just enough ground to beat the cover. He made it in the league match months before; now he had again brought his side back to near parity with Harlequins at a crucial time. Webb too, as before, stayed coolly precise for the conversion to level the scores, with scarcely ten minutes to go.

Once more Bath had defied all Harlequins' attempts to bury them, digging their way out to launch the counter-attack. Or, as Robert Armstrong described it in *The Guardian*, Bath had been 'like a bull terrier refusing to let go of an ankle'.

Now it was to be 20 minutes of extra-time with the players already clearly exhausted after the busiest season English rugby had known. (Paul Ackford, in his second first-class game in six months, affected to weep uncontrollably at the prospect.)

Guscott, foreshadowing the drama yet to come, went near with a dropped-goal attempt in the first period; Pears and fly-half Challinor twice each missed similar attempts. With Fred Howard eyeing his watch and both sets of players perhaps mentally prepared for a share of the cup, the final match-winning moment of wizardry was upon them.

Of all ironies it came when, for once, Bath and Nigel Redman won the ball at a shortened line-out. Hill fed Barnes who took a look at his tired three-quarters and another at the posts. From the Harlequins' ten-metre line he fired over a remarkable, impertinent, utterly Barnesian dropped goal. It was the final kick of a remarkable season, and it had won the cup — and the 'double' — for Bath.

After the ball was over . . . Barnes's match-winning drop goal in the 1992 Pilkington Cup Final.

Eddie Butler wrote in *The Observer*: " . . .the mastermind of so many of the West Country team's triumphs, Stuart Barnes, had done it again."

Other press comments are also worth recalling. Gerald Davies, the former Welsh wing, writing in *The Times*, described the moment as a magnificent justification for the 'sheer impudence' of a dropped-goal.

"It can create a piece of unforgettable rugby magic. It did on Saturday."

Stephen Jones put the moment in context in the *Sunday Times*: "The final act may have been out of the blue and it most certainly added up to one of the most dramatic moments that Twickenham has seen. Yet it also represented a magnificent achievement by arguably the greatest side that the world of club rugby has seen."

David Hands in *The Times* wrote: "A quite magnificent climax to the most intense and demanding eight months the game has known . . .played out to the last gasping breath and drop of sweat."

Harlequins, the cup-holders, had been deprived of their beloved trophy by the team that played their heart out the season through. But both sides, whatever their motivation for a game or for a season, had done the game and their club's great honour.

There was one bizarre tailpiece, or rather headpiece. It emerged that Nigel Redman, Bath's electrician and lock, had severed an artery in his scalp just 48 hours before the Final in an accident on a building site. Hence his heavy bandaging covering the stitches for the Twickenham game. But he made no excuses for being outplayed by the man of the match, Ackford (who incidentally may have ended Redman's longer-term England hopes by his display).

But Redman was understandably pleased that his vital flick back to Richard Hill in the last minute had given Stuart Barnes his chance to win the game. "I always felt we could win the balls we needed to," joked Redman afterwards.

There was one daft note about it all. BBC television, to the disbelief of the game's followers, had chosen not to show any of the epic game live. After that, it would have fewer defenders in its attempt to hold its rights to coverage of the sport. Bob Burrows, ITV head of sport, said of the BBC's 'highlights only' decision: "I wonder the sponsors don't ask questions about that." Perhaps they did. But he added to what should have been the BBC's discomfiture (they preferred Rugby League on the day) by boasting that ITV, given the chance, would have shown the Pilkington Cup semi-finals live too.

As for Bath, it was the by now familiar return

They're happier than they look, honest – Glen Leat (left) and Clive Banks, literally the men behind *Ere*, the club fanzine.

to the adulation of the Georgian city and its people. But there was one farewell imminent.

Jim Fallon, the 'powerhouse' wing as people liked to call him, had decided to turn professional. A fortnight after the Cup Final, he withdrew from the England 'B' squad training session at Bisham Abbey for the New Zealand tour, and went north to join Doug Laughton's Leeds. He was going where earlier in the season Jeremy Guscott decided not to tread. And Laughton was of course the man who had signed Offiah and Davies (successes) and John Gallagher.

Fallon, an important extra ingredient in Bath's brilliant back-play of the 1991-92 season, widely tipped for an England cap, and now 27, explained: "It is a big decision to make, but sudden sums of money have to be thought about."

A fortnight after the Cup Final therefore he'd gone. Bath's unofficial fanzine, *Ere*, ran his picture on their front page showing him holding the paper and saying: "And I said to Doug Laughton I'll sign but you must get me my copies of *Ere* on time."

Inside, it said:

"We all would like to see Jim do well as he gave all Bath fans a lot of pleasure during the last couple of years, but anyone expecting an automatic try machine may be slightly disappointed."

It added that although his qualities may have been exceptional in Union 'the attributes which made him a star can be found in many players in the northern game'.

Meanwhile, Bath could now happily contemplate a season when they had overcome remarkable extra odds to take cup and league. All they thought they had to worry about — other than replacing Fallon — was how to defend their trophies in the 1992-93 season, with its major changes of laws.

A Hat-trick of Championships: 1992-93

AMAZING, what a difference a few law changes make to the game of rugby. Once again, too, head-shakers were yearning for former, and in their view better times. Here's one such wistful enthusiast, fresh from watching Bath on the Rec, not liking what he saw, and writing to the local paper:

"When I played rugby it used to be a game to take part in and not to watch . . .we used to go dressed for the game to the ground and . . .after the match was over we went our respective ways — putting on your coats oftentimes over our mud-slashed frames. It was a rarity to have a pavilion, and hot baths and refreshments were unknown.

"Now what do I see? Huge stands, huge attendances, players found everything, not wearing anything they paid for, with trainers to look after them as though they were prize fighters or gladiators, the spectators howling out exhortations and menaces. It seemed to me more like a Hippodrome than a match, and then the press criticisms and reports — we had nothing like that in the old days."

He recalled too when three-quarters used to bolt for the line, 'not prance around'. And they knew all about the hand-off:

"A man who tried to kiss them — this is what modern tackling looks like — would have a hand placed under his chin, and would have gone to grass like a dog."

But this critic was also nostalgic for the days

All smiles from Robinson and Hill, 1992.

when 'we never had more than three three-quarters, sometimes two'. That's the trouble with changing the rules — there's always someone around to insist the game was so much better in an earlier generation.

The man who wrote that letter to the *Bath Herald* (which closed in the 1920s) had left for India in the 1880s and on his return to England was saddened to see what had happened to the game: his letter was published on 5 February 1910.

But in truth his words have been heard many times over the past decade or so on many a ground and in many a clubhouse. They have been echoed throughout these pages by some among old players, the press, and supporters.

So Harry Barstow, Bath club historian, who unearthed the letter from the unhappy spectator from the year Edward VII died, and published it in a 1990 club programme, was one who seemed frequently uneasy about the changes threatening old traditions after the 1992-93 season. Writing at the end of that season he recalled the 1970s, when, he asserted, London Welsh were 'perhaps the best club side in the world' while Bath were struggling.

"Yet the Welsh kept the fixture going. Why? In a word, friendship. We still keep it going. But for how much longer will we enjoy that kind of freedom; the freedom to do our own thing, if only occasionally?"

The answer — in two words — was, no longer. Club treasurers apparently viewed revenue more kindly than less tangible benefits such as 'friendship,' because the clubs themselves were keen to move the Courage Clubs' Championship from its limited competition of each club playing another in the same division in only one League game a season to a home-and-away arrangement.

As well as giving more prominence and impetus to the league programme, there would be three more home league games to generate big crowds. That was the theory and the hope. But there had to be some savage chopping of the clubs from the leagues to attain the goal. Four clubs would be relegated from the First Division, seven from the Second, and nine from the Third where narrowly missing promotion (one club to go up) might also guarantee narrowly missing relegation. The teeth-gnashing at the end of the new season as sponsors and treasurers alike saw their protégés slipping down a division was predictable — the gnashers had usually asked for it as members of the senior clubs' association, which wanted the new league structure.

Just as significant were more than 30 major and minor changes in the rules of the game approved by the International Rugby Board. They were designed primarily to speed up the game, cut out delays and time-wasting. The most easily understood of the new laws (even for travellers home from India) was the increase from four points to five for scoring a try.

Almost as obvious were sensible changes to avoid what had become the boring routine of kick-offs being put out of play behind the opponent's goal-line. If that happened under the changes, a scrum back on the halfway line with the opposition put-in would result. After a score, restarts would always be by a drop-kick. Free-kicks rather than penalties would be awarded for some technical offences, and the side taking the kick did not need all its players to be behind the ball.

Another tedious ploy for spectators was properly ruled out — the dummy pass from the base of the scrum, previously used by scrum-halves to catch opponents offside by deluding them into thinking the ball had emerged. Nor could a player run back into his own 22 to kick directly into touch.

There were also important changes to the line-out, allowing a side to take the throw from anywhere between where the ball had gone into touch and its goal-line (but only if the player throwing in himself retrieved the ball). A further change — insisting that line-out jumpers use either both hands or the inside arm to catch the ball — was 'to be reviewed in one year's time.'

More controversial was the other one-year experiment to encourage teams in possession to use the ball, instead of perhaps constantly mauling in order to gain ground by a succession of scrums. When the ball in a ruck became 'unplayable' or the maul stopped the referee would order a scrum to the team not in possession at the start of the maul.

This was the most unsettling of the new rules for players and spectators alike. Sides renowned for their marching, maul by maul, and scrum by scrum, into opposition territory, had to move it out instead or find their advance arrested by the whistle and subsequent scrum.

Bath had often progressed in the past by such methods — so had every side with a strong pack — but other than in their comparative doldrums of 1987-88 they always had the flair behind the scrum to vary the game. Not surprisingly, teams like Gloucester and Orrell in the First Division — and newly-promoted West Hartlepool — who relied so much on forward power, with little pace behind the pack, were expected to feel the impact of the new laws most keenly.

For Bath, after the usual pre-season tour — this time to Italy where they beat Record Cucine Casale and Benetton Treviso — there was optimism about the new laws. "All of them suit Bath rugby," said captain Andy Robinson. "We're a side who can play off the cuff, stay on our feet and release great runners from second phase.''

Bath looked stronger even than they had done in winning the league and cup 'double'. John Hall was back after his season's absence from injury, spurred by the success of Steve Ojomoh in his stead, and David Egerton would be competing again for a back-row place. Sean O'Leary, the former Cambridge Blue, Wasps and England 'B' lock, like Webb, a surgeon, had also joined amid hopes that he would strengthen the line-out jumping. (O'Leary was also a survivor of the car crash which killed his Wasps' colleague Raph Tsagane near Bath on their 1990 Easter tour.)

Among the reserve players there were good reports of the performance of a fly-half from Aldermaston, Craig Raymond, on the Italian tour, and Audley Lumsden was again in contention. Adedayo Adebayo, fit again, would take the place of the departed Jim Fallon.

But as the team prepared for the opening Courage League match, the first home game of the new season, there was a large gap in the roof of the stand. It seemed symbolic of the back-stage committee problems which would surface again before many weeks went by. The hole, or rather the non-arrival of the new press box intended to fill it, had provoked a resignation or two. Chairman Roger Berry, from an old Bath family, had sought to remove secretary Clive Howard, but instead it was Berry who went. The grounds committee chairman, John Roberts, and a former club captain from the 1950s, went as well.

As for the game, against Harlequins, which was what the spectators (and the press) wanted to see, both sides were comparatively much changed from the riveting Final of only five months earlier. Harlequins fielded only eight of the Twickenham side. Halliday and Ackford had retired, Skinner had returned to Blackheath, Luxton had gone to Richmond. Langhorn and Fox were in the back row, with Sheasby and Winterbottom absent. Alex Snow, from Heriot's and Simon Dear were the locks, with Nick Edwards out of early season contention. Harriman was back on the wing, Mark Evans (like Dear, from Rosslyn Park) replaced Halliday and Glenister was at scrum-half.

Bath had four changes from the Cup Final team. John Mallett was at prop for the injured Ubogu, and John Hall was whisked in from a second-team game to replace Andy Robinson whose late withdrawal meant Hall's first league match for 18 months. Adebayo was in for Fallon, O'Leary for Haag.

For the unfortunate David Pears, Harlequins' full-back, it was an unhappy start — and virtual end — to his season. A couple of weeks earlier he had ended a sevens game in a neck brace. Now, after a collision, he was taken off with his upper jaw broken in three places. He had earlier kicked a penalty, which, with a similar effort from Challinor, was all Harlequins managed. Webb, in prime form for Bath, kicked five penalties, and converted Guscott's fine try, made for him by Hill's pass to Barnes on the blindside whose scampering run prised the opening. As a match, it was a drab beginning, with the crowd and perhaps the players still adjusting to the new rules.

For Bath, who were never in danger, there was at least the satisfaction of beating Harlequins yet again. The Londoners, as so often, looked as if the league programme had taken them by early-season surprise: they were losers against Wasps the following week, too.

Ubogu was back for Bath, again at The Rec, the following Saturday, when the league opponents were London Irish. Iestyn Lewis stood in for an injured Guscott, and Robinson was still absent. The Irish, as in the previous season, played adventurously, but lost by five tries to one, Ubogu scoring two of Bath's tries, the others coming from de Glanville, Clarke and Barnes with Webb kicking four conversions and two penalty-goals.

Webb, unfortunately, was not in such sound form a fortnight later when Bath were away to Northampton, widely tipped as likely championship contenders themselves, and bubbling with bright young talent such as the precocious backs Beal, Dawson and Hunter, and a rugged pack marshalled by Shelford. Bath had Robinson back and omitted John Hall, with Ojomoh switching flanks to accommodate the captain; Haag accompanying O'Leary in the second row.

It was not Bath's day. The pack was out of sorts faced by the vigorous Northampton tackling and referee Fred Howard was in the midst of minor controversy half-an-hour into the game. Swift had linked with his forwards in a flowing move only for a Northampton defender apparently knocking-on to interrupt the move. But there was no whistle and Beal kicked the loose ball ahead, chased by de Glanville in vain. The winger scored and Bath were struggling to come back.

In the second half Bath robbed MacNaughton to set up a chance for Guscott who put Clarke over for Bath's try. But although the scoring difference between the sides was finally a penalty for John Steele, Bath could not complain. They had given a less confident performance on the day than they would have wished, and lost 11-8. It was to be their only league defeat of the season.

The selectors' answer to the setback — and the signs of rustiness in the two preceding league

Even the policeman is a Bath supporter – and the game was at Bristol! Clarke scores for Bath in the 1992 league win over Bristol.

games — was typically ruthless in its lack of sentiment. Out went two of the previous season's successes from the pack, Martin Haag and Steve Ojomoh, and the new man, O'Leary. Hall and Redman were back for the game at home to Orrell two weeks after the Northampton defeat, and with them was the Bodmin lock, Andy Reed, who had played only three previous league games over the two previous seasons.

The reward from the changes was immediate. Orrell, clearly struggling to adapt their game to the new laws which had done them no favours, were comprehensively outwitted and suffered their heaviest league defeat against Bath, 39-3. John Hall scored two of Bath's five tries, Redman, Webb and Hill scoring the others, with Webb also converting four and kicking two penalties.

A week later it was Bristol's turn to take their largest league defeat from Bath. It was a game which illustrated the opportunities of the new laws, and the tactical futility of playing as if there had been no change. Bristol's pack toiled away dutifully making useful inroads into Bath's defences only to lose the ball in second phase or by losing the put-in. By contrast Bath scored four tries brilliant even by their own high standards. Webb, back on the Memorial Ground, had an outstanding game. He and Guscott and Barnes

and their colleagues took opportunity after opportunity to run from deep at Bristol, and Clarke, Webb, and Swift (two) were the try-scorers.

For some of the Bristol crowd it seemed like injustice as the territorial pressure their team imposed had scant reward, compounded by missed penalty chances. Webb by contrast kicked two penalties and converted all the tries. Other Bristol supporters wisely realised the confidence which imbued the whole Bath performance under the new rules which was in itself a stark lesson to the home team. Bravely though Bristol played at times, they were too often left behind by Bath's speed of thought and movement.

If the 31-8 defeat was a blow to the crowd, it was no comfort either to Bristol's coaching trio, Rob Cunningham and Dave Robson, and fitness and goal-kicking coach — also formerly helping at Bath — Dave Alred. But it showed them how far Bristol still had to go to compete with their johnny-come-lately neighbours. As Bryan Stiles remarked bluntly in his report in *The Times*: "The honest tradesmen from Bristol were exposed to the telling difference in class."

Meanwhile the Pilkington Cup beckoned, with Bath drawn away to Waterloo, who were going well in the Second Division. In the circumstances both clubs agreed to cancel a friendly they were due to play a fortnight before the cup match.

Before then Bath had a tough away league fixture at Welford Road against the current leaders, Leicester. The Midlands were murky and wet, the ground muddy and unforgiving for handling errors. At the start the fists were flying — mostly, apparently, in Ubogu's direction, perhaps also to make Leicester's point about having a tougher pack — and both captains were spoken too after only five minutes. Webb kicked an early penalty after a punch by a Leicester player on Ubogu, and Liley soon equalised for a Bath high tackle. But the longer the game of attrition went on, it seemed clear that whichever side scored the first try would have a rare advantage worth holding.

Halfway through the second half, the scores were still level at a penalty apiece when Barnes applied one of his magic potions to set up a score for Bath. Misplaced ambition by Kardooni led to Bath smuggling the ball. Hill fed Barnes and the fly-half drew the opposition who smothered him just as he threw a high ball to Guscott whose instant transfer let Adebayo in on the left wing. Webb missed the conversion, but Bath soon struck again. From a scrum Hill and Clarke and Guscott were all involved before Redman barged through to score an unconverted try.

Leicester on the day had missed Richards, no doubt, but it was a notable win for Bath, 13-3, which confirmed that, defeat at Northampton notwithstanding, they were still on course for another league championship.

There was also the Pilkington Cup, due to be played at Blundellsands the week after the Leicester game. Two other matters had occurred, however, whose bearing on the result of the cup game will long be the subject of debate wherever two or three Bath supporters are gathered together. There can be little argument, perhaps, about the first occurrence. Barnes, whose claims to an England recall were ever more vigorously debated in the media as the season ran on, was chosen to play for the Barbarians against Australia on the same day as the cup game.

"It's out of the question," said Jack Rowell, when Barnes told him. But as Rowell said, it's an amateur game, and it was obviously an important stage for Barnes to make a point to the England selectors. Ben Clarke was also chosen for the same match. They were to play: Andy Reed was away on Scottish international trial duty and Ubogu was also absent. Craig Raymond, David Egerton, Sean O'Leary and John Mallett were their respective replacements for the Waterloo game, one a full international and another an England 'B' cap.

Meanwhile back at the clubhouse the reverberations of the committee rumpus as the season started were growing louder. Expensively, Bath had been forced to call an extraordinary general meeting to consider demands for the removal of the entire management committee — and that included Jack Rowell. The request for the meeting, organised by Frank Cottle, was signed by the necessary 25 members — although it later emerged that at least one club stalwart signed under a misapprehension, which added to the air of tragi-comedy about the whole affair.

The club had made a loss in the year the team did the double, and for that and other largely arcane reasons of intense interest to some but of little moment to a majority, the rebels wanted heads to roll. They also wanted confidential details of the sponsorship deal with SWEB made known. But the players stepped in to have their say. Andy Robinson, as captain, told a press conference in advance of the extraordinary meeting the SWEB deal was 'perfect'. The players were happy with the appointment of the new chairman, John Gaynor, and the revised executive committee had already taken more decisions than he had known in his time at the club.

Robinson, on behalf of the winning team, was saying enough of rebellions, let's get on with playing, and forget the differences in the best interests of the club. "Poor decisions have been made by the management committee in the past and we have to own up to those mistakes. But now we must plan for the next five years and set our sights on making Bath a major investment concern."

In the event, Frank Cottle's initiative proved stillborn, with the ruling that the management committee could only be ousted at an annual meeting, not an extraordinary one, and Stuart Barnes, like Robinson, expressing his backing for the revised set-up already running the club. And the day when a chief executive, or a full-time administrator, would eventually be responsible for running affairs seemed nearer as a result of the controversy. (Stuart Barnes's name was mentioned as one long-term possibility.)

Jack Rowell allowed himself a rare, and stinging public comment, reported in the *Bath Evening Chronicle*. It was high time certain people 'buried their egos,' he said, and concentrated on giving the club's chief asset, the players, the backing they deserved.

The timing of the extraordinary meeting — almost on the eve of the Waterloo cup game — was indeed itself extraordinary, as *Ere* pointed out in advance of both events:

"How are our players supposed to continue maintaining such high standards and retain the 'double' under the black cloud of internal rifts and extraordinary general meetings? They should have nothing more to think about than winning the next game."

The 'next game' was at Blundellsands, and Bath lost. They were out of the cup. If indeed there was an element in the post-match inquest of an Ollie telling a Stanley what another fine mess he'd got them into, it wasn't exactly clear who in the committee episode was Laurel and who was Hardy. But the rumpus must have been a distraction for the senior players in particular, and added point to the quibble of one correspondent who acknowledged Bath as the finest team in the land, rather than the finest club.

But on the day the players lost the game, not the committee. Waterloo's stand-off, Paul Grayson, soon to leave for Northampton, kicked three penalties, his third a few minutes before the end giving the Merseysiders their 9-8 victory. Earlier a Swift try and a Webb penalty had given Bath a brief lead.

It was a great day for Waterloo, and their performance in giving Bath what David Irvine in the *Guardian* rightly described as 'their most embarrassing defeat in a decade' could not be gainsaid. A Bath side with 11 internationals offered no inspiration in response to Waterloo's tenacity and tackling, with the experienced Peter Buckton outstanding in the back row, which disrupted any semblance of Bath rhythm.

But it was still surprising that a team with players of the pedigrees and experience of Hill, Guscott, Webb, Robinson and Hall — to name but five — should have been so bereft of counters on the day, Alan Pearey assessed it thus in the *Evening Chronicle*: "It was by some distance the most abject Bath display I've seen in my two-and-a-quarter years here."

No wonder the Bath dressing-room was locked for some time after the final whistle, while Nick Allott, the Waterloo captain and survivor of the Waterloo win at the Rec in that first league season, explained: "Our game plan was to harass them as much as possible and see what happened."

In Jack Rowell's words, the atmosphere on the Bath team coach home was 'funereal'. The rest of rugby was delighted, but the result was such a surprise that Barnes admitted he hadn't even bothered to inquire about the score when his Barbarians' game finished. Undoubtedly his influence was sorely missed on the day, not that any particular blame should be shouldered by his stand-in, Craig Raymond, surrounded as he was by the regular back division.

Incidentally the result also gave currency to the rumour that Bath only nowadays lost cup games in Barnes's absence. Not so. As a later chapter

And sometimes he's earning a living – building society manager Stuart Barnes, 1992.

will show, there was a common factor concerning Bath's cup defeats since that 1984 trophy but Barnes wasn't it.

Perhaps in retrospect the Waterloo defeat was the kind of salutary shock which, whatever it did for the players and their coaching team, was a useful reminder to their mass support that although the team's achievements over past seasons was immense, they could not, should not be taken for granted.

There was no great consolation in seeing Bristol and Gloucester also leave the competition at the same stage, but there was perhaps a glimmer in seeing Orrell also bettered at Blundellsands in the next round, and Harlequins being given a close run there too (not without controversy — some Harlequins players having used illegal long studs which the referee forced them to change and for which they were gently admonished later).

For Bath and their fellow Westcountrymen that annual round of Divisional Championships now

Chilcott's the one playing hooker: rehearsal shot for Cinderella at Bath Theatre Royal.

cropped up. Instead of being an unfortunate diversion from the more serious business of winning cups, the competition suddenly seemed as if it might be worth winning, for pride's sake, at least. And that, with the help of 'imports' from clubs outside the big three, like Chris Clark, a prop with Swansea, and Nick Beal of Northampton, was what the South-West did, under Gloucester coach Keith Richardson, for the first time in the championship's history. That win is dealt with in more perspective later. For Bath the contest for the league title, which resumed in early January, was now even more important, given the lost battle of Waterloo.

The seven-week interruption to the league programme, covering the divisional games, Christmas and New Year, would be followed by another five-week-break, and then by a gap of four weeks — international and cup games intervening. Three league games in 16 weeks was an odd way to run a competition. It was no great surprise therefore that the sponsors Courage, as well as the senior clubs, should have opted for a more coherent structure to the championship henceforward, whatever the temporary mayhem in terms of relegation in the current season.

On 9 January, 1993, Bath faced Rugby in a Courage game — their first competitive fixture

since the Waterloo defeat at the end of November. Bath had Chilcott (playing broker's man in *Cinderella* at the Bath Theatre Royal), Reed, and Clarke absent from the pack, with Hilton, O'Leary and Egerton deputising. Dawe went off after quarter-of-an-hour, to be replaced by Atkins. No matter — they ran in nine tries, with two each for Adebayo and Barnes, and a first for Bath by O'Leary, to one from Rugby in a 61-7 victory.

If the result again suggested that Rugby were out of their class in the higher division (they would be relegated) it was also a reminder of the strength of the Bath squad which would be an important asset in the increased demands of the Courage championship from the next season on.

Meanwhile the current competition was developing into a race between unbeaten Wasps and Bath, two points behind but with a considerable advantage in scoring differential. But any smugness was again gently removed when Bath saw an intended friendly with Exeter cancelled, as they had probably expected. It clashed with a cup day, Exeter, not Bath, were still in the cup.

Gloucester at Kingsholm were the next league hurdle, and Bath were missing Hill and Barnes. Ian Sanders deputised at scrum-half and at stand-off, Mike Catt. Both were starting a league game for the first time. Sanders's kick into the box as

Barnes on the burst in the 1993 league win over Rugby.

Surging Guscott against despairing Rugby, 1993.

Bath attacked early in the match enabled Swift to collect and score his 350th try in senior rugby. A brief genuflection of joy from the winger was the only difference from the others he'd scored over the years. It was the only try of the game.

Gloucester, not free from relegation worries, were rarely a threat and while they missed kickable penalties, Jon Webb was at his surest in kicking five. Bath were below their best but Gloucester were never serious contenders for the points.

Afterwards, the story goes, Mike Catt having left the field delighted Bath had won and that he hadn't let the side down in Barnes's absence, still felt the adrenalin coursing through him as he sat in the dressing-room, only to realise that an extremely tall man he had scarcely heard speak until now was delivering the biggest rollicking to the team Catt had ever heard. Bath had won but not won well, and Catt realised that Rowell was right. But what if they had lost, Catt wondered?

The capture of Catt, incidentally, said something about the two clubs who had just met. He had been on extended holiday from South Africa in the Stroud area and got in touch with Gloucester, offering his services. He heard nothing. So he tried Bath. Gareth Chilcott was promptly in touch with him and arranged for Catt to turn up to train. His potential was immediately recognised. There were jokes at Kingsholm's expense about someone letting the Catt out of the bag. Whether he would return to Bath for later seasons — he had dual nationality and was quickly starring for England Under-21s — was for the future. Certainly Jack Rowell assured me that he considered Catt 'exceptional'.

Catt also played against Swansea in a 13-try record defeat for the Welsh club at the Rec the following Friday evening. Swansea, with five men on international duty, fielded some regular backs but a second-choice pack, and it showed as Ben Clarke scored four tries, and Swift and Adebayo two each in the 79-3 victory — a superb display of attacking rugby. But it was also a reminder of the loss of clout the Anglo-Welsh encounters now carried.

It was Bath's turn to do themselves less than justice in a defeat by 27-17 at Cardiff on the next cup day. If Bath had been surprised by Waterloo, their experience was modest beside the embarrassment of Cardiff, beaten at home in the cup by St Peter's, a Cardiff junior side they underestimated to the extent of consciously resting some star players. Cardiff v Bath, therefore, was now reduced to a mutually unsatisfactory consolation fixture compared with the clubs' great games of the not-so-distant past.

But Bath next faced the match billed as the

Jon Callard, Webb's shadow, perseveres in a night game against Swansea, 1993.

likely championship decider, at home to leaders Wasps, a fortnight after that Cardiff game. There was added savour before the contest in the inevitable and continuing rivalry between Andrew and Barnes — the one so long the man in possession for England but now discarded in favour of Barnes. Each was chosen for the Lions' tour.

If anyone had hoped for a classic game they were to be disappointed. It was an often ugly struggle which did little credit to either side, unless there was an unspoken agenda among the forwards to see who wouldn't prove the bigger cissy on the day. The desperate edge to the first quarter-hour was grim watching, with the forwards indulging in the tedious macho-man

Punch-ups between Wasps and Bath players in the grim league 'decider', March 1993.

contests they apparently find so absorbing but which does nothing for the paying spectator.

Jack Arnold, one of Bath's veteran members, writing in a later club programme, called the opening 15 minutes 'a disgraceful exhibition.' John Mason in the *Daily Telegraph* sighed: "Punching, gouging, spitting, kicking, raking, trampling, elbows, knees, feet — oh for the sight of a good honest fist."

The two captains, Dean Ryan and Andy Robinson, were warned — and both had been to the fore in the scrapping. Soon afterwards, Fran Clough got up from a tackle by Guscott as the ball went into touch and charged the Bath centre. After a word with the touch-judge, referee David Matthews dismissed Clough.

Thereafter the game settled down into uneasy tension, as Bath early behind, went 11-3 down by half-time. A try carved out by Andrew for winger Phil Hopley looked at the time, and on later TV evidence, to involve a clear forward pass, but it was a neatly-worked move.

Later Clough was to claim Guscott had trampled on him as the two came away from the tackle. Television evidence suggested Guscott had

not been particularly careful as he got to his feet, but trampling seemed an over-statement. Eddie Butler in *The Observer* was particularly hard on the referee blaming him for the general chaos of the opening stages. But it was not Mr Matthews who gouged and kicked players.

Bath slowly took charge of the game, as Webb made up for earlier misses by kicking four penalty-goals, and Barnes dropping a notable goal under pressure to confirm Bath's lead in the closing stages. Then the forwards set up an attacking position with Ubogu and Clarke and the chance to put Guscott in for the decisive try. (Nigel Starmer-Smith on TV described the Bath try as being scored 'ironically' by Guscott: presumably a reference to the Clough incident. But the gratuitous comment sounded like another attempt to rewrite a game — forward passes as well? — involving Bath and a London side.)

Wasps defended ferociously. But their intimidatory tactics (matched on the day by Bath — "Why did Bath persist in the macho stuff against 14 men?" complained *Ere*) were noted by reporters of their subsequent league games against Northampton and Orrell, with Ryan and flanker

Guscott's tackle on Fran Clough which immediately preceded the incident which led to Clough's dismissal: Bath v Wasps.

Emeruwa again prominent — Northampton prop Baldwin had his nose bloodied in the first minute.

But as a result of the 22-11 Bath win, they were now level on points with Wasps but ahead because of their scoring points advantage. That was further enhanced by a rather happier victory at West Hartlepool, two weeks later, at the end of March, after a narrow win in a friendly at Pontypool.

For Jack Rowell it was a particularly happy homecoming to his native town, and the local club offered rather special hospitality to welcome — what was he? the wizard from West Hartlepool? — their famous rugby son. The night before the game ten members of the West Hartlepool Grammar School side first XV of 1954-55 greeted their old teammate. The stories swapped that night included the local legend that even when he was 11 Master Jack Rowell, goalkeeper of Lister Street junior school soccer team, was so tall he could touch the crossbar.

Rowell was himself touched by the generosity of the greeting. "It was wonderful," he said.

West Hartlepool, remarkably, had risen through three divisions, and in their year in the top flight had scored first in every one of their league matches to date. They did the same with a converted try after only four minutes against Bath. But by half-time Bath were 13-10 ahead, and by the end had won 38-10, Barnes collecting three tries, and Jonathan Callard, making a rare appearance in place of Webb, described as unavailable, scoring two.

Bath's coach-travelling supporters had a great time too — a local landlord opening specially for them as they arrived. "When can we go again?" asked Bath's telephone 'club call' announcer Peter Hall, in the programme. The answer appeared to be not for the foreseeable future. West Hartlepool, unlucky perhaps to arrive in the First Division as four clubs were due to drop, would have to try again.

For the North and the strength of the game there, it was good news that Newcastle-Gosforth (who pipped Waterloo, in spite of losing their last game) would take the one promotion place available. Good news for Jack Rowell and Bath too, surely: for if he was the wizard of 'West', he might too be regarded as a guru from Gosforth? He could hardly choose the year of his old club's

He's behind you! Ben Clarke frightens a London Scottish attacker in Bath's league game which doomed Scottish to relegation, 1993.

first appearance in Courage Division One to retire as Bath's coach . . .

Next, though, (on the day of the aborted Grand National) Bath were hosts to London Scottish, also fighting for survival in the top flight. They had been cruelly robbed of key players at vital times, including the new Scottish flanker Ian Morrison. He and fellow internationals Derek White and Paul Burnell were missing from their pack against Bath. But Damian Cronin was back on the Rec, smiling and combative, and celebrating his selection for the British Lions with his Scotland second-row partner, Bath's Andy Reed, now his opponent.

Jon Webb, not chosen for the Lions, was again absent from the Bath line-up, this time officially dropped with Callard preferred. Webb had not been at his most confident in recent games, and his omission was no great surprise, given Callard's excellent form in other matches. But it was also evidence again that past good form was no guarantee of a player keeping a place.

The contrast in atmosphere after the last home league game against Wasps was marked — there was more good rugby and style from both sides

in the first 15 minutes than the earlier game had offered in its full 80 minutes. If the final score of 40-15 perhaps was a trifle harsh on the Scottish, consequently relegated, Bath for considerable stretches imposed sweeping control of events. The pack in particular, with the cantering Ubogu and the marauding back row of Hall, Clarke and Robinson, provided some classic displays of how to make the most of the new laws, providing quick second-phase possession.

One marvellous move from broken play involving Guscott, Clarke, Hall, Swift and Callard ended with the latter scoring a try; another saw Adebayo, as he was tackled, slipping the ball inside for Clarke to score in the second half, almost a re-run of a first-half try when Adebayo that time fed Ubogu.

The same day, at Orrell, Wasps won by 11-10 to keep themselves in contention against a home team safe from relegation but still, apparently, lacking the tactical nous required to win. It meant that all now depended for the league title on the last day of the season, with Bath away to relegated Saracens, and Wasps home to Bristol.

Precision: Jonathan Webb places the ball for a kick at goal in one of his last games for the club.

A win for Bath would be enough to secure the championship once more.

Any hint of complacency was unlikely, given Saracens' earlier shock to Bath's system in 1990, when Andy Robinson's brother Sean kicked vital points for Saracens in their defeat of Bath. This time Sean was not playing. But there may have been an uneasy thought or two for Jon Callard. He played out of position at fly-half in that earlier game. Now he was again switched from full-back to play on the left wing — not the easiest of positions for anyone not accustomed to it (ask David Trick).

A change was necessary because of injury to Adebayo, a hero for England's unfancied sevens squad which had so surprised the rugby world by winning the inaugural world sevens tournament at Edinburgh the previous weekend, under the captaincy of Andy Harriman. But Adebayo's injury meant at least that Bath could also accommodate Jon Webb again at full-back for what was announced as his final game for the club.

Bath — like other sides playing important games that day — were granted the release of their four British Lions (Barnes, Guscott, Redman and

Reed) from pre-tour training to play. Perhaps the exhuastive two-and-a-half-hour session on the Friday sapped the stamina of the two Lions' forwards in particular? The game was never the easy canter some less-informed observers had imagined it would be. Saracens had something to prove to themselves, for their club and for others — and for Bath.

At the end of the 80 minutes, however, as David Hands wittily put it in *The Times*: "Bath had survived, yet again, their annual examination by rugby's equivalent of the Monopolies Commission."

An early dropped-goal by fly-half Gareth Hughes put Bath on their mettle but Webb missed three penalty-goal chances before Callard went over in the corner for an unconverted try, and Barnes kicked two penalties to give Bath an 11-3 half-time lead. The expectation was that Bath would then, as so often, increase the pressure and the points. Rather, Saracens, with their scavenging pack and veteran Lee Adamson outstanding in reportedly his last game for the club, pressed for much of the second-half, and when Hughes dropped a second goal Bath supporters blinked a little harder. Worse was to come for their side,

Jon Webb running out for his last home game for Bath at the end of the 1992-93 season.

as the Saracens pack bamboozled Bath over the line for captain and scrum-half Brian Davies to touch down for a try converted by Andy Tunningley and a 13-11 Saracens lead with about eight minutes remaining.

Bath had scarcely been out of their own half in the second session but didn't concede a single penalty. (Saracens' coach John Davies remarked later: "That's down to self-discipline, a very good captain who is near the action at no.6, and experience.")

But the sign of a side of high skill and confidence (simply fear of losing, claimed Andy Robinson later) was also the way Bath struck back so soon after the second Hughes goal.

First Barnes put over a penalty to restore the lead, and then with one of his rare pieces of quick possession in the second half, Barnes, as so often, like Horton before him, the inventive match-winner for Bath, sent a steepling kick into Saracens' half. As full-back Tunningley took it so Guscott tackled him and the ball spilled from his grasp: de Glanville briskly scooped it on to his wing without attempting anything himself — more evidence of the quickness of thought and action that was a feature of his game. Callard was away for his second try of the game to complete a decisive movement, stunning in its speed.

Chris Rea in *The Independent on Sunday* called it 'the most sumptuously timed movement of the

game and, in the circumstances, of the entire season.'

Even though Barnes missed his conversion that effectively was that. Saracens had again shown they were good enough for the top division. Bath, below their best, had produced vital scores when only minutes from losing the Courage trophy.

As it was, Wasps, beating Bristol 7-6, and so winning yet another league game by a single point, finished with the same number of league points, but Bath had a colossal scoring difference of 195 points, and were the only side in the division to concede fewer than 100 points. Wasps had proved remarkably tenacious all season but their weakness had been an inability to pile on the points — four clubs beside Bath scored more points than them, including relegated London Scottish. Nevertheless, it was a season when a deducted point — perish the thought — could not have been overcome in the face of Wasps' challenge.

Were there again a few mutterings about it being a pity someone else couldn't win for a change? Rob Smith, Wasps' coach, was generous in answering such criticisms: "Bath are superbly well-organised. They have helped improve every club in the country."

After the game several Bath players, including three Lions (Reed declined), chose bungee-jumping to celebrate. It shook them and probably didn't do much for the heartbeats of the Lions

Andy Robinson holds the trophy as Bath celebrate the retention of the courage Championship.

management either — but it was certainly a new and exciting way of giving thanks.

Less sensationally, the third successive Courage League title, and the end of the fixture pattern that had held sway for the competition so far, also seemed reason enough for Bath politely to inquire about holding the particular trophy in perpetuity — with another to be found for subsequent seasons.

Bath's record was awesome. In the decade from the close of the 1983-84 season they failed to claim either cup or league, or both, in only one season.

And although there were, as always with Rowell sides, new names in the team or its fringes — the revelatory lock Andy Reed for one — Chilcott and Redman, Hall and Hill who were in the 1984 cup-winning side that started the habit, were also in the 1993 side that continued it.

They were a reminder too of others who had graced the Rec, and earlier honours winners: Trick and Trevaskis, Palmer and Martin, Horton and Halliday, Lee and Cunningham and Simpson and Spurrell and the rest. The second generation of Bath's winners included Barnes and Swift, Guscott and Egerton, Dawe and Cronin and Robinson. Ubogu and Clarke, de Glanville and Callard, Fallon and Adebayo, were a third generation. Webb had been a bonus, and in his three full seasons with the club he shared in three league titles; as good a time for a great full-back (and — no dodging the word — a gentleman) to leave the game as might be imagined.

Callard, so prolific a scorer over the season in bread-and-butter friendlies, had shown, in his three league games with which he closed the season with five tries, his eagerness to reclaim his place from the England man. There were one or two other names joining the club, including prop Chris Clark from Swansea and Mike Lloyd, a left wing from Bristol, to compete for places in the new, 18-match, home-and-away Courage leagues.

But in all the controversy and speculation that continued around the movement of players from so-called smaller clubs to the elite, there was the odd absurd story linking Bath with dodgy deals. One such implied that Bath had hi-jacked 'a Scottish international', Andy Reed. It ignored the fact that Reed had to fight over three seasons to claim a first-team place at Bath: only thereafter did he become an international.

The absurdity of that implication, though, illustrated again that Bath had no need to offer illegal cash incentives. A player might be helped in finding a job. But what Bath had to offer — and potential recruits knew it — was simply the coaching genius named Jack Rowell and his assistants. Bath-bred players had been stars of his teams from Beese and Palmer to Hall and Guscott. But he continued to recruit, legitimately, from the whole of the region for his teams.

Other sides were catching up as the new league demands began — a smaller division would be a more exacting division. Harlequins would have to apply themselves rather more assiduously, in the wake of Winterbottom's retirement, to maintain their top status. Bristol, beginning to bristle with young talent such as Kyran Bracken and Simon Shaw, hoped at last to start restoring their great reputation.

As for Bath Jack Rowell and his coaching team believed the home-and-away programme offered the kind of fresh challenge that had always been welcomed during his time. He considered it reminiscent of the early 1980s when tough games with the Welsh clubs helped to fashion the Bath side.

Rapidly, too, the game was changing. Purists argued it was imitating Rugby League with defences blocking the midfield, and in its recent rule changes. But Bath, with more than 355 points and more than 40 league tries, had averaged 30 points a league game, in adapting much better than most other senior sides to the changes. Rowell said: "Technically we've taken on the new laws and our rugby's come a long way."

With Bath's home league record of only two home defeats in six seasons, there was a confidence in the club which suggested that however hard it might be to approach, never mind emulate, the successes of the past decade, as other clubs approached their standards, it would nevertheless need a fine side to oust Bath from the top perch in English rugby.

It is now time, in the next few chapters, to look more closely at the players mentioned above — and others — who brought the trophies to Bath in that decade of victories.

Andy Robinson and Jeremy Guscott.

The Players: Full-backs

THERE are still plenty of Bath fans who smile with pleasure at the memory of the piratical figure of Jim Waterman at full-back for Bath just before the decade of glory began. His incursions into the line, imaginary cutlass flailing, sometimes with inspired results, brought excitement to a game.

But the Waterman impatience to start the action — and perhaps grab the element of surprise for his side by initiating it himself — was a touchstone prized by most of his successors in that position at Bath. Only Charlie Ralston perhaps, decorous in his occasional deception, and another occasional player, Phil Cue, were more reminiscent of the earlier days of safety-first full-backs. (Both were near the end of their careers by that time.)

For Bath's first four Cup Final successes, the full-back was the Cornishman Chris Martin, fast and hefty, who was one of the club's several finds at Bath University. Born in Truro and starting his rugby with Penryn (whose coach rang Jack Rowell in advance to advise him to latch on to Martin) he made an immediate impact on fans — and more importantly, opposition teams — when he first made the team at Bath.

His bursts into the line fuelled by his 14 stones broke many an initial attempt at tackles and set up tries for his team and his crunching tackles were deadly and invariably perfectly-timed. He was also something of a fitness freak, who either delighted or irritated spectators, according to taste, by his occasional full somersaults and backflips when regaining his feet. It was perhaps ironic that successive injuries to his shoulder ended his career prematurely.

His international appearances were not his happiest games. After he spilled the odd high ball in internationals, opponents in club games hoped he would do the same for them. It rarely happened. Instead time and again he would punish them for their cheek by huge kicks downfield or counter-attacking.

Rather, the weakness in his game, according to many who saw him frequently, occurred on occasions when even from the touchline it was obvious that he had started to think. Instead of using his natural instinct he seemed to wonder what might happen if something went wrong.

(And as a mathematician he presumably calculated the risks accurately . . .) His pauses were almost always the signal for him to get into problems — letting a ball bounce once too often or seemingly being caught in two minds about what to do. If he simply didn't hesitate, he seldom went wrong.

In sum, it was his slow reaction to a situation that sometimes caused his temporary undoing — and the end to his international career.

The season after his four international caps, for a home game against Wasps, the Bath team as listed in the programme began: "Christ Martin." Was it a devout offering of thanks, or a subliminal supplication from someone who didn't feel easy with him in the side?

It was, of course, simply a gremlin from the misprints department who played such a diverting role in club programmes (more usually in those produced by Bristol, I should add in fairness) in those years. (There's another collector's item from that same season when Rosslyn Park at Bath fielded a winger named "M.Ossiah." It was only a wonder, perhaps, that he wasn't M.Essiah — although he probably became that later, at Central Park, Wigan.)

After successive shoulder dislocations Martin talked of converting to a flank forward, but his last appearance for the team in a club match was on the wing — when again unfortunately he was injured in making a tackle. Happily, 12 days later he was fit enough to make his last appearance on the Rec in that charity game in autumn, 1988, against Public School Wanderers when Bath's internationals were paraded, and he scored a try playing on the left wing.

With his speed and tackling skills he could indeed have been a useful wing. But at full-back, if he never fulfilled the hopes he may himself have held for an international career, he was still a formidable force for Bath, and he took genuine good wishes from everyone when he emigrated to New Zealand. He was also, incidentally, one of those stars whose reputation scarcely carried into the new league system: after four successive appearances in the Cup Final sides, he played only in Bath's first two league games in 1987-88) before injury ended his season.

In the circumstances Bath were fortunate that Phil Cue, unwanted by Bristol, had joined them the previous season. He was inevitably called on to stand in for the injured Martin, and later for Barnes at fly-half. He made eight league appearances out of 11 games played that first Courage season, and played in all three games in the unsuccessful cup run that term. His kicking was not always as reliable as he or his side wished on a couple of crucial occasions. But for a player who had seen the best of his career at Bristol he was surprisingly valuable to Bath in the emergencies they faced.

But Bath had a new find from the same doorstep from which they had plucked Chris Martin: Audley Lumsden was another of the club's harvest from Bath University. He excited first his coaches and then the crowds at his early first-team games — a handful in the 1986-87 season, an increasing number the next.

For the second league season, 1988-89, with Bath determined to make up for their loss of determination the previous campaign, Lumsden was first-choice full-back. So often Bath had found a new player whose impact on the game seemed almost immediate — Hill, Egerton and Robinson in their time had a similar effect — but Lumsden, raw and inexperienced though he might be in match conditions, was a vital new ingredient to Bath's mix.

Was he occasionally too adventurous? Even conservative watchers overlooked any such reservations in the general delight at the extra dimension his exciting running from broken play and deep positions provided, as well as his brave tackling. It was the unorthodoxy of his approach that added spice to his skills at speed, and made him potentially an unpredictable surprise weapon in Bath's armoury for the Cup Final that season against Leicester.

The chance to play on the big occasion against the venerable Dusty Hare would have given Lumsden an opportunity to reveal his capacity for brilliance to a wider audience. There were already those who were earmarking him for the 1992 World Cup squad — he had already represented England 'B'.

It was not to be, as we have seen. He scored three tries in nine league games that season, and five tries in four cup matches. The sight of Lumsden's exciting support play, overlapping and initiating, stays vivid in the memory. The sight of Lumsden at Twickenham that day wearing a surgical halo round his head instead of playing remains a vivid but poignant symbol of the halt to a career that may have led to great things. Might it still do so?

Slowly, in spite of that broken neck vertebrae,

medical and specialist care and treatment brought him back to match fitness. With great courage and selfless help in coaching young players as he recovered he began his comeback, at first with Bath. He went on to Oxford University and was picked for the 1991 university match — only for that Dubai sevens to give him a broken ankle.

For 1992 he was again shrugging off injury to appear for Oxford at Twickenham, but on the right wing, and he was soon appearing in Bath Spartans, Bath's third string. ("I would really love to play for Bath again," he said on the eve of the university match.)

It was all part of his remarkable determination yet to succeed at the top in a game he loved in spite of the cruel injury it had brought him. Bath, he has said, has always been a special club for him. (Indeed it had helped in finding him assistance both in his rehabilitation and in his education.)

But to reclaim a first-team place Lumsden would first have to displace not Jon Webb but the man who came to Bath after that Cup Final when John Palmer made his unexpected fifth Cup Final appearance in Lumsden's place.

Jon Callard was another in the tradition of running, adventurous full-backs Bath ideally sought — and usually found. In his first season he played in all 11 league games and scored six tries, and in all the cup games (two tries) culminating in his share in the hammering of Gloucester at Twickenham.

Then came Jon Webb. And although initially, as Webb took time to regain his confidence, Callard remained first choice, Webb's chance came when Callard switched temporarily to fly-half when Barnes was injured. He didn't get his place back. Webb was in, with Callard making only two league appearances in the 1990-91 season. But the following term — remember Heatherley and the deducted point — Callard was injured when the odd chance to deputise for Webb came his way and he shared in neither the cup run nor the league win.

It must have been as disappointing in its way as the problems that afflicted Audley Lumsden earlier. But although Callard's name was linked with Bristol the former Newport player seemed determined to take his chance of winning back his place when, at the end of the 1992-93 season, Jon Webb retired from the first-class game to concentrate on his medical career. Ironically, he had also stood in for Webb in the final game for the South-West's 1992-93 Divisional Championship side. But before the end of the 1992-93 season Callard had at last won back his place from Webb on form — and scored tries to celebrate his return.

Full-back Jon Callard, 1991.

a player who took confidence from the confidence around him. In a bad side his own game would, one suspected, have deteriorated rapidly. It did so in the Bristol team that shed first its nerve and then Webb. "I'd had enough," he told *Rugby World.* "I was fed up to the back teeth with the whole thing, was getting no enjoyment from playing at all, so I did what any sensible person would do and jacked it all in."

And that would have been that — he had spoken frequently about the great relief he felt having made the decision to give up rugby at that time.

But it was flair and pace and confidence which distinguished his play when he first came into the game. Bath restored that confidence. He was again 'a class act,' as Jack Rowell described him.

Webb often told, too, how Bath took his game and his skills apart and examined them and repaired them. And his wife Amanda — like Graham Dawe's wife Liz before her — was the catalyst in persuading her husband to take his chance with Bath. Mrs Webb explained to the *Western Daily Press*: "For him to have given up at that stage I felt would have been a waste of everything he had achieved before. I didn't want him to look back and say, I wish I'd given it one more go."

The rest (as Nigel Starmer-Smith might have, must have, said on the box) is history, with his pace in hitting the line providing England with something extra which the unlucky Hodgkinson lacked.

For Bath Webb played some immensely confident games — one against Harlequins in the league in his first full season at the Rec was outstanding, and so was his return to Bristol in Bath's 31-8 win there in the 1992-93 season. But that remarkable pressure kick from the touch-line in the closing moments at The Stoop to convert de Glanville's try and give Bath the 18-18 draw was perhaps his most vital contribution to Bath's double triumph that season.

That alone should be sufficient cause for faithful Bath supporters to include Amanda Webb in their seasonal prayers . . .before they wish many happy returns to the full-back slot for patient Jon Callard — and the indefatigable Audley Lumsden, who took a job at Millfield School (where Gareth Edwards was once a pupil) in 1993, confirming his commitment to Bath.

Plenty of people at Bath would be glad to see him reclaiming that position permanently — if Bath were fortunate then Callard was unlucky to have found a player of Webb's talent squeezing him out. And Lumsden remained to fight for his place, too.

Which brings us to the talents of Jon Webb himself. Enough has been written about him and said by him concerning his feats for England in Grand Slam and World Cup successes. Nor need much more be said about his play for Bath.

Webb, whose physical appearance — seemingly so fragile as to catch the eye on a chill winter's day as being almost translucent — was so deceptive given his achievement, was essentially

The Players: Wings

LOVERS of the English language as well as rugby had much to savour in the early 1980s, as the game provided outstanding players whose names seemed entirely apt for their positions. A game of rugby Happy Families could hardly have devised anything better, for example, than Hare and Dodge for two of Leicester's outstanding backs.

And Trick and Swift as the names for international wing three-quarters seemed similarly made for a side managed by an Ollie Onomatopoeia. (Only Buzza, fittingly with Wasps, and Hunter of later aspirants have even half-suitable names.) By happy contrast, several England forwards of the same period were also aptly named . . . Pearce, Brain, Boyle, Rendall, Probyn, Skinner — all sounded menacing and painfully to the point — and there could be no comfort for opponents, surely, from someone called Winterbottom.

But enough of such linguistic indulgence. Trick and Swift were only two of several fine wingers to play for Bath in recent seasons. Those with long memories will recall the eccentric Ian Duckworth, who missed an England cap only because the selectors couldn't find him when he was needed as a replacement for an England side in the 1960s. They weren't the only ones. Duckworth was sometimes as elusive off the field as he was on it. But his name on the team-sheet was enough to put a few score extra on the meagre attendances at the Rec in the mid-1960s.

By the time Jack Rowell had the team in hand there was also the remarkable Indian summer of the prolific Derek Wyatt, capped for England years before when with Bedford, but who threatened all club records of his day with his running on the Bath left wing. His huge frame and galloping style meant that once he got up a good head of steam he was most difficult to bring down.

But by the time Bath reached that first Cup Final the regular wings were David Trick on the right and Barry Trevaskis on the left.

Trick was rather special. When he first burst on the scene he seemed an almost impossible opponent for other teams to lay their match-winning hands on. His change of pace, sidestep and ability to accelerate suddenly through half a gap made him one of the most exciting wingers in the game.

He had been a national sprint champion as a schoolboy, as well as a schoolboy rugby international, and he first played for Bath while still at Bryanston School, in Dorset, in the late 1970s, before becoming a regular when a Bath University student.

But he was much more than sprinter — ask Bristol and Cardiff, Gloucester and Llanelli, Pontypool and Bridgend. Some of his greatest performances were against Welsh sides in the seasons when such matches were among the highlights. (He had a particularly good game against a man called Swift in one game at the Rec against Swansea, I recall . . .)

Twickenham scarcely saw him at his best, although his try against London Welsh in the 1985 Final was typical of his deadly finishing with only two or three defenders to beat. Indeed he suffered from the tendency of the Bath side to keep the game tight in the later 1980s in particular. The despairing cry "Give it to Tricky." was commonly heard, and the expectation of something unpredictable and match winning on rare occasions when he was given the ball placed a heavy responsibility on him. It wasn't surprising that he couldn't always deliver the goods — increasingly his hands proved fallible.

Indeed his disillusion with the game meant that at one stage he withdrew for a time and gave sprinting another chance. But he came back to delight the crowd on many more occasions.

Maybe his defence and all-round play was never strong enough to sustain his game once the edge had gone from his speed. But when it's remembered that he is over a year younger than Tony Swift who carried on playing for five or more seasons after Trick effectively bowed out, then his comparatively early departure from the game can be seen as the premature loss it was.

In his three Twickenham Finals he scored only that one try in games which seldom came his way, but he kicked — winningly — three conversions and a penalty goal in that second win against Wasps.

But the facts that reveal most starkly his comparative starvation in his last full season with the club are that he scored not a single try in any of his nine games out of the 11 played in Bath's first league season or during their three-game cup run which ended in the defeat at Moseley. It was a sharp reflection also of the neglect of one of the club's most potent attacking weapons in the side's generally poor showing that season.

The next season, 1988-89, he played one — his last — league match (no tries) for the club.

It was therefore a little ironic that within a season or two Bath's back play was flourishing as handsomely as when Trick had first come into the game. By then others were scoring tries in Trick's place. Nevertheless he was one of the most popular as well as one of the most exciting wingers Bath has seen. It was a pity England never used his talents at their peak.

He had toured Argentina with England in 1981 and scored a try in one game from deep in defence — a feat he repeated many times for Bath. He also scored three fine tries for 'an England XV' against Fiji in the 1982-83 season and his England chance seemed imminent.

So it was. But as the former England hooker Peter Wheeler has recalled in his autobiography, Trick wasn't told he was playing out of position, on the left wing, until two days before the game with Ireland in Dublin. Curiously, too, he displaced another right winger out of position on the left — Tony Swift, then of Swansea. It was not a good day for Trick, whose positional play was not surprisingly adrift. He won his only other cap on the unhappy tour of South Africa in 1984, where Swift was also capped again.

Next year Swift had joined Bath and played initially on the left, with Trick, retaining his right-wing place — they were in the 1985-86 cup-winning team together. Then came Trick's season 'out' and Swift claimed the right-wing slot with Barry Trevaskis, much dogged by injury, back on the left. And although Trick returned for the start of league rugby Swift was effectively his successor.

But before looking at Swift's contribution to Bath's more recent successes, Trevaskis deserves broader mention. He was another of Bath's useful haul from Cornwall, having played for Falmouth as a teenager, then moving to Bristol in search of greater challenges. But although he was a Cornwall county player, he never made much headway at Bristol and by 1980 he had switched to Bath where he quickly made an impact on the left wing. Indeed, in 1982-83 (a year when Bath

The long-running wingman: Tony Swift.

failed even to qualify for the John Player Cup) he scored a record total of tries for the club, 32.

Trevaskis was the quiet man of the side and soon also found himself the only uncapped back in the team. But he had no inferiority complex as a result: his wing-play, direct and disciplined, was in contrast to Trick on the right, but as his scoring record showed, nonetheless effective, particularly from short range.

He will also be remembered for that heart-stopping moment when he tackled Alan Morley who hadn't the ball, which gave Barnes and Bristol the chance to beat Bath in that first Cup Final, which was of course missed — happily for Trevaskis's peace of mind in the years to come.

Injury which seemed to dog him increasingly as he reached his thirties meant he missed part of the second Twickenham Final, and he was effectively displaced by Tony Swift for the third. But with Trick absent and the switch of Swift, he reclaimed his place on the left for the club's fourth successive Final, in 1987.

But the start of league rugby again saw him

Winger Peter Blackett, 1991.

crowd to his efforts on the left wing. His thick-thighed chunky body was a powerful force going to the line which helped compensate for lack of any great speed.

The barrister from Ghana with the flamboyant dress sense scored seven tries in the 1988-89 cup run in only three of the five games, and was the first of Bath's succession of black wingmen to appear at Twickenham.

More unlucky was Peter Blackett, the Bath boy who took Sagoe's place on the left wing the following season. He had already played one league game in the opening Courage season of 1987-88, but his most notable contributions came in the third league campaign, which Bath won, when he appeared in nine of the 11 games, and scored two tries including that notable match-winner in the game at Bristol.

Blackett played in all the cup games too in the run-up to the final against Gloucester, only to injure himself in a midweek hammering of Cheltenham. His season was over, alas, and with it his chance of a Cup Final place.

Thereafter, his role with the club was essentially a valuable reserve as other, younger claimants to the left-wing place emerged. But his match-saving tackle at Northampton was vital to Bath's league championship run.

His replacement in that Cup Final against Gloucester was another schoolboy international, still a teenager 'reckoned to be as speedy as Chris Oti' said the reports, the Nigerian Adedayo Adebayo. He too had been at school in Devon, but not West Buckland. He was from Kelly College, and then went to university at Swansea.

In his first season, 1989-90, he played three league games — two of them in the centre — before coming in on the left wing after Blackett's injury and scoring two tries in the final league match of the season, a 26-15 home win over Leicester. Hence his place at Twickenham — where he was the only Bath back not to score any points — was assured.

The next season, still a student, he began as first-choice left wing (although playing as a makeshift centre, not very happily, in the home cup defeat by Leicester, with Peter Blackett returning on the left wing), and scored five tries in his five (out of 12) league games, before universities' rugby claimed him for most of the second half of the season. Luckily for Bath, they had another Devonian, Jim Fallon, waiting in the (reserve) wings.

As it happened any competition for places between the two for the left-wing place at the start of the 1991-92 World Cup season was quickly and sadly ended for Adebayo long before any league or cup games were scheduled. Making his

injured and he had to wait until the second season of Courage games, in the 1988-89 season, for his only league appearances for the club, scoring one try in his five games. His age and his injury record also told against him that season and although he played in two games in the cup run the younger Fred Sagoe was preferred to him for the Final, with Trevaskis on the replacements' bench.

Later he played again for Cornwall and moved briefly to Clifton for league rugby. But his contribution to Bath's early successes before the onset of the leagues was bigger than his comparative lack of fame suggests.

Fred Sagoe was another product of that remarkable rugby nursery in Devon, West Buckland School, who came to Bath late in his career after earlier spells mostly at full-back with Rosslyn Park, Bristol United, and Clifton.

He played two league games that first Courage season and six the second. And although his stay with Bath was brief, he quickly won over the first appearance of the season, against Cork Constitution, he was seriously injured and was out for the rest of the season.

By the time he was to play again for Bath, the club had won the double, and Jim Fallon had departed. Adebayo, still a student, this time at Bristol, came back after intensive treatment and recuperation and almost a year away, to claim his place on the left at the start of the 1992-93 season.

Understandably in his first few games he lacked some of his former speed and confidence. His tie-breaking try at a wet Welford Road in November 1992 did his side a deal of good — and probably restored much of his self-belief. By mid-season he was recognisably the hard-tackling, fast-moving wing who had first appeared in Bath colours, and won England 'B' and international sevens recognition.

Jim Fallon had made a comparatively quiet start to his Bath career, early-season injury and Adebayo's good form keeping him out of the league and cup games. But he was proving a consistent try-scorer in friendlies. In March 1991 he made his first league appearance, in the home defeat by Wasps, but by season's end he had played in five of the 12 league games, scoring one try.

In the following season of the double his hard running seemed to have extra impetus. His upper body strength and full stride enabled him to break tackles even when it seemed he must be stopped. And when he was halted it was often close enough to the line for his colleagues to pick up and continue the attack. With Tony Swift he was a particularly happy combination, the one pounding down his wing, the other darting — as Gloucester needed no reminding.

But Fallon's attributes were increasingly seen in midfield breaks or decoy moves in which Tony Swift also play his part. Both wings played in all 12 league games in 1991-92 and in all cup matches. Fallon scored seven league and five cup tries, Swift eight in the league and two in the cup.

It was a great season and it was also his last for Bath. Fallon, already well into his twenties, chose the professional game. Otherwise, who knows?, he might have been competing with Hunter or Tony Underwood for a place on England's left wing the next international season.

In some ways Fallon was a late developer. He had played for Richmond for some seasons and represented the South-West early in his time with the London club without hinting at his outstanding if brief contribution to the country's leading club. Not a natural footballer, he owed much to the coaching of Rowell and Brian Ashton to bring out the best in him.

Winger Jim Fallon, 1992, the year he switched to Rugby League.

But if ever there was a player who benefited and blossomed in the glow of the good playing habits around him, Jim Fallon was that man. Whatever happened to him in Rugby League his place in Bath's folk memories was secure.

Fallon was a West Countryman who went north. His senior partner in that great double season, Tony Swift, did the journey in reverse.

Like John Horton before him he was a Lancashire lad whose playing successes were largely with Bath. He played for the famous Fylde club (there's another whose location the parochial ones haven't a clue about. "Where's that then?" "It's at Lytham St Annes." Where's that, then?").

But all Swift's caps were won with Swansea, with all bar one on the left wing — even though he has claimed: "I can't play on the left to save my life." He moved job and rugby to Bath, where he was at first preferred to Trevaskis on the left wing, before claiming the right-wing berth as his own on David Trick's departure from the big-match scene.

David Trick, 1988.

He played in every league season (Barnes, Hill, and Guscott are the other current Bath backs to do the same), and in seasons 1989-90, 1990-91, 1991-92, and 1992-93 he played in every single league game, also ending as leading try scorer in three of those seasons, sharing the honour in one of them. It was a remarkable record of high skill as well as of personal fitness for someone who was described as a veteran for at least those seasons in the 1990s.

Yet, as I've mentioned, he was older than David

Trick — and Simon Halliday, to name but two of his contemporaries who had earlier blown their own whistle. Over the seasons, his general game, and his defence in particular improved. But above all, in the view of many of the more knowledgeable Bath supporters, it was his ability to read a situation in a split-second — the sort of second sight shared by a Horton or a Barnes (not, alas, by a Chris Martin) which enabled him to carry on for so long at the top of a demanding game.

No wonder Swift admitted to Steve Bale of *The Independent*, writing about the long-lasting powers of Swift and Fran Clough (both Lancastrians) that he would have liked to have played on the right wing in a good England side.

He could be as clinical a finisher as an Alan Morley, a great chaser of the kick ahead, possessed of speed off the mark and superbly balanced running with the ball in hand.

But there was probably another, more prosaic reason for Swift's great Indian summer of seasons that began, significantly, from 1989. That was the year he was persuaded to wear contact lenses. He had been forced to recognise there were times the previous season when play would switch suddenly on the other side of the field. "By the time I cottoned on to what was happening, I'd be several yards out of position."

Hence a Swift visit to the optician. "He thought I was joking when I told him I was a rugby player," he reported later. "And when he found out I was in the Bath first team he just did not believe me. My sight was that bad."

Certainly his vision in a game showed no sign of deterioration by the time he claimed the 350th try of his career. Ever the classic poacher of tries, he scored that in typical fashion at Kingsholm in the 1992-93 season by timing perfectly his follow-through for the kick behind the defence by scrum-half Ian Sanders, judging the bounce and collecting the ball to score the game's only try.

On that kind of form Tony Swift looked good for another 50 tries for Bath at least. And when he did eventually follow his contemporary class of the Tricks and Dodges and Hares into retirement himself he would leave behind memories of a winger of high class — and an unenviable act for his eventual successor to follow.

The Players: Centres

BATH have had some outstanding centre three-quarters during the Rowell years. Early on, Mike Beese, capped for England while with Liverpool in the early 1970s, came to the Rec and delighted the crowd with his willowy strength and skills. But it was a schoolboy from Prior Park School in the city, soon to be a familiar name in the Bath back division, who was cause for special pride, long before any cups were won.

John Palmer may have been from Wiltshire — like so many of Bath's recruits in the Rowell years — but the Melksham-born prodigy who had played for the county at soccer learned his rugby in sight of Bath Abbey, and was still at school when he first played for the club.

At the time he seemed a player who could become a regular for his country. It never quite happened. In his early days he was essentially a fly-half, but because of the presence of John Horton, and Palmer's capacity to adapt to almost any position, he began to be used more and more as a centre three-quarter. By the time, late in his career, that he again played some games at stand-off he showed that Bath and England might indeed have 'lost' a great half-back. (John Horton, one of his admirers, acknowledged to me that Palmer was probably a natural fly-half who had to become a centre.) But by then the edge of his pace, and even his appetite for the game was ebbing. And it is as a centre that he will be remembered.

Palmer, in the words of the old watchers, had a beautiful pair of hands and was a magnificent kicker of the ball from those hands. His balance and ability to change pace and to time his passes perfectly, were other assets. But it was his capacity to see openings, and add abrupt changes of direction, so wrong-footing his opponents, followed by sudden acceleration, that made him so exciting a centre, deft, darting and at times dazzling in his creation.

As a place kicker he was rather less reliable as he knew well, but he scored more than 1000 points in his Bath career, many of them from penalties and conversion kicks.

In harness with the emerging Simon Halliday, three-and-a-half years his junior, he was at his creative peak. That notable victory against Cardiff (the night of Terry Holmes' most famous crooked feed) saw the pair at their conquering best — a performance to make old men weep in their beer at the memory. And Palmer was at the heart of the matter. But then the big Welsh games invariably saw him at his best.

He lacked the sustained speed that would have put him into an even higher class and perhaps his tackling sometimes let him down. His occasional fondness for over-elaboration with Halliday irritated crowds when it ended in failure (but enraptured them when it worked, of course). Nor, he will admit, having put out a cigarette, was he the keenest of trainers. Yet his play was redolent of class.

Taciturn off the field, John Palmer was never less than articulate in his game. And it was typical of his whole career that his last serious match for the club should have been in his fifth Cup Final at Twickenham, standing in for Lumsden at full-back. Indeed, in his few Courage League games — seven in its first season, three in its second — 'JP' played at full-back, fly-half and centre: adaptable to the last and demonstrating the utility value which had also probably undermined England chances in the past.

England never used him properly, his two caps in South Africa in 1984, and one as a replacement against Ireland, piffling recognition of one of the cleverest playmakers in the English game in the early 1980s; his ability to play anywhere in the back division meant he stayed on the bench for the Grand Slam season of 1980, for example.

Perhaps, too, he suffered from the selectors' weakness in those years for picking centres on the strength of someone having just caught their eye in the Varsity Match, rather than someone who was to be seen prising open the Pontypool defence on a wet day in Wales . . .

Yet not even a starring role for Oxford or Cambridge was enough to guarantee selection on obvious merit — as one of Bath's Oxford Blues, Simon Halliday, born in Wales, but educated in Somerset and a Minor Counties batsman for Dorset, who joined Bath in 1982, was to discover.

It was not only the perversity of national selectors that kept Halliday out of major honours early in his career with Bath. After a handful of games with Harlequins he stayed in the West Country and his striding centre play in partnership with John Palmer impressed all who saw him in action. Alas, a bad fracture in his leg in a county game at Bridgwater in 1983 put him out of action for England — who seemed poised to pick him — but more seriously, for Bath too.

In his place came one of rugby's sturdy journeymen, and only a few months older than Halliday. The red-headed Alun Rees, although of Welsh parents, was born in Bristol and although his early career was with Ebbw Vale and Avonmouth, he joined Bristol only to move to Bath while still 21. His strength in defence was his particular asset. He was never a great try scorer, but his surging runs and resistance when tackled was often a catalyst for others to build opportunities.

In Halliday's absence through injury Rees took his chance, playing in the 1984 Final against his former club, and winning divisional honours. More, he performed so well that he eventually kept the recovering, fretful Halliday out of the Bath side for a time.

Perhaps Halliday's return to claim his place was inevitable even without the Horton controversy that indirectly helped Halliday's cause. But Rees was a tough-tackling centre whose best days were spent at the Rec and should not be totally overshadowed by the bigger names who surrounded him.

Simon Halliday reclaimed his place amid fears that perhaps his lengthy lay-off from first-team action and the seriousness of his injury (which was to continue to nag him for the rest of his career) had robbed him of his searing speed. Not so. Palmer once again had his ideal complement in the comparatively uncomplicated running of Halliday.

Halliday was another popular player at the Rec, as he added an extra ingredient to the side's attacking play.

The ploy close to the opposition try-line, where Richard Hill would miss out his inside centre to find Halliday bursting through to take the pass and score by the posts, was for some seasons a party piece. But because it was never overdone, opponents still had to guard against Bath's other attacking options. It was dramatically used in the 1987 Twickenham Final against Wasps. Cling as they could to the marauding Halliday, Wasps' defenders were thrown back by his momentum as the near-14-stones centre hurtled over.

Years later Jack Rowell remarked to me of that try: "That was running into the valley of death. It takes a special man."

Halliday's great pace opened up space consistently and provided many scoring opportunities for teammates. Undoubtedly, his injury, plus reluctance or unavailability to go on overseas tours — including the 1987 World Cup — cost him many England caps. And another factor was the curious way the selectors chose to shun players in Bath's successful side for some time in the 1980s.

Halliday's last game for Bath, in the Gloucester Cup Final, was also justification at the last for his long and visible advocacy of the expansive game — even though he didn't score a try he was given the sentimental consolation of a conversion kick. In his league seasons with Bath he played in 24 of the 33 Courage games but scored only three tries in them.

He had given up the game because of the injuries which continued to pursue him, and there was an eyebrow or two raised when 18 months later, (after a short, readable spell as a guest columnist for the *Bristol Evening Post*), he played for Harlequins. But if some Bath players were a little miffed at his rugby resurrection, well, as they constantly reminded us, it was an amateur game — and one or two now with Bath had been known to change clubs themselves.

Perhaps though Jack Rowell spoke the thoughts of more than a few when he said to me, albeit with a smile: "I always thought Hallers was to a certain degree a closet Harlequin! — and I mean that in a nice way! But he gave so much to Bath and was an outstanding rugby player."

As it turned out, Halliday must have found the contrast between the dedication for every match which was the Bath philosophy a little odd when faced with Harlequins' cup fixation. But he had the special experience of making two farewells to the game in two Twickenham Finals two years apart. It was also a kind of strange rugby justice that, having played in five winning Final sides for Bath and then changing clubs, he should end his career by losing to Bath in his sixth and most exciting Final.

But when Halliday departed he had left behind him a centre who was already becoming one of the best-known names in world rugby, a Bath boy whose early experience playing alongside Halliday was an important factor in his development as one of the most exciting centres in the game.

Jeremy Guscott began his time with Bath early. The son of a Jamaican father and an English mother, he was seven years old when he played mini-rugby there, and even though he played soccer as well at Ralph Allen School rugby became his choice. "It was the first thing I was good at," he has recalled. "It was exciting to run with the ball." It was also one of the few qualifications he took with him when he left school.

Guscott played with the local junior club, Walcot, before returning to Bath. By the time he broke into the side he was first a bricklayer, later a Badgerline bus driver — and a promising new partner for stockbroker Halliday.

Simon Halliday.

Centre Jon Bamsey, 1988.

The arrogance that was to be a feature of his style on the field was apparent even in those early appearances. One minute he would puzzle the impatient in the crowd by some sudden switch that led into a cul-de-sac; the next time the groaners would be about to give voice again only to turn to cheers as they saw Guscott had insinuated his way through the close tacklers.

Nevertheless even after he had made his place safe in the side as John Palmer prepared to leave the game, Guscott still had a few problems. Later, in March 1990, he was famously dropped for a Pilkington Cup semi-final even though he was now an automatic England choice. Jack Rowell paternally explained it away as relieving the pressure on someone who had suddenly become the club's most widely-known player (yes, better-known than Chilcott . . .)

Guscott readily acknowledged his occasional past local difficulties too. "Anyone getting big-headed or too full of himself (at Bath) soon gets put in his place," he told James Belsey in the *Bristol Evening Post*, just before Jack Rowell dropped him.

Twenty months later he was even more forthcoming with Simon Barnes in *The Times* when he recalled how his teammates had at one time in the mid-1980s reacted to his 'strut and swagger.' David Trick, no less, gave him some necessary advice. "I took heed. I benefited from it enormously. It made me a better rugby player, and it also made me a better individual socially.''

The result was that, ignoring the Rugby League temptations, he stayed with the club he first sampled as a scampering seven-year-old. No longer laying bricks or driving buses, he became a fashion model and also a sales executive for British Gas. Rugby was his passport to the good life with his wife Jayne.

On the field enough has been talked and written about his international career. For Bath he tackled and kicked prodigiously — there is much more to his play than the ghosting runs that so tantalise opposing teams.

Was there still the occasion when he seemed, selfishly, to make it to the line himself when a pass to a better-placed colleague was the more obvious alternative? Perhaps. But part of the beauty of rugby for the romantics who follow it occurs when such individual skill — or arrogance — ends in that same individual scoring: aesthetics as well as aggression have had their reward.

But, say the sterner critics, the team should come first. I would simply argue that the occasional mistaken piece of selfishness in attack has been amply compensated by the defences he has opened up for others, as well as himself, to score. For England, the Guscott glide was never more gloriously seen than in the try he fashioned for Rory Underwood in the 1993 Calcutta Cup match — but a chance made for him, crucially, by his MC, Stuart Barnes.

Which brings me to another point: it is precisely because of Guscott's original, graceful talent that he insists, occasionally, on going it alone. And does so with a languid assurance about it that can prompt such extreme reactions. Averagely-talented players falter without arousing the same, occasional, obloquy.

The real test for his Rec critics, such as they are, is to ask if they would prefer that he was playing against, rather than for Bath — or England?

All that said he is largely one who builds from the ideas made possible by those around him. He at times has surprisingly little influence on a tight game for one so talented and is rarely a rescuer of lost causes. Nor is he a playmaker like a Palmer. Guscott needs a Barnes (or a Horton). Then he will snap up what others might have thought an ill-considered trifle — only Swift had a better tries total for Bath in the League than Guscott.

That aspect of Guscott's play was typically evident in the bruising struggle at a wet Welford Road in the 1992-93 season. With only minutes remaining in which to break the deadlock Barnes pointed the way for Guscott twice to make tries for others: first a quick flip for Adebayo to score

after an overhead floated pass by the fly-half; next a wriggling break by Guscott, after Barnes again gave him the opportunity, with Redman scoring. That, emphatically, was Guscott the team-player.

Bath will miss him when he's gone . . .

After Halliday's departure, Jon Bamsey, from Weston-super-Mare, frequently partnered Guscott in the centre. Bamsey, strong and possessed of a mighty left-footed kick, played eight league games of the 12 in the 1990-91 season and in emergency was used at full-back or even fly-half. But with the arrival of Philip de Glanville, aged 20, as the previous season ended, Bamsey's chances became more limited.

The first de Glanville (meaning Glan's place) was one of the Normans who did for Harold at the Battle of Hastings. Nine hundred years or so later the rugby-playing de Glanvilles had their place at Loughborough where Master Philip was born.

Then they came to the West Country, and de Glanville came to Bath via Tavistock in Devon (he and his father once played for Tavistock 2nds on the same day), Bryanston in Dorset — David Trick's training school — and Durham University. He also sampled Bristol briefly before opting for Bath (as he was about to go to Oxford University). He played five league games in his first full season.

By the 1991-92 season he was well-established in the side, his courage taking him into the heart of the action as he scored important tries including the vital score against Harlequins which gave Jon Webb his chance to give Bath the draw. Physically smaller than Bath's other successful centres, he was an elusive runner who also benefited from the attention given to Guscott. His play was recognised by England, too, and he made two appearances on the wing in full internationals as a replacement in the 1992-93 season.

His positional play, speed of pass, tackling, and courage were noticed early by many good judges (Peter Sibley and the former British Lion John Taylor among them) but it was too soon to predict how he would eventually compare with the three big names in Bath's centre frame from the winning Rowell years.

Another promising centre, from Wales, was Iestyn Lewis, one more recruit from Bath University, nephew of Bath's former scrum-half, Steve Lewis.

The younger Lewis, who was also given some opportunities on the wing, was one of a host of ambitious young centres who had come to Bath over the years. Some of them, although failing to grab a regular place in the first team, provided useful cover when bigger names dropped out. Padfield, Cundy, Hoskin, Westcott and Heath-

Jeremy Guscott.

Typical de Glanville opportunism – snapping up a loose ball after Fallon is tackled.

erley come to mind. There were others.

But the names that will set the arguments going wherever two or three Bath fans are gathered together in future years, and the chat turns to centre three-quarters, will be Palmer the play-maker, Halliday the runner, Guscott the mover. A few old heads will still recall wistfully a centre named Beese, while a new generation may be adding a Norman named de Glanville to the debate.

The Players: Half-backs

IN THE beginning was John Horton. Or at least it seemed like that for many Bath followers with memories going back 20 years or more.

There were others who had important parts to play in Bath's slow yet certain transition from a rather dull, run-of-the-land rugby side to one which had — if not weight up front — plenty of wit at the back. There was Peter Sibley and Mike Beese and Jim Waterman. But the modest master of ceremonies who kept the party going was the neat and nimble Horton.

He came from the heart of Rugby League territory, St Helens in Lancashire and Cowley School in particular, nursery of considerable talents in both rugby codes (and some who played both, such as Ray French). Indeed, Horton himself thought seriously about going to Rugby League straight from school but decided to try for an England cap at Rugby Union first, something his admirers thought (wrongly as it turned out) would not be long in coming.

He played briefly for Sale and for his native county before moving to Bath in 1973. Bath must have thanked the rugby gods many times over for the teaching job that brought him to the Rec.

In his early seasons Horton's defensive skills as much as his attacking ploys were of great value to the club. His prodigious kicking from hand gained swathes of territory that put attacking opponents right back where they came from — and kept Bath in many a game, or from heavier defeat, time after time.

Richard Hill, whose career was starting as Horton's was close to ending, and partnered him in two Twickenham Finals, has reminded me not just of the repeated sidesteps that were Horton's hallmark but also the fly-half's particular skill and accuracy in his long, rolling touch-finding kicks that could bring despair to opponents.

Nevertheless it was his jinking runs, his little chip-and-gather stratagems, and sleight-of-hand with the ball, setting up attacking opportunities and chances galore, that made Horton at times a minor genius in displaying the skills of the playmaking fly-half.

Many who watched the modern Bath's less successful early seasons, when Horton was playing, thought their admission money worthwhile, even if Bath lost, for the chance to see the little stand-off (he stands 5ft 6in) plying his trade. That his trade involved deception and improvisation as well as that mighty, ground-gaining tactical kicking merely added to the joy.

Horton helped Lancashire win the County Championship in the days when the title still meant something. And it was in the early and mid-1970s when the inveterate Horton-fanciers, particularly in the North, reckoned he was to be seen at the height of his playing powers. Indeed, there were and are good judges around who maintained he was at his best before — not when or after — he was first picked for England, in days when he had speed to add to the novelty and freshness of his ideas.

Brian Ashton, later to coach Bath's backs, like many who saw him when he first played for Lancashire, considered Horton was at his best when still in his late teens and immediately after — and Horton believes his own best days were around that time too.

England, alas, never used him on a consistent basis, and although he was first capped as late as 1978 and was also the Grand Slam stand-off in 1980, popping over his inevitable quota of dropped-goals, England never saw him at his inventive best. Those were days when playing to order for fly-halves rarely meant flights or even runs of fancy.

Neil Bennett and Alan Old, safer, solid kicking stand-offs both, were generally competing for the position, with Les Cusworth and John Horton, the smaller playmakers, never given the chance of seasons of security in the role such as Rob Andrew was to enjoy a decade or so later. Nevertheless, Horton was the first of Bath's modern-day internationals and gained 13 caps.

Of course, he was never the tackling fly-half that most clubs insist upon. Like Barry John, Horton reckoned it wasn't his job to grapple with a galumphing lock. He preferred to stay intact to clear the danger.

But when he had to tackle — because there was no one else — then Horton did tackle on a notable occasion or two (maybe even three or four?) both for Bath and for England. (And given the bad injuries Stuart Barnes has suffered in making tackles over the seasons, the sense of Horton's philosophy can be understood even by those who don't share it.)

Mention of Barry John is a reminder that Horton was much admired by Welsh clubs, and was sometimes likened to a Welsh mould of half-backs. He preferred to claim he was a Lancashire breed of stand-off, prevalent after World War Two in both League and Union: two of his Lancashire and England predecessors, Martin Regan and Tom Brophy, both moved to Rugby League. Horton himself also rejected overtures in his Bath heyday in the 1970s from Salford, who had former England caps such as Keith Fielding and Mike Coulman.

At Bath a few spectators became impatient at times when his ideas went awry, or became as they thought too elaborate, but it was rare for him to have a bad game.

As the main architect of Bath's enterprising back play in the late-1970s, overlapping into the arrival of Jack Rowell, it was justice that the little man was still in the driving seat for the first two of the club's Twickenham Cup Final triumphs. And when the comparisons began between the younger Barnes and the seasoned wizard of St Helens, the older man had the first laugh.

Horton's match-winning contributions that night at Bristol when he pulled the game round for Bath in the final quarter-of-an-hour was enough to show the doubters — and they were there — that the old trickster hadn't yet exhausted his repertoire.

But the parting of the ways was near, as described in an earlier chapter. Talking with me, Jack Rowell has insisted that if Horton had stayed with Bath, he would have started the next season a first choice, and Barnes, the new recruit, would have had to earn his place.

Horton, though, his confidence in the Bath selectors shaken by his omission in that last season at the Rec, was looking further ahead. Having been the chef for many of Bath's diets of comparative hard tack in bad times and fine feasts in good, it was hardly surprising that Horton should decide he was not going to share the kitchen with another.

Undoubtedly his earlier thoughts about retiring — which helped precipitate Barnes's decision to go to Bath — complicated matters. And other pressures may have added to Horton's soul-searchings.

What few people in the game knew — never

John Horton.

mind those outside it — was the pressure Horton had faced in going on the South African tour of 1984, from his employers, Kingswood School. As a Methodist foundation (owing much to John Wesley) it was inevitably caught up in Horton's decision to go, with the headmaster Laurie Campbell receiving calls and letters expressing delight at Horton's selection — or criticising the head for allowing Horton to go.

Campbell, himself opposed to Horton's acceptance, and the school governors, supporting the head's stance, said they deplored the decision to tour South Africa and regretted the decision 'by a member of staff of Kingswood School to join that tour.'

The tale began with Horton asking the head's permission to tour. Campbell said he needed time to consider the matter and 'the RFU would have to wait.' A few days later, Campbell addressed the 45 members of staff at the school about the issue and later the school's three senior forms. He said there were two possible Christian responses — that contact with South Africa was better than absence, in the sense that good must always confront evil; or that international sport was morale-boosting propaganda for the apartheid system. Campbell, although taking the second view, said that 'out of respect for liberty of conscience' he protected Horton's right to make his own decision, but with 'as much information as we could give him.' Horton decided to tour, Campbell accepting his decision with regret. Horton repaid the school the cost of replacing him temporarily.

What Campbell called 'the John Horton affair . . .how a headmaster acts in the political education' of his staff and pupils clearly made more ripples for the player than were faced by, say, John Palmer, teaching at King Edward's School, Bath, who was also on the tour. But Horton has said that he believed he was treated fairly at all times and that his headmaster acted entirely properly. If, Horton said, a majority of his teaching colleagues had also opposed the tour, then his decision might have been different.

Horton believed his headmaster — 'a great character' — acted fairly and with good sense; and Horton stayed at Kingswood for another four years until he moved to Bloxham School, Oxfordshire, where he became director of physical education.

The dilemma — to tour or not to tour South Africa — was not one that Stuart Barnes was called on to face. But, like a few other prominent players before him, he always made it clear he would not have played there under apartheid.

In style on the field, too, Barnes was different from Horton. If Horton was the jinking, witty 'man with an educated rugby boot' as John Stevens described him, and an artful dodger in avoiding the opposition's big guns, then Barnes, scampering and scheming, was willing to go where the action was at its most hectic. It was from such positions that he made tries for others as he broke through the gain-line, or scored them himself, memorably the match-winning score in the 1989 Cup Final against Leicester.

In that stratagem of darting into dangerous areas, too, he was strikingly different from the man who was preferred to him in the England side for more than 50 internationals, Rob Andrew. If they had been pre-war cycling enthusiasts, then Andrew might have been riding a sit-up-and-beg model, while Barnes would have been whizzing into the traffic with his dropped handlebars.

But Barnes and England deserves almost a chapter in itself. Before that, though, it is right to assess his outstanding contribution to Bath's continued success story under Jack Rowell. At first his play was understandably more tentative than he might have wished. But it did not take him long to stamp his mark on each Bath game as firmly as Horton had done before him. Barnes was the playmaker, the chooser of options, the man in the cockpit as Jack Rowell calls him. He must decide where to go — and where Bath's play is to go — often in a split-second of judgement.

It is tribute to the soundness and speed of Barnes's thought that his absence so often meant that the team faltered. Important games were narrowly lost with Barnes in the side, but the coincidence of defeat in games he has missed assumed what for the club were alarmingly high proportions. They included the cup defeats at Moseley and Waterloo, sandwiched in time by the title-robbing league defeat at Saracens in 1990.

His influence as playmaker seemed hard to replace. If that was eloquent of his value to the club it could equally suggest that his colleagues, without perhaps realising it, found it difficult to perform without the usual leader of the band deciding the repertoire.

England did not have that problem. For the most part the England selectors avoided it simply by not choosing him. And for the rest Barnes himself decided he didn't wish to be chosen.

That conflict had its origins in the England tour of New Zealand of 1985 when Barnes, playing in both internationals, was one of the few successes — only to find Andrew preferred to him first against Romania and then for the Five Nations Championship the next season. Instead he went on the replacements' bench.

What followed was succinctly explained to his friend Tim Davey in the *Bristol Evening Post*, as Barnes prepared for the 1987 Cup Final against Bath, while his rival Rob Andrew prepared both for the Final and the subsequent World Cup in the Antipodes.

"Basically, I quit England after spending four years sitting on the replacements' bench at internationals. In 13 games I managed to get on just four times as a substitute and on each occasion played out of position," he said. "Now while it is an honour to play for your country, you want to play in your right position, so there did not seem a lot of point doing something unfulfilling when you're also having to take two or three days' holiday from work to do it."

And the alleged snub to his country in saying he didn't wish to be considered for selection? "It is also slightly disappointing that an amateur sportsman cannot do what he wishes. It is only

Barnes the boot.

a hobby, albeit a serious one.''

More, he had no longer thought he was even worth his place on the bench (where he sat in all 23 times) — an added irony.

Five years later he told Steve Bale of *The Independent:* ''In the end I was kept on the bench even when I was playing badly, and by then I wouldn't have felt aggrieved if they'd dropped

It's a try for Barnes.

me. But I still believe that, if I'd been given chances and second lives, like others, I would have established myself.''

Briefly, Barnes said, he was again officially back in contention. But he failed to win his international place and by the time he was Bath captain he bowed out of 1989 divisional rugby as well — ostensibly, as was noted in an earlier chapter, to give others a chance of catching the selectors' eyes.

Jack Rowell had never agreed with Barnes's abdication from England squads. But Bath's continuing and rarely-interrupted success of which Barnes was so integral a part meant that for all who thought his attitude either wrong, or even arrogant or petulant, there were many more who took him at his own valuation — as probably the best and most consistent fly-half in

England, one moreover who was helping his club win more cups than any other.

But by the time he told England manager Geoff Cooke he was again prepared to offer himself for selection, and with the 1991 World Cup soon to arrive, Cooke let him sweat — preferring to stick with Andrew as first choice and the Cumbrian Harlequin David Pears on the bench.

There was perhaps further irony for Barnes in seeing Pears play at full-back for Harlequins, rather than as fly-half, in the 1992 Pilkington Cup Final. The winning dropped-goal at the last gasp when others had failed merely compounded it. Gerald Davies, found the winning kick a reason to purr publicly about Barnes in *The Times:*

''His impudence has won many a match and many a divided heart, but has, at the same time, kept him out of the England team.''

But if the sorcerer had to serve his apprenticeship all over again, then Barnes proved his willingness to do so by accepting captaincy of an England 'B' team tour to New Zealand that summer (coached by Jack Rowell), and coming close to leading the team to victory over (the also reinstated) South Africa at Bristol the following autumn. He topped it off with a key performance for the Barbarians against Australia in November (as Bath lost in the cup at Waterloo), in which he made a try possible as the tackles went in on him: a classic example of the difference between his game and Andrew's.

Poor Andrew, meanwhile, having returned from working and playing in France only to find himself barred from Courage League action for 120 days under a rule intended for quite different targets, was dropped by England after the 1993 defeat by Wales. In yet another twist of irony, Andrew almost echoed Barnes's thoughts of eight years earlier but not voiced at that time, wondering why he should have been dropped and wanting clear-the-air talks with the England management.

As for Barnes, the Calcutta Cup match that year at Twickenham was the first time he had started a Five Nations game even though he was first capped in 1984. It was only his fifth start for England — yet of the team, only Winterbottom and Rory Underwood had played for their country over a longer period, Nevertheless it was a surprise, he told Robert Armstrong of *The Guardian:* "I decided to have one last crack at getting back but I cannot say I really expected to be selected again."

A few people may have been ready to jeer if his appearance had been an anticlimax. But he could hardly have been pushed into a more public challenge to show what he might do on the international stage. He replaced a man with 50 caps, in one of only two changes from a side beaten in Wales, and the selectors were taking a deep breath themselves because, if he did strike sparks, a wider audience might wonder why Barnes had been buried all this time. But the story of his comeback triumph is now rugby history.

John Mason in the *Daily Telegraph* summed up Barnes and the game thus:

"Being the generous extrovert he is, he brought not a spark to Twickenham, but a bonfire, a roaring conflagration in which Scottish hopes perished. From the ashes, English back-play, at last, flowered."

The highlight was Barnes's second-half break from his own 22 when he took a high pass from Morris over his head and, perforce, standing still. Then — to quote Frank Keating in *The Guardian* 'he broke from defence like a full barrel down a pub chute to fashion that voluptuous try.'

He gave the accelerating Guscott a beautifully weighted pass. His Bath colleague glided 50 metres through the Scottish cover to feed Rory Underwood at just the right moment. It was the kind of try for which the England backs — and the England crowd — had been yearning. Barnes had struck the sparks as he said he would.

The rugby writers were properly appreciative, and some didn't hide the tone of justifiable we-told-you-so in their praise of Barnes's vision. It was inevitable probably that the England management were more sheepishly circumspect — or perhaps kind to Andrew — in assessing his contribution. But an absurd note, surely, was struck by that recent England player, Paul Ackford, lately turned analyst. He told his *Daily Telegraph* readers:

"Part of the reason for Barnes's success was the novelty factor . . .defences are not sure what he is capable of. Opponents will have a better idea of what he can do next time, after the video tapes have been analysed. All players get a honeymoon period of two or three games before they get sussed . . ."

If Barnes had been 20 years of age, such a view might have been valid. But he was 30 — and if opponents hadn't learned enough about him from seven Twickenham Cup Finals, tours of New Zealand, games against Australia and Courage League clashes they never would — the Welsh, who did know him, had wondered for years why, like Horton before him, Barnes wasn't picked more often for his country. And as for Scotland they had Bath past (Cronin) and present (Reed) players in their second row as well as a former Bath player as their recent, retired captain. Indeed, Ackford's grudging reservation was more insulting to Ian McGeechan, on his last game as coach, than it was to Barnes.

The subsequent game in Dublin was as much an anticlimax for Barnes and the losing England side as it was a triumph for Ireland and their fly-half Elwood.

But to judge Barnes without giving him a run of at least a full term of Five Nations games would merely have been to complement the mutual neglect that had robbed England of his services over so many seasons. The Lions' selectors underlined that view by picking him for the 1993 tour to New Zealand.

In a career encrusted with irony it was almost forgotten that the Essex boy who went west had also qualified for Wales, had captained Welsh Schools, and been selected for a Welsh senior squad while at Newport, his first club. Then he opted for his England qualification.

Arguments about the respective merits of Andrew or Barnes as an England fly-half will continue wherever rugby people chatter.

Andrew for a long time seemed like an under-achiever who eventually made good with some solid performances for his country. But his game always seemed more limited than Barnes's could be. Both were fearless tacklers, Andrew perhaps was the more consistent kicking from hand, but seemingly reluctant to dare. Barnes by contrast was ever prepared to scuttle his way through the closest cover and to vary his game more judiciously than his rival. He also — dangerous fellow — occasionally took risks.

Spurned by England, and in turn spurning England, Barnes poured his skills and his spirit into the Bath club. One of the other views which didn't endear him to the establishment was his often repeated opinion that playing and winning with friends and regular teammates was satisfaction enough in an amateur sport.

(Not all Barnes's critics were in past England camps: in his time he was reviled and spat upon by diehard Bristolians — he still lived in the city although, in his latest job, he managed the Stroud and Swindon Building Society branch in Bath. "The whole problem with my move was that it was between rival clubs. For a lot of people it was merely an excuse to have a go at me.")

Jack Rowell was in no doubt at Barnes's value. "As a team member, as an outside-half and as a captain, there has been none better at Bath, and we've had some very good ones."

As for Barnes's international career there was yet more irony in his eventual recall. By then the scrum-half who had partnered Barnes for several seasons, and Andrew through Grand Slam and World Cup games for England, was no longer first or second choice for his country. Dewi Morris had replaced Richard Hill, 18 months Barnes's senior. Like Andrew later, Hill perhaps suffered from playing according to a rigid England game-plan which was now being re-drawn.

Hill had been paired at half-back during Bath's glory years with two outstanding outside-halves; all three had been capped for England. But Hill, whose total of caps outnumbered theirs combined, played only with Horton at full international level, in their two games in South Africa in 1984.

If Chilcott was the only other Bath player to appear in every Twickenham Cup Final for his club, Hill (who had to be replaced during the Gloucester match) could, if he wished, have countered the jest about Chilcott being the only player on the field for all of every Final by a boast of his own.

Hill was the only Bath player selected in the same position for every Final (Chilcott, of course, propped on both sides of the front row). It demonstrated the value to his side of a player whose sheer consistency at times may have led

Richard Hill.

some to take his skills too much for granted.

Richard Hill joined the club the season before their first cup win. Although Birmingham-born he was another of the recruits from Wiltshire — he was at school with David Egerton at Bishop Wordsworth's, Salisbury. But if, as it turned out, it was an opportune moment for the young university student to arrive at the Rec (he was at Exeter with David Sole, later to follow him to Bath), it was also auspicious for the club. His speed, accuracy of pass, and strength with the ball were immediate assets that at once solved what had become a position where new strength was needed; before him, only the former Oxford Blue, Steve Lewis, had played there consistently.

To have remained first choice in the position in the subsequent ten seasons is tribute enough to the durability as well as skill of a player in so exposed a position.

Hill's tenure was not without its hard times,

however. His captaincy of England for a few games in the mid-1980s ended when he was, perhaps unfairly, apparently blamed for not being able to separate warring packs in the game against Wales.

The red-haired scrum-half could be fiery enough himself on the field too, but as he admitted, his game was the better when he learned to keep his temper — as well as opponents — in check.

But of all the weapons in Hill's armoury none was so telling as his speed of pass, the product of many hours of practising passing, passing, and passing. It was a service which meant that his outside-half had so often an important split-second extra in which to act. No other scrum-half in the English game could rival it, and it was a leading reason for Hill's recall to the England side in good time for the 1991 World Cup.

When he did finally lose his place — when he was already just over 30 — it was apparently because his game for England was considered too predictable — the same argument that was soon to lead to Andrew's omission and Barnes's recall. In both cases it seemed the players were dropped because the very consistency of performance demanded of them had forbidden variety.

Generously, his predecessor and successor in the England side, Dewi Morris, acknowledged Hill as the biggest influence on his game, particularly his passing and kicking. They had worked together on summer tours to Argentina and Australia. "I'm very grateful for that," said Morris, and only curmudgeons might hope he would continue to take lessons in passing from the Bath man.

Bath too had much to thank Hill for, not least in partnering two great stand-offs so admirably: inevitably, he occasionally had spells when he was below his best form, and captaincy, as he himself conceded, seemed to detract from his general play — he appeared a better player without the extra responsibility.

He probably had many competing memories of his decisive play for the club. But most regular supporters will find it hard to forget his huge, fast pass in the second Wasps Final, of 1987, which gave Halliday the chance to crash over and break Wasps' resistance at last. But of his own many tries for the club none was more needed, more hard-won than his decisive late score in the 1989 cup-tie in the mud of the Rec against Bristol.

If Hill will be a difficult act for anyone to follow, it must also have been hard shadowing him all those seasons with only rare opportunities to replace him in big games.

When injury did strike, Chris Stanley was the first of the competent second-strings who did duty — including three stints on the replacements' bench for Twickenham Cup Finals.

Then came policeman Steve Knight, whose father Terry and younger brother Jamie (also a scrum-half) also had close Bath links.

Steve Knight played effectively as a constant stand-by for Hill, and had his deserved 20 minutes of the high life when he went on in the second half of the 1990 Final against Gloucester. Knight was a player who could probably have found a regular first-team place at other senior Courage League clubs (he was even a reserve for England 'B') and he had considerable popularity among the Bath crowd.

By the 1992-93 season, a third player had become first choice as Hill's occasional stand-in. He was Ian Sanders, another of the club's Cornishmen, whose chip into space gave Tony Swift his 350th try in the Courage League game at Gloucester.

But who would, who could, eventually replace the man who set daunting standards behind Bath's winning packs for so many seasons was a question still open to answer as the season ended, with Hill still Bath's first-choice scrum-half.

The Players: Front Row

ONLY two players have played in all seven of Bath's Twickenham Cup Finals. They are Gareth Chilcott and Richard Hill. But Chilcott, as mentioned in the previous chapter likes to joke that he's the only player to have been on the field for 'all' of the seven: Hill took a knock and gave way to Steve Knight late in the 1990 Final against Gloucester.

But that the prop forward was one of the two whose winning appearances have spanned nine years was tribute enough to the fitness and form of the former British Lion. Other players may have appeared in that 1984 Final who were also with the club at the time of the 1992 triumph, but Trick and Lee were no longer in contention, and Redman and Hall had missed Finals because of loss of form (Redman), suspension or injury (Hall).

Given Chilcott's own early record when he was the man opposing fans loved to hate and Bath fans almost despaired of because of his disciplinary record, the conversion to cuddly Coochie ('Mr Chilcott to you,' as his ghosted book put it), star of World Cup commentary team and pantomime alike, seemed something of which the followers of St Paul might have been proud.

Yet the playing career of the man who has come to symbolise the Bath team spirit could have been so different: with Welsh ancestry he was nevertheless Bristol born and bred — a Bedminster boy and proud of it.

But he has admitted that his academic skills at Ashton Park Comprehensive were such that during English, his worst subject, he might be sent off to help the dinner ladies lay the cutlery. "Ashton Park was a good school and it was me that couldn't be bothered, not the teachers," he told *Bristol Evening Post* columnist Rebecca Gooch in 1990.

His problem was that he was only interested in sport and didn't bother about study which he lived to regret: if it had been different he might have become a sports teacher, his idea of a perfect job. As it was, he became a lumberjack and a french polisher, a road digger and a security guard. Then with the help of that keen Bath-supporting businessman, Malcolm Pearce he took on first a

uniform, and then a directorship in a limousine hire company. Plus some modelling and the panto. But back to the rugby.

His rugby at Ashton Park School, first as a hooker and then as a prop won him a place in the Bristol's Schools under-15 side, and a chance with the junior club, Old Redcliffians, better known as Old Reds. Indeed, that's where he had his first sending off. But it seemed natural to try his luck with his own city team, Bristol. He attended a training session which he didn't enjoy. "No one spoke to us new lads." So, still only 18, he tried Bath instead, and never regretted it.

Even though he had left school at 15 without a certificate to his name, and found himself in training with men from universities, he was neither put-off nor patronised. Instead he was coaxed and coached — and won a place in the front row of Jack Rowell's burgeoning Bath pack at the start of the 1980s.

Chilcott himself also gave much credit to his captain of those days, flanker Roger Spurrell — although in doing so he did himself few favours with his critics. "We worked together rather well," he said. "He'd start the trouble, I'd finish it."

But the pattern of the problems from his early reputation was set when he was sent off for kicking Bob Hesford in a game against Bristol and was banned for a year. Hesford was one of those who spoke up for him at an appeal and the term was reduced by seven weeks.

In 1983 he was again dismissed after a free-for-all at Exeter; he was accused of head-butting. Two weeks were added to his automatic 30-day ban. As well as the bad reputation it gave both Chilcott and Bath, the offences also cost his club an important member of the pack for weeks on end.

Chilcott was a fierce, formidable forward who anchored the set scrums and was no slouch in the loose. His reputation was only partly due to his disciplinary problems — the reasons opponents respected him was because of his considerable scrummaging skills. Unusually, too, in the modern game, he could perform either as tighthead prop or as loose head — an adaptability that helped win him a British Lions tour place.

He also won 14 England caps (four as a

Easy now, Gareth . . .Chilcott points the finger in a league game against Moseley, 1991.

replacement) between 1984 and 1989, in spite of being dropped after the notorious punch-up in the 1987 Welsh game (Chilcott was not himself directly involved but his reputation seemed to count against him). But as the Bath-baiters (crowds at Kingsholm and the Memorial Ground to the fore) labelled his game as barbarian-like, the more certain it was he would never play for the Barbarians. Nor did he.

His last sending off, more serious in the context both of match and career, was by Fred Howard at Kingsholm in the league defeat by Gloucester. He was dismissed for punching. He had not been the only offender. But he had ignored the referee's proper catch-all warning and was out for nearly two months.

Since that time his career was trouble-free and he consciously stayed aloof from trouble which would once have tempted him. As the 1992-93 season began he was announcing his biggest regret: "My indiscretions on the rugby field when younger."

By then, too, speculation about his retirement from the game had been going on for two or three seasons. But his play had justified his continuing selection — and as Bath discovered in that league defeat at Orrell in their last 'double' season his loss through injury during a game visibly weakened the pack's scrummaging strength to the point where it may even have decided the outcome.

Strong as he has been on the field, he has increasingly become a growing favourite off it, with an avuncular, almost cuddly style.

Some of that improved reputation within the game has also come from largely unsung gestures. Reporter Kevin Coughlan, the nearest to a Devonian Irishman I know (but who like Palmer and Cronin, was at Prior Park School, Bath) has told in a Twickenham programme of Chilcott's ready agreement to go to Brixham for a coaching session with the lads who had beaten Bath in a friendly a few seasons earlier. It was, said Coughlan, who made it, an impertinent request given Chilcott's commitments for England and Bath and that he had just started a new job. But he agreed, and he and Coughlan set off on a late Tuesday afternoon for the 200-mile round trip.

"After two hours of forthright advice on scrummaging and line-out techniques and the virtues of good rucking — 'a legal way of softening up the opposition,' he beamed — there was the obligatory drink in the bar. But when a Brixham committee member quietly offered some expenses to cover his travelling costs, the answer was simple and direct. "No, that would just upset me . . .I was given a lift. It's been my pleasure to help out."

That natural friendliness of spirit was also evident when he became a member of the 1991 ITV World Cup commentary team where his knowledge of the forwards' trade tricks was a worthwhile contribution. With the help of frequent appearances as a guest pundit for HTV in their Bristol studios, too, he has become more relaxed and cheerful in the role.

In the circumstances it should have been no great surprise that he also went where Ian Botham and Frank Bruno had trodden and became a pantomime star.

Whatever it did for Equity's qualms, it certainly did plenty for the box office at Bath's handsome Theatre Royal, when Chilcott was signed up as a villainous broker's man for Christmas 1992, with co-stars Rolf Harris, Lesley Joseph, and Sylvester McCoy, in Cinderella. It was a taxing change for him — and he did miss a couple of Courage League games — and he was generous in his public thanks to his stage colleagues for their help.

An experienced theatre critic, Helen Reid of the *Western Daily Press*, who must have seen as many pantomimes as Chilcott had played cup games, didn't much care for the production, but liked the stars. As for Gareth Chilcott he was indeed 'a hit'. Said Miss Reid:

"He may sound like a West Country I-Speak-Your-Weight machine but he has a good sense of timing and a very solid (!) stage presence."

Whatever his future, Bath supporters will always remember the mighty efforts Gareth Chilcott contributed to his club's success against the great Welsh club sides and in cup and league during the Jack Rowell years.

And when, at a break in play, the croak of a Coochie clearing his throat is no longer to be heard, then autumn, winter, and spring on the Rec won't sound quite the same.

But if Chilcott took the prisoners, there was a trusty colleague close by equally experienced in laying siege to opponents' defences. Richard Lee, like Barry Trevaskis in the backs, was one of the Bath stalwarts who rarely won headlines yet was a most valuable member of the earlier cup-winning sides. He too joined the club in the late 1970s, and became an essential part of Jack Rowell's strategy for building a strong pack as the bedrock of success.

"When I first joined we lived off scraps," Lee has recalled, "then we became more forward-dominated. Now we have the right balance of forwards and backs. On our day we feel we can beat anyone." He was speaking then before the 1989 Cup Final against Leicester, a game which marked his return to Twickenham — for the 1987 Final David Sole's emergence meant that Lee stood down.

But his loyalty and perseverance were only two of the qualities that marked out Richard Lee, one

Spot the prop of Bath's 1992-93 pantomime.

of the game's honest journeymen. His solid scrummaging, strength in tap penalty moves, and week-by-week consistency led to more than 300 appearances for the club. Yet his switch from junior rugby to Bath meant considerable sacrifices in time and travel. He was a journeyman who did indeed journey to ply his rugby skills.

With his father, Morris, he ran a dairy farm at West Buckland, Devon, not far from the Somerset border (and in kicking distance of the school that nurtured Victor Ubogu, Steve Ojomoh, and Fred Sagoe) and the never-ending cycle of farm work meant extra strain on them both as Richard went to Bath for his vital training sessions.

He played in Finals against Bristol, London Welsh, Wasps and Leicester, and was first-choice tight-head prop for the first three Courage League seasons. But supporters with a long memory will never forget in particular his tie-saving tackle on Gloucester's John Gadd in the 1985 John Player Cup semi-final at Kingsholm. It was crucial. But even that is played down in the modesty of the player's own memory: "Minutes later I went over the top and gave away the penalty which could have cost us the game."

Much has been written about the man who for a couple of seasons ousted Richard Lee from the Bath front row in the mid-1980s. David Sole, born in Aylesbury, came to Bath's attention — like Richard Hill before him — when he was at Exeter University. He had also been close to Bath at the Royal Agricultural College at Cirencester (where Ben Clarke was later to follow).

When he first arrived at Bath, a surprise for spectators was his comparatively modest build compared with the solidity of his peers, Chilcott and Lee. But his speed about the pitch spoke of unusual mobility and was allied to scrummaging techniques that promised to live with the best: so they did.

As he pressed for a first-team place, so he benefited from the generosity of Malcolm Pearce whose dairy business found a place for him. Bath did likewise by switching the versatile Chilcott to tight-head in place of Lee so accommodating Sole on the loose-head. After being on the bench for the 1985 Final it seemed likely he would be in the Twickenham line-up if Bath made it again the following season.

Indeed, he had already claimed his first Scottish caps in 1986 when that nasty injury received in the cup game at Moseley ended his season. Bath were lucky to have Richard Lee on call.

When Sole did make his first Twickenham appearance for the club in a Final, in 1987 against Wasps, he and his rival Jeff Probyn entertained themselves but not the crowd or the referee with their tussle. Worse, an early knock meant that Sole — who had played only with special permission from the Scottish authorities who wanted him under wraps for the 1987 World Cup — went through much of the game dangerously unaware of what was going on.

Next season Sole, who lived in Wiltshire and also ran a wine import business, upped sticks and joined Edinburgh Academicals. He was the first of Bath's Anglo-Scots of the glory run to claim a Scottish cap. And much has been written and said — a lot of it by Sole himself — since then; he became an outstanding Scottish captain.

Bath enjoyed him — he enjoyed Bath. But he left just as his best rugby was beginning, and as Bath were going through what can now be seen as one of their least impressive periods, of which the uneasy second Final against Wasps was a warning pointer.

Sole's departure meant he also missed the start of the Courage Clubs' Championship. That was a blow. His subsequent success, though, reflected well on his time at the Rec — even if many listened in fascination as they heard Sole's Scottish accent, scarcely noticed in the West Country, become so authentically honed in the years that followed.

In Sole's absence, the faithful Richard Lee reclaimed his place, and it was three seasons before a new rival to the old guard of props seriously emerged. It was Victor Ubogu — the man who was at school just down the road while Richard Lee was milking his cows at West Buckland.

In his schooldays, the Nigerian was clocking around 12 seconds for the 100 metres and was a winger, until the school's loose-head prop was crocked and big Vic was switched. After Birmingham University he went to Oxford and played in the 1987 Varsity Match. As a student he had experience with Moseley and Richmond and spurned Harlequins ("The atmosphere was not serious enough.").

Earlier Oxford Blues — Halliday, Barnes — suggested he try Bath. He quickly made his impact even though his first-team chances were strictly limited initially. But he proved an ideal man on the bench to cover back or front-row injuries, and his first league appearance in the 1988-89 season was as a replacement. The following season with Chilcott suspended, he had more chances and in season 1990-91 he made more league appearances than Chilcott or Lee. 'Victor' as the crowd called him, had arrived.

He is quick to point to Jack Rowell, Chilcott and hooker Graham Dawe for assisting his education in the subterranean world of the front row, essential for someone who was to switch from loose head to tight-head prop, where he also played for England in the autumn of 1992.

Heads down: Lee, Dawe, and Ubogu.

A few wiseacres mutter about his scrummaging abilities in literal comparison with the old heads. But in a changing game where more emphasis was now given to mobility rather than the successions of scrums which dominated the scene for so long, Ubogu's virtues were particularly valuable.

Ubogu is an exciting player to watch because of his zest for the game, his speed about the pitch, and his irrepressible urge to run the ball or set others running whenever he can — what Mick Cleary in *The Observer* called 'that demolition-ball style of his, would-be tacklers simply rebounding off him.'

His Devon schooling apart, he is one of the few Bath first-teamers without a local claim to adoption by geography: after a time working with Malcolm Pearce he moved to Barnes, and ran a family security agency in West London. but he is a Bathonian simply because he has caught the crowd's delighted attention by the energy and exuberance he brings to his rugby.

In the gallery of fine props Chilcott and Lee typified for Bath the best of the old school techniques, beloved of the Rendalls and the Probyns, the Blakeways and the Cottons. Victor Ubogu, like David Sole before him, was of a different mould but one from which, increasingly, the props of the future seem likely to be cast.

There have been numerous men in between the established props but only two or three with a claim to a regular place, reflected in their Cup Final appearances.

Rob Cunningham, first-choice hooker at the time of Bath's first Final against Bristol, was by then the oldest member of the side at 33. He had also played in a previous John Player Special Final. Although Edinburgh-born and a player with Boroughmuir, he had moved to Newcastle University and became a member of the successful Gosforth side of the late 1970s (shades of Rowell and Uttley).

He was in Gosforth's losing 1980-81 side against Leicester, and scored their only try in their 22-15 defeat. For Bath, he is remembered almost as a caricature of the Englishman's idea of a Scot — dour, uncompromising, a growler rather than a smiler. But he was a fully-committed competitor on the field, and only injury in the first game of the following season's cup run robbed him of a second Cup Final appearance, in 1985.

Later he coached first Richmond, and then Bristol where he regularly fulminated about the vagaries of selectors, of the South West or from England, who he claimed ignored his young — and old — thrusters. Rob Cunningham knew plenty about the caprices and cruelties of selectors. Fourteen times (or was it 15?) he sat on the bench for Scotland sides in which Colin Deans reigned as hooker. Never once did he get his chance even through injury — he must go down as one of the unluckiest replacements in the game's history.

His replacement for the 1985 cup run, culminating in the win over London Welsh, was the much younger Greg Bess, yet another graduate to Bath's playing force from Bath University. Bess filled in skilfully for Cunningham until he in turn was displaced by the man who was to make the role his own for much of Bath's great seasons.

Elsewhere I have told how at Christmas 1985, Liz Dawe persuaded husband Graham, the Launceston captain, then 26, to have a crack at big-time rugby. He had been playing for Cornwall and was twice picked as a non-travelling reserve for England, against Canada and New Zealand. He was honest in admitting why he initially sought to join Bath's Cornish contingent. "My reason for joining Bath was to play for England."

He achieved that ambition — if not as often as he would have wished, against stiff competition from Brian Moore and John Olver. But he soon became a vital member of Bath's match-winning pack. Whenever Bath's commitments permitted, too, he continued to play for Cornwall — and there was the likelihood that when he did finally bow out of the Bath front row (he was 33 at the start of the 1992-93 season) there would be another season or so of rugby back in his beloved Cornwall.

Yet the adopted Bathonian, and adopted Cornishman, was Plymouth-born and lived near Tavistock on the Devon side of the border. But the family farm in the Tamar Valley was an increasing commitment after Mr Dawe senior retired.

Dawe was a hard competitor who has been

Hooker Greg Bess, 1984.

known to go a step too far for the liking of opponents or referees — 'Typical Dawesey' say the fans in exasperation, admiration, or admonition, according to taste.

Perhaps part of his aggression — particularly against a team like Harlequins — came from his farming background. Helping deliver a cow by Caesarean section in the early hours of the morning was not always the best prelude for a big match. But it was also a rather different preparation from the suit-and-tie office job of say, the Harlequins hooker — or of some of his Bath colleagues. Perhaps that's why the Chilcott-Dawe-Lee trio was so firm a foundation for so many Bath victories. They were all tough lads who had earned a living with their hands — and brawn: two farmers and a former lumberjack.

Might Dawe have played more for England but for his unfortunate part in the famous Cardiff punch-up? Almost certainly, and he has admitted it was the lowest point in his career. As it was, he eventually fought his way back into contention with good performances for the England 'B' side and went to New Zealand with them in the tour Jim Fallon 'missed' of 1992.

Bell-ringer, cattle-breeder, sheep-shearer, pint-downer — Graham Dawe was all of these but for Bath his contribution over league and cup triumphs, had been consistently committed (how could anyone not be who made a 300-mile round trip to train or play two or three times a week?) and uncompromising in his specialist role and general play.

Dawe's deputy at first was Greg Bess, who stood in for him when he was injured in the 1987 Final, but Bess himself soon had to give up the game because of injury. Thereafter Dawe's shadow at Bath was Jimmy Deane, who came through the club's youth side, and although small, was remarkably brisk about the field. Over half a dozen seasons he played in a handful of league games — some as a replacement, but missed the cup action.

His later, younger rival was Colin Atkins, a member of the brave Headingley side that lost at Bath in the cup in the 1989-90 season. In a sense he did a Fallon in reverse by leaving the Yorkshire city after taking a master's degree at Leeds University. ("You see kids playing rugby in the streets but they've all got 'Leeds RL' shirts on. It's nice to be where people are interested in proper rugby. It's a major part of life down here," he told Bath's programme editor, Ken Johnstone.)

Injuries marred his early career at Bath but he made his first league appearance in the 1991-92 season and was a candidate to step in when 'Dawesey' finally returned to fleecing sheep instead of rival front-rows.

The Players: Locks

IF THE freemasonry of the front row is one about which referees seem sometimes to know little, and spectators even less, then the engine-room (donkey engine?) of the second row is almost as big a mystery. There is less mystery about the mastery some players can establish at line-outs — but the scrummaging art remains little known.

Nigel Gaymond summed it up thus: "I just do the donkey work . . .You're left in no doubt at Bath what is expected of you. Jack Rowell gets worried if he sees me with the ball in my hands too much — it gives him the feeling I am not working hard enough elsewhere."

Gaymond was another of those players who came to Bath from Bristol, where he made more than 60 appearances over several seasons without particularly exciting the Memorial Ground. But at Bath he moved into a higher gear, and after joining in 1981 he quickly claimed a first-choice place. Gaymond was born in Manchester, but had been at Bristol Grammar School and taught locally. He played in the first two Cup Finals when in his 30s, before emigrating to Canada and becoming a Canadian citizen.

He was one of Bath's uncapped forwards. But he was appreciated by the crowd at the Rec — not least for his beef in the charge at tap penalties. Then, with the ball in his hands, Gaymond won even Jack Rowell's approval.

His partner in those first two Finals was his teenage namesake, Nigel Redman, whose selection ahead of the Irishman Ronnie Hakin effectively closed the latter's career at the Rec. Hakin was brisk in the loose and helped show the Rec what lock forwards could offer in open play. But his latter days were increasingly injury-prone and Redman was given his big chance.

Redman was another of the Welsh-born Bath contingent, but his upbringing and early rugby came in John Cleese's home town, Weston-super-Mare, and his local club suggested he move to a bigger club after he won England colts' caps. He thus came to Bath in 1983 and quickly won recognition.

His whole-hearted play made him much admired at Bath and beyond. Only his premature baldness had misled opponents and opposition fans, too — his 30th birthday falls in 1994. His

dozen England caps — plus one as a replacement — stretched from 1984 to 1991 and included appearances in two World Cups.

But in an era when height was considered a major benefit at the line-out in international rugby, Redman was realistic. Even after his first cap he confessed that at 6ft 4in "I am not quite tall enough for international rugby." No matter, he never let England down in his games for his 'adopted' country and his scrupulously fair style of play meant no lessening of his physical presence about the field. 'Ollie' — as he was known at the Rec — was a central figure in the club's league and cup successes.

His partner in the 1986 and 1987 Cup Finals was John Morrison, who preferred to be the front jumper, with Redman jumping at no.4. Morrison (whose first names implied Scottish ancestry: Johnstone Stewart Charles) was born in Kent, but like Egerton and Robinson who were to follow, had learned his rugby at the prolific producer of quality players, Loughborough University.

He handled well, was mobile, and made an ideal partner for Redman. It was towards the end of their first season together, which ended in the 1986 Cup Final against Wasps, that the pairing of the two was hailed as one of the revelations in Bath's success. Morrison, still 22, and Redman at 21 had together overturned the accepted notion that experience was vital in the second row. They provided strength and stamina allied to superbly-balanced scrummaging.

They were together again for the second Final against Wasps, too, in 1987. But by then there was a surprise rival for their places, another of Bath's increasingly unlikely Anglo-Scots — Damian Cronin, the lock his future Scotland teammates were to nickname 'Del boy.' He was a gangling 6ft 6in high, and raw with it. He learned his rugby at the same academy as John Palmer — Prior Park School — and played for the Essex junior club, Ilford Wanderers.

At Bath he had a few games in the second half of the 1985-86 season and began to impress the doubters when he played a whole string of matches the next term. He stood in for an injured John Morrison in an early cup game, and appeared for the Anglo-Scots. But injury kept him

Nigel Redman.

out of serious contention.

Injury again disrupted his season in 1987-88, as the Courage League began, but he played in three league games, playing usually as middle jumper, with Redman moving to the front at line-outs, and won his first Scottish international caps. Nevertheless his rise to claim a regular place in the Scottish pack was a surprise to many who had seen few of his games for Bath.

It was a pattern repeated a few seasons later with another of Bath's Anglo-Scots, Andy Reed.

Cronin's adoption by Scotland came after David Sole discovered that although Cronin had been born in West Germany — and his father was Irish — his grandparents on his mother's side were from Lothian. That, under International Board regulations, was good enough for Scotland.

His selection also encouraged him to discover how he might like life north of the border. He moved briefly that summer to Scotland, perhaps to join David Sole at Edinburgh Academicals — and to settle in the hotel business in Dingwall, near Inverness, which even Sassenachs might have thought rather a long drive from Edinburgh . . .

By the end of the summer he was back in Bath. "It was just too quiet for me," he confessed. He worked in catering, including managing a restaurant for Malcolm Pearce; he also managed a bar for Roger Spurrell. Later he was to go into the weight training equipment business — which caused some knowing smirks: by his own admission he was not the most diligent of trainers.

He played, though, in five league games in the 1988-89 season, and after a powerful display in the penultimate league game, in which he scored two tries against Waterloo, his credentials for a place at Twickenham in the Pilkington Cup Final were hard to gainsay, in spite of the rota system for the three Bath had diplomatically claimed to be operating.

"I would have been disappointed if I hadn't been picked for the Final," Cronin admitted at the time. "I played a few games at the start of the season but wasn't playing well. Then I had a good trial, got back in the Scottish team and since then it's been going very well. I'm a lot fitter."

Some loss of form by Nigel Redman meant he was the unlucky one to be dropped. Cronin, partnered Morrison, whose 26th birthday, like his own, had preceded the Final by only a few days. As it happened, even Redman's admirers (which meant most Bath supporters) conceded that on the day Cronin's selection was justified. He had an outstanding match.

He played in all bar one of the Courage League games in the 1989-90 season, Redman and Morrison each playing in half-a-dozen. Cronin and Redman were partners in all cup games, including the triumphant Final over Gloucester.

John Morrison decided to go at the end of that season, still ambitious for further honours to add to his England 'B' selection, switching to Bristol. Injuries and a struggling side brought him disappointment. Like Gaymond before him, Morrison was a better player for being at Bath. At Bristol success eluded him as it eluded the club.

Cronin, too, was nearing the end of his time at Bath. He played only three league games in the 1990-91 season, and the next season went to London Scottish. briefly he lost his place in the Scotland side. But his old Bath pals were delighted and perhaps surprised to see him burst back so convincingly into the Scotland XV for the 1992-93 season, and even more so as Andy Reed was beside him.

Tourist's eye view of the terraces of Bath, from the stand side, as Cronin leaps in the line-out against Bristol at the Rec.

For Bath a cheerful Cronin at his best, jumping, shoving, and hurtling, was a considerable player. Unfortunately his best was seen too infrequently for many supporters — and some of his team-mates. Travel to the Scottish district games and trials inevitably took time and concentration which might otherwise have been given to Bath. But at that occasional best, such as his Cup Final against Leicester, then he could win his place in any 'big occasion' Bath team of the past decade or so.

With both Morrison and then Cronin gone, another of Bath's Cornish contingent took a regular place for the 1990-91 season. Martin Haag was another of that county's adopted sons. He had played for St Ives and the county before serving his apprenticeship with Bath before making his first Bath league appearance (part-nered by Mark Jones) in that 'second team' league match the week before the 1989 Cup Final.

In his first two seasons as first choice alongside Redman, which included the double triumph of 1991-92, his speed in the loose allied to the conventional skills of a lock forward made him an exciting player. Facially he had a certain resemblance to the young John Palmer (and there were some who thought he could even have become a useful centre three-quarter if he had taken the fancy to play there). England 'B' honours followed.

By the start of the 1992-93 season, however, he had lost his place to another of the game's medicine men, Sean O'Leary. In spite of the Irish name, O'Leary had been on the fringe of full England honours in his time with Wasps. By joining Bath he was returning to the West Country — his early days were at Plymouth.

Steve Bale in *The Independent* named him as one of 'four players to follow' in the new season. He noted Bath's 'one persistent problem, line-out possession' and suggested the arrival of O'Leary might be the last piece in the Bath jigsaw if O'Leary could at last fulfil his potential.

Perhaps it was the change in the line-out law which took the edge off their game for O'Leary and Haag. Perhaps too, for O'Leary, travelling from his work at Slough told against him as he struggled to win a place with Bath. He was dropped after the third league game of the 1992-93 season, defeat at Northampton, but was recalled for the seventh game, against Rugby, when he scored one of Bath's nine tries. To compound his troubled start with Bath, however, he was also in the side knocked out of the third

Martin Haag on the charge, in a 1990 league win over Liverpool St Helens.

Lock John Morrison, 1988.

Lock Sean O'Leary, newly recruited, 1992.

round of the cup that season at Waterloo. The jury was still out on Bath's newest recruit.

The man who ousted him was not Martin Haag, but another Cornish import, Andy Reed from Bodmin. Reed, who had been with Plymouth Albion, had dipped his toe into the Bath waters for a couple of seasons, and made a few league appearances without creating many ripples.

The oft-repeated legend has it that a Scottish official visiting Cornwall saw Reed wearing a Hearts soccer scarf, asked some questions about his ancestry, and so Reed began playing for the Anglo-Scots. He had already claimed a Bath first-team place alongside Nigel Redman, surprising opponents as well as Bath followers by his speed about the pitch and his jumping skills. Almost from nowhere Bath had a formidable new lock, albeit still willing to learn — another of Jack Rowell's hunches coming good. And Ian McGee-chan, the Scottish coach, had yet another player whose accents were decidedly from south of the (in this case, Devon) border, courtesy of Bath.

The one long-distance runner, in terms of service to the club, was Nigel Redman, the promising teenager of the 1984 Cup Final, and long since established as one of the key members of the Bath pack.

The disappointments and successes over the seasons of all these locks, however, were set in perspective by the death in October 1992 of Mark Jones, who came to Bath in the mid-1980s from Taunton and played three dozen games over four seasons, including three league games, for the club. He became a solicitor and after failing to claim a regular slot at Bath moved to Swansea and later to Clifton. All three clubs were

Lock Andy Reed, 1991.

represented at his funeral: he was 29. Andy Robinson organised a memorial game on an April Sunday in 1993, in aid of cancer research.

The Players: Back row

FRONT five, or back row: which is the more vital ingredient of a successful pack? The question itself is probably invidious. Each unit is dependent for team success on the other. But an effective back row is crucial for launching a club to consistent performances both within a game or within a season.

By the time Bath won their first trophy, in 1984, that necessarily dynamic back row that spoiled and harassed, scrapped and mauled, drove and created was already in full career: Hall, Simpson, Spurrell.

The 'baby' of the trio was John Hall who was also to span the years to be a member of another, later formidable back row. His crushing power in the tackle overthrowing an opponent was often the signal for Spurrell to be in there wresting and wrestling the ball away, for Simpson to set up the charge.

Hall was the nephew of one of Bath's former internationals, the famous Alec Lewis, and grandson of the pre-war scrum-half Harry Vowles. He went to school at Beechen Cliff in the city, and won an England Colts' cap while playing for the local Oldfield club. He was at once an automatic choice for Bath, and for season after season his mighty presence was of huge importance for his club.

As for England, his qualities were recognised with caps as he reached his 22nd birthday. It was not long before his status as a world-class blindside flanker was also acclaimed. Yet he was missing — when the time came — both from England's World Cup games of 1987 and 1991 and their Grand Slam successes.

Bath, not England, is the prime topic in this book, of course, but a combination of problems undermined the international career of a player who could have raised England's back row to greater heights if he had been consistently fit and consistently selected.

The selectors were wayward enough in their selection policy largely to ignore Hall after the 1986-87 season, when in spite of some injuires which meant he played in only three games of the opening Courage League season, and seven in the second, his form was undiminished.

In the circumstances it was not surprising that at the start of the 1989-90 season, he announced that, like Stuart Barnes, he had decided to concentrate on Bath, rather than his country, but for somewhat different reasons. Hall declared he was turning his back on divisional and international rugby for the immediate future. "I am very happy playing for Bath," he said, adding that too many demands were made on players.

As it happened, that season was the start of a particularly unhappy spell for Hall. He was sent off in the league game against Rosslyn Park and had scarcely returned when he was dismissed again at Plymouth and given a 90-day suspension. He missed the cup semi-final and final against Gloucester, and played six league games. But back he came again for 1990-91 and even stormed back into England contention with an outstanding display against Argentina early that season, only for injury again to rob him of an opportunity to wrest the no.6 spot from Mike Teague.

Even so he had his fullest league programme in that season for Bath missing only one of the 12 games and scoring three tries. He was selected for England's close season tour, but not for the first time withdrew because of his troubled knee. That was to keep him out of the 1991 World Cup and the whole of the 1991-92 season. Infection was the complicated extra factor.

"I was rushed into hospital, put on a drip, and there I stayed for two weeks. I lost two stones and my leg just wasted away. It was horrendous," Hall has recalled.

Inevitably some wondered if that was to be the end of his career. He was as uncompromising in his answer to those jeremiahs, in an interview with Mick Cleary of *The Observer*, as he was on the field: "I could hear them all right, writing me off, talking of me either in the past tense or as a liability. I had no option. I had to stuff it up them."

But before continuing the John Hall story it is time to go back to that successful back row

Taking a breather! Hall, left, and Egerton.

that helped see Bath home in three successive Cup Finals. Paul Simpson, who had a brief England career, where he was shuffled around the back row sometimes in exchange for Hall, was either flanker or no.8 for Bath but it was in the latter role that he was seen most often at his best.

Although born in Leeds he was another recruit from a Wiltshire schooling — he was at what is now the John Bentley Comprehensive near Calne. But while at Newcastle University he first made his impact with Gosforth and was on the bench for their 1981 Twickenham Final, before returning to the West Country and Bath. 'Simmo' quickly became a favourite with his strength on the burst and his determination in defence.

Nowhere was that better seen than in the 1986 Final when Bath were so shaken by the early concession of points to the cock-a-hoop Wasps. If Bath were to claw their way back it had be done in the pack. Simpson epitomised that massive effort that shut Wasps virtually out of the rest of the game, and scored a typical try.

The cheerful Simpson was another who found the disciplines of training less than congenial, and as he went past 30 his chances as first-choice no.8 diminished: he played only 11 league games in three seasons.

But by the time David Egerton had displaced

him, Paul Simpson had still one last half of glory to contribute to the club when he came on as replacement for the injured Egerton in the second period of the 1989 Leicester Final. His sudden presence seemed visibly to galvanise and encourage the rest of the pack — and deflate Leicester's in a way that had a decisive effect on the final outcome.

But if Simpson inspired his side that day, then the first cup-winning captain that Bath had was an inspiration for all his seasons.

Roger Spurrell the Cornish flanker was hardly the man to invite to take tea, perhaps, with one's maiden aunt. He was, though, the sort of comrade to be beside at the siege of Mafeking or on a sticky outpost of the North-West Frontier — or a muddy pitch at Neath.

Others may have seen him as a latter-day, rugby-playing equivalent of a buccaneer or an adventurer under Drake's flag, not above crunching glass to give the enemy an extra fright as he went into battle.

David Sole, more soberly and accurately, has described him as 'one of the hardest and most courageous men I've ever played rugby with.' Few who played (or saw) Bath sides Spurrell led in the early 1980s would disagree with that verdict. Jack Rowell too lays great store on the contri-

Bursting through . . .Paul Simpson.

bution Spurrell made in transforming the forward play of his early Bath sides.

Spurrell was the man who went grubbing where the boots were flying, and would emerge many more times than the opposition with the ball. He was a magnificent ball-winner, whose face was for ever bearing blood and bruises from his pitch battles. But he was more than a ball-winner; he was simply a winner.

In retrospect it seems absurd that other than a standby squad call, he never received any international recognition. Perhaps it was to do with fears for the susceptibilities of maiden aunts . . .An altercation with Bob Weighill of the RFU at the second Twickenham Final, and a brief appearance in the columns of *The Sun* probably didn't help either. And playing for his native Cornwall was probably the 'international' recognition that satisfied Spurrell.

Spurrell's parents farmed on Bodmin Moor, but he admitted that as a teenager he went off the rails and was 'into the wrong things.' But at 17 he resolved his problems by joining the Army and becoming a paratrooper, and a physical training instructor. Then he farmed near Bodmin again, and when the family farm was sold took a small farm of his own and had what he once

described as 'the best 12 months of my life'. Bath was still to come.

He was playing rugby for Plymouth Albion, like other Bath recruits, when he and his friend and opponent Simon Jones, were dismissed. It was after that (and I hope Alan Watkins doesn't read this and draw some significant moral lesson from it) that Spurrell joined Bath at Jones's persuasion.

He was first a shepherd in the Mendips, later a club owner in Bath, taking over the former public conveniences — a couple of pitches' length kick away from the Rec and known as the 'Bog' Island club. And in ordinary life as on the rugby field he was unsparing and unhesitating in his courage — once notably diving into the Avon in an attempt to save a drowning canoeist.

He led Bath to their first two cup wins, and played in the third. But the next season, 1986-87, was his last, and he made only three early season appearances, and at 31, his last for Bath. A new young ball-winning open-side flanker was at hand.

Spurrell may not have been one of Bath's many capped forwards of the Rowell era. But with Horton and Palmer in their very different ways he was one of the chief-on-field catalysts that allowed all that followed to happen. And if the world had to win a game in order to save us all from conquest by aliens, then by heaven, perhaps even Bob Weighill would have wanted Roger Spurrell at his peak, bloody no doubt, but never, we can be sure, bowed, to play for our lives.

It was also entirely in keeping with his rumbustious image that he should also have figured in *The Guardian* diary column a year or two ago in its Great Corrections of Our Time.

"We are asked to point that the correct name for the company run by former Bath rugby player Roger Spurrell is Balls For You and NOT as published in the *Evening Post* on Thursday and Friday."

The man who had taken over from Spurrell was Andy Robinson, nine years his junior, and from Taunton, where he had been at Richard Huish School before going to Loughborough University where he became captain of their XV. He played for Bath while at Loughborough and won his place in his first full season for the club. His impact was as immediate as his arrival, and there was no gainsaying him. Although smaller and lighter than Spurrell (he had once thought of becoming a hooker because of his lack of height), he was a ball-winner in similar mould.

Robinson was playing for England in only his second senior season — he had a notable game against Australia on his Twickenham debut in 1988 — and was named Player of the Year in the 1989 Whitbread/Rugby World awards.

It looked as if Robinson's explosive mix of strong defence plus alert support play, linking with his half-backs and back row, would assure him of an international future. It was not to be. His games in the 1989 Five Nations Championship season were his last senior caps; thereafter Peter Winterbottom was back in favour.

Like Nigel Redman before him, Robinson was to discover that his lack of height counted against him in international rugby, at least so far as Geoff Cooke, his England manager, was concerned. Cooke had famously and publicly written off the international prospects of the Leicester flanker Neil Back as being too small, during the 1992-93 season (and later sought to qualify his comments). Back, at 5ft 10in, was an inch taller than Robinson.

For Bath, Robinson was an effective captain on field and was not afraid to speak his players' minds in the various problems that dogged the club off the field. Whether it concerned failure to register a player, or committee squabbles, Robinson — like Barnes before him — was determined that the opinions of the senior playing strength of the club should not be overlooked.

His first seasons as Spurrell's successor for Bath were outstanding, when he was widely regarded

Andy Robinson with the 1993 courage trophy.

as the English game's outstanding open-side flanker. Robinson was the burrower and the digger, ever scrapping and striving for possession and a constant provider and instigator in the loose, and outshining Winterbottom in his early clashes with Harlequins.

Robinson taught at Writhlington School, Radstock, before following John Palmer to King Edward's School, Bath. Robinson's father, Ray, once a Somerset scrum-half and rugby coach, although stricken with illness, was a frequent spectator in his son's seasons with the club, following play from his wheelchair on the touchline with the help of a friend's commentary.

Robinson's fitness was also remarkable: after playing eight league games in the first Courage season of 1987-88, he played in every league game in the next four seasons (the 'second team' Leicester game of 1989 apart). It was remarkable testimony to his consistency. That total of 45 games from a possible 46, incidentally, was most closely matched by Graham Dawe (44), and Stuart Barnes and Tony Swift (42).

Robinson's colleague at no.8 in his first Twickenham Final, against Wasps in 1987, was also making his first Cup Final appearance. David Egerton was the man whose impact against John Scott and Cardiff one night at the Rec had the England international asking who this fellow was?

Egerton, from the same school as Richard Hill, Bishop Wordsworth's at Salisbury, and another of the side's Wiltshire recruits, was at Loughborough University and although working for British Aerospace in Bristol found little joy at the Memorial Ground. (Whisper it, but his father had made him a member of Wasps at birth . . .) Instead, Egerton sought to make his way at Bath. He too, like Robinson, quickly became a favourite with the crowd at the Rec. His height (6ft 5in) added a useful extra at lineouts, and his control in the tight brought him many pushover tries.

He too was early recognised by the England selectors but although chosen for the 1987 World Cup squad played in none of the games. When he did play for his country he was chosen as a flanker as well as no.8 or as replacement (his 12-seconds appearance against Fiji being something of a record in brevity in international contests).

But if selectorial whims didn't favour him, Egerton suffered more from injury. His career for Bath and his chances for England were damagingly interrupted by a serious back injury. "There was a time when I thought 'That's it — I'm finished," he admitted. Continuing injury problems meant he played in only four league games in the 1990-91 season, and didn't reappear the next season until February, in time to play in four more league games. But he was no longer first choice at no.8.

Steve Ojomoh was another to come to Bath from Nigeria, via the fringes of Exmoor and West Buckland School. He had declined a sports scholarship in the United States and first played for Bath at the start of 1989-90 season after success as an England Colt. He took his chances in Egerton's absence and showed himself a prom-

ising no.8 — a performance in a league match in October 1990 at the Memorial Ground in particular being outstanding for his tackling and line-out work. "Bath are always looking to players to provide a different dimension. I'm hoping to offer that," he said. "I can't just come in and make up the numbers . . ."

But with Ojomoh learning his craft, John Hall out for the season, and Egerton's future uncertain, a new no.8 with a known pedigree also appeared at the Rec at the start of the 1991-92 season.

Before the Bath crowd had time to assess him, Ben Clarke was suspended after being sent off in his second match (at Cardiff), missing the start of the league programme as a result. Clarke had already made an impact at Saracens, as Bath remembered only too well. But if there was any complacency he may have felt on arriving at the Rec, the shock of the early suspension must certainly have removed it. He soon dispelled any doubts the connoisseurs of no.8 play might have had by his commitment to Bath's success.

Nor did Clarke's arrival mean Steve Ojomoh was necessarily out of the side; he switched to blindside flanker in Hall's absence and with Robinson appeared in the Twickenham Final against Harlequins. (Ojomoh also played in eight league games that season.)

Thereafter Clarke's game moved on even further. The new laws, as Stuart Barnes observed, suited him to perfection. "With his fast, hard running, his dynamism and fitness, he repeatedly makes ten to 15 yards for us, time and again."

It was perhaps a dynamism Bath missed — from Clarke as well as Barnes, both absent — when they went down at Waterloo in the cup in the 1992-93 season.

Clarke himself praised Andy Robinson and John Hall for their help in lifting his game to the point where he soon became a powerful force in Bath's back-row and overall play.

Which brings back John Hall on the scene. After his season's absence and those doubting voices he knew his return to the side would hardly be automatic. Clarke was at no.8, flanked by Robinson. Steve Ojomoh was blindside flanker for the start of the 1992-93 season and Hall admitted that Ojomoh's progress to England 'B' and 'A' honours was a big incentive for his own return. "I doubt I would have trained as hard if I'd been guaranteed my place at Bath."

But Hall was in the back row for the opening two league games of the season in place of an injured Andy Robinson, before dropping out for the match at Northampton. Thereafter he was back as first choice with Ojomoh the unlucky man. The irony of the competition between the two went further — Hall was made captain of

Another cap for Bath and England, Ben Clarke, 1992.

the England 'A' team, with Ojomoh at no.8, and they played together at the Rec when the England 'A' side hammered the Italians 59-0. But Geoff Cooke, in further explaining his prejudices against flankers without those extra inches, announced that Ojomoh — all 6ft 2in of him — was being groomed as a flanker for the senior side. But that was for England and the future to decide.

David Egerton and Steve Ojomoh were for the moment on the fringe of the first-choice side — but the advent of an extended league programme for the 1993-94 season suggested that Bath's selectors, if not the players, would be happy to be so spoiled for choice. Gareth Adams, another undergraduate at Bath University, was another flanker waiting his chance.

Ojomoh — if the club could keep him content — and Clarke, in particular, could be the basis of a powerful back row in the best traditions of Hall, Simpson, Spurrell; Hall, Egerton, Robinson; or Hall, Clarke, Robinson.

Hall, the Bath boy bred in the club's traditions almost from birth, was the constant factor, note, in three fine back rows of the Rowell era.

Nor can any review of Bath's back row players during their years of success omit Kevin Withey, the reserve flanker whose taste of the big-time in the 1990 Cup Final led to his move from Bath to Newport; or Nick Maslen.

Ten of Bath's stars played in the club's league games in each of the first six Courage seasons. Maslen played league games in each of the first five seasons — the only reserve to do so. He became captain of Bath United but also filled in worthily when called if one or more of the international back-row men was not available.

The Coaches

JACK Rowell was perhaps as surprised — and as pleased — about Bath's achievements as anyone else. "If someone had said when we won the first cup that we'd win ten trophies in the ten years I wouldn't have believed it. We worked hard at it, but I never thought we'd get to where we are now." After he talked with me, an eleventh trophy was won — on the last day of the 1992-93 season. So how was it done?

Bath rugby, he said, had to be a way of life. In the past, with only one cup won, he had said: "Bath is a smashing club and a smashing city and I derive enormous pleasure from doing the job. But if you don't enter into it whole-heartedly there is always someone else who is a little more hungry for success and will turn round and beat you." Jack Rowell and his team had not assuaged that hunger, it seemed.

But he has acknowledged the immense and continuing contribution from those who have worked with him and the players.

Dave Robson, a former prop with the club, mostly with the United side, was there when Rowell joined the club.

Increasingly Robson, a good technical coach with the forwards, became also the talent scout and the Mr Fixit of the coaching team. He had an excellent eye for a player's potential and was early in realising that if players were to come to Bath they would need help in finding jobs. Not all would commute like Richard Lee and Graham Dawe from their West Country farms. Robson was also the 'organisation-man' of the coaching trio that dominated the early years of Bath trophy-winning.

The third was a physical giant of a man. Tom Hudson, former Olympic athlete, was a physical education lecturer at Bath University.

His rugby claim to fame, before Bath, was that he helped Carwyn James prepare the Llanelli team that famously beat the All Blacks in season 1972-73. He was fiercely merciless in the routines and challenges he set the Bath players as he built their strength and their stamina to the point where Dave Robson could confidently assert that no previous Bath side could have lived with the Bath of the 1980s.

Between them the three made an awesome coaching team with an awesome record. Then, for two of them, it all fell apart.

There were signs of strain before the break came.

Hudson and Robson, unlike the more taciturn Rowell, were keen to say their piece from time to time, to the occasional embarrassment of Rowell. Hudson's remarkable ambition for the club was made publicly clear 20 months before he walked out.

In February, 1988, with the first Courage League season already near completion, he was saying: "If I had my way we wouldn't take part in the league . . .Apart from the cup, Bath should be looking to play European fixtures, say home and away against the top five French clubs, while retaining the Welsh links. We can't afford to lose those. League rugby will inevitably mean more matches when we should be cutting down. It's fine for the Second and Third Division clubs and below, but at the top it's superfluous."

This was startling stuff, not necessarily eased by Hudson's reassurance that this was not club policy — or even views necessarily shared by players or spectators. He went on: "Until league matches are played on fixed dates, the competition means very little. And even next season I doubt whether any league game will match our semi-final with Leicester for atmosphere."

On one hand he was on the side of traditionalists who sought the retention of the Welsh games. But on the other he outpaced the game's rulers in his apparent wish to have Bath playing in the knock-out cup, in Wales, and in Toulouse and places east.

If it seemed to have more than a touch of the maverick in its viewpoint it also sounded a little like Bath arrogance (or sour grapes?) when the club's first league season was proving less than successful. That it wasn't Bath, but one of the coaching team offering his own thoughts aloud, didn't matter to a wider audience.

But it also seemed to envisage taking the game away from the central core of English rugby. Bath's games with European sides were an important (and continuing) aspect of the club's development but underestimating the introduction of the league structure, regardless of its misbegotten beginnings, made Bath (or Hudson) appear like the only soldier in the regiment who didn't know he was out of step.

It was perhaps predictable therefore, that the break when it came (while Rowell was temporarily absent) should concern a clash of dates with a fixture for a Romanian team and Pontypool.

Coach Dave Robson.

The matter was resolved, as noted in an earlier chapter, by the club fulfilling the two fixtures in successive days.

But Hudson had gone, and Robson followed. Rowell stayed. He at least had not forgotten the adage mentioned at the start of this chapter: Bath rugby had to be a way of life.

The departure of his lieutenants was a blow, and it thrust immediate extra responsibility on Rowell himself. But it has seemed unlikely that he has quite forgiven them for going, not because of himself but for the players and the club. As one close observer of the Bath scene put it to me: "For Rowell, the players and the team, not the coaches' ego, come first."

Perhaps the parting was inevitable, as Hudson in particular seemed eager for a wider canvas. If it had not come then it may not have been much longer in coming for some other disagreement, with Rowell in a different corner from his aides who perhaps sought greater recognition for their part in the club's success.

The rift was a shock to the club's following. It seemed that at the best there would be hiatus, and at worst Bath would fall flat on its face. Nothing of the sort happened, and the team went on to win the Courage Clubs' Championship, and do the cup and league 'double' next.

Jack Rowell got on with his task at the club, and people like John Palmer, Simon Jones, and Gareth Chilcott were glad to help. What the episode finally showed, three seasons later, was that the club was indeed by now bigger than any individuals. But also that Jack Rowell was pre-eminent in the players' eyes and the one who had their essential respect.

From the old days of Bath the public schools in the South-West provided a constant supply of players both as boys and masters. And it was from such a source that the new name on Bath's coaching staff was found. Brian Ashton came to King's School, Bruton, in Somerset, after years teaching (and coaching rugby) in France, Italy (that European dimension again?) and his native Lancashire. He was also a notable scrum-half for Fylde and Orrell (and was preferred to Dewi Morris in a 'best of Orrell' team I saw in a match programme there a few seasons ago). He was also about to win an England cap on a tour of Australia in the 1970s when family bereavement properly took priority instead.

This cheerful physical education and history teacher found himself at the heart of the sparkling back play that took Bath to its 'double' of 1991-92, working closely with Barnes and his colleagues. The Lancashire link for Bath thus remained strong: Ashton remembered Horton at his best — before he came to Bath! And he taught Tony Swift at Hutton Grammar School, near Preston, when the future England winger was in his early teens.

Tom Hudson's successor at Bath University, Ged Roddy, was also his successor at Lambridge training ground. Roddy also worked on individual training and fitness programmes for the players which kept the poor lads at it even when they were not in squad sessions. Simon Jones was with the forwards, and at least temporarily, carried out the Mr Fixit role. Increasingly too it seemed that Gareth Chilcott might have an influential coaching part to play.

John Kimberley, Alistair McKibben and others too numerous to name took care of coaching at other levels within the club. It seemed in safe hands as the start of another huge leap forward in the game's competitive structure — home and away league games — posed new challenges to Bath.

There were other safe hands at work on the players too — Julie Bardner and her fellow physiotherapists Fiona Phillips, Heather McKibben, and Rebecca Williams. Members of the team were in attendance at all training sessions and first team and United games.

Julie Bardner, mother of four children long grown up, was recruited as successor to Gareth George by Dave Robson who had been to her as a patient. Now her skills and those of her colleagues were an important factor in the fitness and good repair of the squad and a special kind of professional dedication perhaps. "Though I'll admit Lambridge on a wet January night can be a bit of a downer!" said Julie. Club doctors and consultants' advice was also available as needed.

Back to Jack Rowell, though, the man who started it all when he first came to Bath around the time he was turning 40 years of age. Now chief executive of Golden Wonder at Market Harborough, and a board member of Dalgety plc, his dedication to Bath in between his business commitments at home and abroad remained remarkable. But the dual interest may also explain his success. "I couldn't be a full-time manager as in soccer, I'd get bored."

And the post-Rowell era at Bath? "As far as I'm concerned we're in it," he said, pointing to the current coaching set-up, the Spartans, junior rugby and colts. As well as the first-team squad the club will be looking to find one or two players a year from the earliest stages who might come through to the first-team squad — the more the better. "So it's not a question of 'that's the Bath first team — where are the other good players?' They'll be here."

Rowell's reputation for finding good or average players and making them even better, and perhaps

Eye on the ball . . .Jack Rowell, 1991.

internationals — has been a major factor in his worldwide reputation as a rugby coach. Players like Nigel Gaymond and John Morrison were early examples. Jim Fallon, helped in particular by Brian Ashton, achieved so much more in his season at Bath than he ever suggested might be possible in his several years in the game before that.

But in the early development of David Sole, Damian Cronin ('lovely chap') and latterly Andy Reed, so that Scotland could claim three international players, Jack Rowell and his colleagues can claim special thanks north of the border: they gave it, too.

He believed he could make average players better players ('two plus two, and it equals five') because the coaching team was forever developing players for two years on, to keep evolving, managing the whole coaching programme together while it fed into different channels. Finding a successor for Tony Swift, for example, was something the coaching team were thinking about well in advance of his eventual retirement.

Another key to Bath's success was to keep the squad element for the first-team games and to judge, aside from league and cup fixtures, which were those which required ten regular first-teamers, and which five: picking the team for the occasion, but attempting to keep all the squad involved.

Every so often special players came along. Rowell considered himself lucky to have such a naturally gifted player as Horton who could run a game, or Trick in his early impact. "A one-off. Anyone who saw him in those early days would agree he should have played more for England." And Palmer and Spurrell and Hall and Barnes and . . .and so on. But the players' gallery of the Rowell years preceded this chapter.

The players respect Jack Rowell. Do they also fear him?

"Well, I hope not, though I think some of them might. But they shouldn't if they work out how committed I am and therefore I want commitment back but not for me, but for the team. What Jack Rowell's all about is the success of that team and the enjoyment that goes with it. You live only once and you get one chance and I'd like to think we made the most of it."

At times that empathy with his players was palpably painful. He once said: "During the match I kick every ball, make every pass, make every tackle, and support every man." But on other occasions he could not bear to watch — and had been discovered wandering in the Twickenham car park or on the Orrell station platform while the vital game went on. He feels every game.

As for Sue Rowell, married to rugby and Jack,

she came to her husband one Sunday morning and said: "Graham Dawe is cooking bacon in the kitchen and Roger Spurrell has arrived with champagne and there seem to be others — did you invite them?" "Ah yes," said her husband.

It is a tradition he started, almost by accident as it might be guessed, after the third Cup Final win. Now champagne chez Rowell to celebrate cup or league success is a regular ritual.

"It's a wonderful day! There's champagne for breakfast, as much as people can drink, with wives and partners, smoked salmon sandwiches. It tends to build up — then on to the coach tour round Bath and a civic reception — yes, we make a day of it."

But when it comes to the players, Jack Rowell had one regret I shared with him. Players, I suggested, don't so much bow out as slowly fade away. John Horton was specially honoured and John Palmer had his surprise Cup Final, but otherwise they just weren't around in the teams any more and no one had apparently said anything about them. I was thinking especially of the Richard Lees and Paul Simpsons of Bath's world.

"Ah, you're on one of my favourite subjects," said Rowell. "I don't know who's going to organise this, but at the end of those careers we should look back and say, 'thanks for this' . . .We should have a special dinner, not the formal annual club dinner, and have some amusing speakers, and the player should be given something like a tankard engraved that he can put on the sideboard and to remember those years with Bath. It's a gap in the club and it's not part of the tradition, not part of the club culture."

It sounded like a gap worth filling.

Which brings me to another thought. One day a woman stopped Sue Rowell in Bath. 'You are Mrs Rowell? I want to talk about your husband." "Why? What's he done?" The woman said: "It's what he's done for the city." "What's that?" And she replied: "Well, the rugby, the big contribution that it's been."

When Jack Rowell's six foot eight inches finally move quietly away from Lambridge and the Rec and leaves the future of Bath's playing fortunes to his successors, it may be an ideal time to add the name of a new Freeman to Bath's small and jealously-restricted roll of distinguished recipients.

But if that would put the city's seal on its appreciation of an adopted son, hardheads could reflect on what might have been Bath's fate as a home of rugby in the tough new world of leagues without Jack Rowell. It was a question which was answered with a unanimous consensus.

Even those who had the odd difference with

him in the past believed the same: without Rowell and the successive coaching teams he had helping him, Bath at the end of season 1992-93 might at best have hoped to cling to a place in the Second Division, along with Bedford and Moseley. At worst they would be in the Third as company for fallen Coventry and Rosslyn Park. The idea of the Fourth (with London Welsh and Mike Hamlin) was beyond contemplation, even for the most pessimistic.

Nor did club historian Harry Barstow dissent, nostalgic and romantic though he may be (even, one sometimes suspected, about nil-all draws in 1902!) The friendly, homely club had for most of its pre-Rowell days been second-best to neighbours Bristol and Gloucester, he pointed out. Why should the situation have changed at a time when both those clubs had a season or two when relegation had threatened? If Bath had

even started in the First Division it was unlikely they would have stayed for long.

But the happy reality was that at the end of the first six seasons of the Courage Clubs' Championship, the West Country could collectively congratulate itself. Of the 21 clubs who sampled league rugby at the top in that time, Bath, Bristol, and Gloucester were among the seven who held their place in Division One unbroken. It was remarkable testimony to the quality of the region's rugby and its traditions, whatever past Divisional Championships might have suggested.

The other four among the successful seven were Leicester, Harlequins and Wasps, and Orrell. All had been Bath's main rivals for honours during the league years, and their record against Bath is worth further scrutiny.

The Rivals:
Bristol and Gloucester

OF THE 12 clubs who began, so tentatively, the first Courage League Division One season in 1987-88, only seven remained in the division at the close of the sixth season in 1992-93.

Those seven could properly claim to be the most consistent sides in that period: all bar Orrell were also in Twickenham Finals during Bath's decade of success.

The end of the first six seasons of the Courage Clubs' Championship also marked the end of the fixture arrangements which had held sway during those years — providing an obvious opportunity to assess the detailed records of those leading clubs during that time.

Given Bath's achievement of four championships in six attempts, it is not surprising to find that Bath easily lead a cumulative table covering those seasons. Wasps, again as might be expected, came second with Harlequins, the habitual time-servers of league rugby, comfortably ahead of Bristol — the only one of the seven to have lost more games than they won.

For the purposes of the cumulative table below I have omitted the first Courage season of 1987-88, not (as some cynics might imagine) because Bath failed to win the title, but because it was the season when not every club played everyone else, and four points were awarded for a win and one point for simply playing. But if that first season is added to the table below, the respective positions of the clubs remain virtually unchanged, with only Gloucester and Leicester changing places.

The league table for the five fixed-Saturday, all-play-each-other seasons, with two points for a win and one for a draw scoring system, is as follows (with the notional addition of the same points system for games played in the 1987-88 season added in brackets on the right.

Seasons 1988-89 to 1992-93 Cumulative Table

	P	W	D	L	F	A	Pts	(87-88)
Bath	58	50	1	7	1,4331	664	101	(114)
Wasps	58	42	2	14	1,071	694	86	(103)
Gloucester	58	34	3	21	1,002	733	71	(84)
Leicester	58	34	2	21	1,163	846	70	(87)
Orrell	58	33	1	24	995	682	67	(78)
Harlequins	58	29	2	27	1,083	873	60	(71)
Bristol	58	24	1	33	899	823	49	(58)

The least successful of the seven — there were no prizes for guessing — have been Bristol for whom the advent of the league system coincided with the decline of a side which had been outstanding for much of the preceding decade or so. Indeed, in spite of their brave, and in some senses unlucky losing Cup Final of 1988 against Harlequins, their league record has been one of occasional brief but ultimately misplaced hope giving way to nervous looks over the shoulder at the threat of relegation.

It was not the happiest of times for a great club, whose style of play, honed under the late John Blake in the mid-1950s (and overused in a thousand headlines since as 'Bristol fashion') set patterns later followed by such clubs as Leicester and Harlequins. The Blake and Sharp traditions were carried on by players such as Alan Morley and Dave Rollitt, Ken Plummer and John Pullin. Later there was Alastair Hignell at full-back, back-row men such as Mike Rafter and Bob Hesford, Richard Harding at scrum-half, soon to be partnered by Stuart Barnes, and an exciting young centre prospect named Ralph Knibbs.

Others, no doubt, will one day chronicle the decline in influence of the Bristol team in the years that followed. But as its old heroes and club stalwarts alike retired — the Morleys, Rafters, Hardings, Pomphreys and Doubledays — so new stars of briefer service, such as Stuart Barnes and Jon Webb, left in disillusion. Faithful club men, too, notably Simon Hogg and Peter Polledri, moved on to Clifton, not always in the best of moods.

There were times when the casual visitor to the Memorial Ground might feel that only three names from the last good days of the club were still familiar — Ralph Knibbs, Derek Eves, and the doughty lock, Peter Stiff, with others coming and going without leaving much mark . . .

In truth, the case of Ralph Knibbs, an exciting, inventive unpredictable centre when he first came into the Bristol side sums up the team's lack of progress. He suffered from the increasing lack of confidence that permeated the team, and the backs in particular, in the late 1980s, and yet he stayed commendably loyal to the club.

When Jeremy Guscott first appeared for Bath,

the odd wag in the Bristol row dubbed him 'the poor man's Ralph Knibbs.' It said as much about the two clubs as it did about the two players that soon it was the Bristol man who had been left far behind in Guscott's slipstream.

Certainly, too, if Stuart Barnes in the mid-1980s had seen the future and decided it was Bath's and not Bristol's then Jon Webb's experience a few seasons later merely confirmed Barnes's prediction. His later games for Bristol were poor as he knew himself, but for a player of flair and confidence to be playing in a team of so little tactical vision seemed to have shattered not only his own belief in his abilities but that of his colleagues.

Webb had become unrecognisable as the player who first burst into the first-class game by the time he was dropped by Bristol.

Long after his career had been revitalised by Bath he told Mick Cleary in *Rugby World*: "I don't particularly want to denigrate Bristol, but they just didn't do things right. They felt that just because I was an international I must know it all. I was left to my own devices . . .At Bath they put you under the right sort of pressure. They take your game to pieces and work on every aspect."

Officials at the club probably didn't realise how much the game was changed by the advent of the league system. Grand plans for a grandstand worthy of the club went ahead (not without some farcical consequences) while the playing side seemed to be left to successive coaches who inevitably suffered by comparison with their neighbour, Jack Rowell. Eventually, Bristol got the message: in a partnership full of irony for their new club, two former Bath men, Rob Cunningham and Dave Robson, came together to see what could be done. But it was bound to be a long road back for a club that for so long — but not for seasons past — had epitomised much that was best in the England game.

As for those Rowell-led rivals, Bath's successes over the same seasons simply made Bristol's comparative decline the harder to bear.

Kevin Coughlan, writing in a Bath match programme in February 1989, for that rain-soaked cup game with Bristol, recalled willing — along with thousands of Bristol supporters — for Barnes to succeed with that injury-time penalty at Twickenham in 1984. He went on:

"While we conceded that Bath had done their homework and made the most of limited resources, it never entered our heads that this team would be unbeaten in cup games for nearly five years and set new standards for the game in these islands.

"Soon afterwards it became my brief — some

would say privilege — at the *Evening Post* to keep a closer eye on this phenomenon. And as they won the cup for a second year, then a third and a fourth, I sometimes got the feeling that our predominantly Bristol readership found it a little hard to stomach reading about one Bath triumph after another. Having lived within earshot of the Memorial Ground for a number of years, I could understand the feeling of hurt pride."

And Bath won that day too, so narrowly, emphasising Coughlan's point.

After decades of being the big brother of the two clubs, Bristol still found it hard to believe the roles were reversed. Their supporters (and their players) may have realised it before some of their committeemen. But the Barnes defection, and Jon Webb's later departure were understandably hard to accept. Webb had become a second-choice at the club. His later successes — like those of Barnes — merely emphasised the wisdom of his decision.

But it wasn't only the two star names who had preferred the Rec and Lambridge to the Memorial Ground.

Chilcott the Bedminster lad, while still with Old Reds, and players like Trevaskis and Sagoe and later Egerton and Reed, when they too were unknown, had also found the attitude to the game at Bath the more testing, having sampled Bristol briefly only to go down the A4. But by the end of the 1980s, John Morrison was one who reversed the trend and Bath reserve players such as James Johnston and Duncan Willett followed with the arrival of new coaching methods at Bristol.

Morrison, though, reportedly likened his switch to the organisation and pattern he found at the Memorial Ground (which was before Cunningham's arrival) to turning back the clock to what Bath's preparations might have been 25 years earlier. But at last Bristol smartened up their act.

There were also, perhaps inevitably, frequent unseemly official spats between the clubs over fixtures cancelled, mentioned in earlier chapters.

The sad truth was that Bristol officials hadn't got the message early enough that the game, whether they or Bath liked it that way or not, had moved on from jolly local derbies at holiday weekends. Bristol might need Bath as an end-of-season attraction; Bath — dare it be said? — didn't really need Bristol. Many mourned that reality, none the less.

But on the field Bristol's players over those same seasons sweated and strove mightily to knock the Bath cocks of the walk out of their stride. In cup and league they pushed Bath close, often raising their game, sometimes losing by only one point, but still losing.

Chris Hewett (a lively flanker himself in his

day), successor to Chris Ducker in covering Bristol rugby for the *Bristol Evening Post*, wrote after the league game at the Rec in 1991 when Bath, minus four first-choice tight forwards, won 9-4 without scoring a try:

"If heartbroken Bristol could have one Christmas wish it would be for someone to build a large estate on the Recreation Ground."

That, he suggested, seemed the only way to stop the succession of Bristol defeats there.

Only once during the six league seasons were Bristol left floundering — when on the last day of October 1992, Bath showed speed and skills in their 31-8 league win at the Memorial Ground beyond anything their rivals could offer.

In one game, the remarkable mudbath of the 1988-89 cup-tie, Bath could not, should not, have argued if the 14-12 scoreline had been in Bristol's favour. But all three cup matches in the ten seasons from 1983-84 went to Bath, as did the six league games. Bath's record against Bristol (with Bath scores first) is:

Cup: John Player 1983-84 Final (Twickenham) 10-9; Pilkington 1988-89 fifth round (h) 14-12; 1991-92 fifth round (a) 15-6.

Courage League: 1987-88 (h) 15-9; 1988-89 (h) 16-9; 1989-90 (a) 14-13; 1990-91 (a) 10-3; 1991-92 (h) 9-4; 1992-93 (a) 31-8.

Bristol may have been temporarily out of fashion: the sooner success over Bath and other top sides returns the better it will be for the English game.

If it took several seasons and as many defeats for Bristol to realise the upstarts from beside Pulteney Bridge were now the leading club in the South-West, never mind the country, then it took a good seven seasons for the message to sink in at Kingsholm. It was then, with Bath having already won the knock-out cup five times that they met Gloucester at Twickenham.

Before that, and unlike Bristol, Gloucester had been a powerful force in the game's new structure with their game, as ever, based on a tough, dominant pack of forwards, and half-backs intent on ensuring that ten-man rugby secured the victories with the emphasis on pushover tries and penalty goals. And the Kingsholm crowd loved it, every mauling rumble of the Gloucester pack, with Hamlin and Hannaford mopping up behind it. The odd try from a Mogg or a Morgan, or a determined burst from the centres, was a mere bonus.

But an inherent lack of pace and invention behind the front ten was grievously exposed on that Twickenham May day when Gloucester were whipped so astonishingly by 48 points to 6. Worse, it came after Gloucester had also faltered in the league when both trophies seemed possibly to be theirs.

It was, in the true sense of that overworked cliché, the end of an era.

But it had been foreseeable in earlier games against Bath, in particular during the previous season of 1988-89 when Gloucester failed to win a home semi-final, losing 6-3. The barrenness of their tactical armoury was cruelly revealed as it seemed that even its key players had largely forgotten the Kingsholm club fielded 15 men. Gloucester simply had no new ideas about breaking down the Bath defence.

As with Orrell, lack of variety and resource on the big occasion was fatal to their ambition.

Nevertheless, Bath had some fierce tussles with Gloucester over the decade and Bath fans were always apprehensive of failure against Gloucester. But it happened only once in the ten cup and league encounters during that time.

Kingsholm had seen little of Mike Teague, because of England calls and injury in recent seasons, but his departure to Moseley of Division Two, and the defections of other players, some seasoned, others somewhat past their play-by date, was a severe depletion of a playing staff recruited locally: England players might be fashioned at Kingsholm but they would not be recruited there.

In all the circumstances the coach, one-time Bath forward Keith Richardson, and his reduced squad found that retaining their place in the top division, rather than battling for honours, had become the main priority for the 1992-93 season. But at least Gloucester had the commercial acumen of one of the game's most wily wheeler-dealers, Mike Burton, on hand in planning how best to come to terms with the changed demands of the game.

In the past, though, just as Yorkshire once upon a time whistled down a coal-mine for a new fast bowler, so Gloucester had metaphorically scanned the local building sites or fruit markets for a likely prop. Now as the lure of both perquisites and playing success took players away the difficulty might be to persuade new players from outside the area to join. Having the Kingsholm crowd at your back when you're winning might be fine: having them on your back when you're not was one of the uglier sounds in the game.

The decade's results for Bath against Gloucester:

Cup: John Player 1984-85 semi-final (a) 12-11; Pilkington 1988-89 semi-final (a) 6-3; 1988-89 Final (Twickenham) 48-6; 1991-92 semi-final (a) 27-18 (aet).

Courage League: 1987-88 (h) 16-9; 1988-89 (h) 19-9; 1989-90 (a) 6-13; 1990-91 (a) 17-15; 1991-92 (h) 29-9; 1992-93 (a) 20-0.

Orrell

IF BRISTOL and Gloucester had long been among the elite of English rugby, there could scarcely have been a stronger contrast than with the more recent pedigree of the Lancashire club, Orrell. Indeed, without the introduction of national cup and league competitions, it seems unlikely that the three — or Bath — would have met.

Orrell's advance into the ranks of the game's leading clubs had been a remarkable achievement. And every time they toppled Harlequins or Wasps or others of that ilk on their exposed pitch at Edge Hall Lane, not far from the M58 (Harlequins still think it's the M6), there is deep, deep satisfaction. If they beat Bath, too, then lad, you're really talking.

One of the constant questions among the Bath fans (and doubtless from numerous other clubs) who never travel north of Gloucester, is: "Where is Orrell, anyway?" Good question. I was born not 50 miles away, and my mother, in her 90s, lived not ten miles away — but I still find the ground hard to find.

I remember once approaching it without benefit of motorways, having just visited my mother. I'm a poor navigator at the best of times. Now I was hopelessly confused, and kick-off time was getting nearer. So I asked two men building a garden wall for help. "Where's tha' come from?" they said. I told them, more or less. "Nay, I wouldn't bother," they suggested. "Bath? Bath?" (complete with hard 'a'.) "Shall we put 'im back on motorway?" one said. Then they told me the way to Edge Hall Lane in their friendliest Lancashire fashion. But I hadn't dared explain I was a Lancashire lad myself. And they were right to be cynical: Bath lost.

Orrell's achievement has been to keep the Union game flourishing, not only when more famous names in the North-West have suffered comparative decline, such as Sale and Liverpool and Waterloo (but don't say that name too often to Bath's players or Orrell's) but because they are surrounded by Rugby League clubs, being almost within cheering distance of Central Park, Wigan.

Nevertheless they have consistently produced England players from John Carleton to Nigel Heslop. But above all they have had a string of mighty forwards, who under coach Des Seabrook could match the Gloucester game most days. Sammy Southern, the colossal lock, Bob Kimmins, who most of us might be frightened of meeting face-to-face on a bright day, never mind a dark night, and Martin Hynes were only three of the formidable forwards who made the basis of much of the club's success in recent seasons.

Behind them players such as Dave Gullick and Simon Langford and Gerry Ainscough (who had an unhappy year at Leicester when Strett won the fly-half spot) over the seasons added steadiness and stability to a back line that indeed had its running stars such as Carleton and Wigan-born Clough. (They once had a scrum-half named Brian Ashton too.) But one of their most successful playmakers was the stand-off Peter Williams who deserved more than his four England caps (including the 1987 World Cup).

What happened to Williams is symbolic of one of the constant hazards of Orrell's team-building. Instead of touring with England one close season, he joined Salford Rugby League club. Williams was only the best-known of several Orrell backs to turn professional, until Nigel Heslop, capped ten times for England on the right wing, went to Oldham in early 1993.

Earlier, lesser-known players such as the backs Fell and Gilfillan also switched, and more recently (also to Oldham) Martin Strett, the stand-off whose goal-kicking, it has to be said, proved so inconsistent in the vital 1991-92 season in particular.

None of these players, with the possible exception of Williams in his first seasons as a professional, had much expectation of becoming stars in their new code. Nor in the case of Strett and Heslop, for example, did it imply lots of money but rather a weekly pay day for playing rugby as well as doing another full-time job.

Of Heslop, Peter Tunks, the Oldham coach, explained that his money would depend entirely on the number of first-team games he played. "It is up to him to produce the goods." A month after signing, in only his third game, Heslop's jaw was broken and he was out for the rest of the season.

But the terms on which players departed and what happened to them thereafter was nothing to do with Orrell; it was the drain on the club's scarce resources which Rugby League represented (it also took young players from their junior sides — Joe Lydon was one such) which was unknown by most others clubs in the top Courage division. Predators from the north only look for 'big' names beyond the north.

There were times, too, when it has seemed as though England selectors, unlike Rugby League scouts, had difficulty finding their way to Edge Hall Lane. Williams was not the first or the last of the Lancashire team to be unfairly neglected at national level. Without the County and Divisional Championship as an extra showcase, indeed, the chances of some Orrell players gaining such recognition might have been even harder. Dewi Morris was already capped at Liverpool St Helens before joining Orrell; and incidentally, although Des Seabrook has joined the chorus from less fashionable clubs worried about movement of players between Union clubs, Heslop, too, only came to Orrell after spells with Waterloo and Liverpool St Helens.

That said, it was the performances of the Orrell team in the League that made them such formidable opponents for anyone with title ambitions. Alas for Orrell that to a considerable degree they more recently began to suffer from the same problem temporarily weakening Gloucester. The law changes impaired the effectiveness of their front five, and before that their apparent lack of tactical options outside ten-man rugby proved fatal to their wonderful chance of taking the Courage title in 1991-92.

For some seasons Orrell had suggested they had the potential to be champions but perhaps lacked self-belief, which caused them to be cautious in games they could have won but instead lost by a few points. In 1989-90 for example they lost six league games, only one by more than six points, and conceded only three tries in them, and also muffed a cup-tie at Nottingham where they dominated but proved tactically inept.

In the 1990-91 season they trounced Northampton 60-0 at home in the league and were favourites to beat them in the cup semi-final away. Instead, bad tactical decisions (or indecision) gave the game to Northampton (not then as strong a side as they were soon to become.) Then, remarkably, Orrell lost their last three league games when second place at least was beckoning.

But the cruellest twist came that next season. Bath minus the deducted point, and already having drawn at The Stoop, went to Orrell on a day when most games were frozen off. Orrell beat Bath and had finished the stronger side. Even defeat at Northampton the following week seemed only a blip on the way to a title. But then, with a trophy almost theirs for the winning, came Orrell's black Saturday at Sudbury when Wasps won 13-12 with Huw Davies's long-range dropped-goal in the final minute. Bath were back in the race. Orrell went on, bravely, to win at Harlequins and Nottingham, but Bath's scoring points difference was decisive, and Orrell finished second.

For a big, confident side, Orrell had again shown a failure of — was it nerve, or tactics, or self-belief at the vital moments? Coach Des Seabrook argued with the latter theory. "I don't think it's a case of inner belief. We always believe we can win," he said after the Wasps game.

Martin Strett can scarcely be solely blamed because of his inconsistent goal-kicking. But it remains largely true that the side too often failed to put the points on the board which their dominance and outstanding defence had earned, by missing kickable penalties. Eventually, though, lack of tactical imagination and of real flair behind Dewi Morris (and his predecessor Chris Wright) was a glaring fault on the big occasions.

Nevertheless that Southern's Northerners had come so close to winning a major title was itself an achievement. No wonder that Wasps' captain Mark Rigby was reported to have 'apologised' to Des Seabrook for the late sting by Wasps. Many must have sympathised as Orrell lost a chance that might not easily come their way again.

Thereafter, like Gloucester, they were having to come to terms with the new laws, and rebuild a side depending heavily on fine servants coming to the end of their careers. That task, and limited tactical ideas, were worryingly emphasised in defeat by neighbours Waterloo of the Second Division who ousted them from the Pilkington Cup in the 1992-93 fourth round, 8-3. They were in good company, Bath having fallen on that battlefield in the previous round.

In the six league seasons under review, Bath lost only once against Orrell, with their biggest win, in the 1992-93 season, drawing attention again to the Lancashire club's future problem. In the cup that remarkable 16-16 draw at Edge Hall Lane is still talked about — it so nearly upset Bath's run of four John Player Cup wins, and the Orrell side that day had lots of flair in the backs.

(It was also the occasion, perhaps not the only one, where the club announcer in the same breath thanked John Player for its sponsorship and said there must be no smoking in the old wooden stand.)

Bath's record against Orrell for the ten seasons is:
Cup: John Player 1985-86 (a) 16-16 (aet); 1986-87 (a) 31-7.
Courage League: 1987-88 (h) 23-18; 1988-89 (h) 36-12; 1989-90 (a) 9-6; 1990-91 (h) 17-9; 1991-92 (a) 9-10; 1992-93 (h) 39-3.

Orrell can be sure that Bath fans who value the friendliness of Edge Hall Lane and the excellent (is it still free?) match programme will hope the club continues to thrive in spite of the Rugby League scouts on the doorstep.

But where's the ground? someone asked again. The postal address is Wigan, but don't go to Wigan because Edge Hall Road is virtually at Upholland. You can see the ground from the M6 . . .but you're probably just as well taking the M58 as if you're going to Ormskirk.

Leicester, Harlequins, Wasps

NOW if only Leicester's backs had been behind Orrell's (or Gloucester's) pack from the mid-1980s on . . .that's how the argument goes anyway to explain the Tigers' comparative failure to build success on the Bath scale to go with all the other delights on show at Welford Road.

But Leicester have been one of the most attractive sides of the whole decade under review, with or without a Hare and a Dodge here or an Underwood or two there. They also have the best record of all the top six clubs against Bath in cup and league in that time. Only once, in the devastating blitz by 37-6 in the 1991-92 season, have the Tigers been totally outgunned by Bath in either competition.

Moreover they hold the curious key to the three seasons in those ten when Bath have faltered in the knock-out competition. Let me explain.

In season 1987-88, Bath won a tensely-fought third-round John Player tie at Welford Road. A fortnight later, in their next competitive game, Bath lost 4-3 at Moseley in the fourth round: Bath out of the cup.

In season 1990-91, Bath won a tensely-fought Courage League game at Welford Road. A week later, in their next competitive game, Bath lost 12-0 at home to Leicester in the Pilkington Cup third round: Bath out of the cup.

In season 1992-93, Bath won a tensely-fought Courage League game at Welford Road. A week later, in their next competitive game, Bath lost 9-7 at Waterloo in the Pilkington Cup: Bath out of the cup.

"Elementary, Watson. If Bath are to prosper in these cup competitions, they must avoid what you choose to call tensely-fought victories at Welford Road immediately preceding a cup game."

"But, my dear Holmes, they cannot refuse to play at Leicester in such circumstances."

"Precisely, Watson. I would therefore draw your attention to that earlier mystery, the so-called Adventure of the Missing Three-Quarter†."

"But Holmes, that young man was the star player and his absence meant his side lost their vital match — you're surely not suggesting that someone from the Bath club should . . .?"

"Rugby football does not normally come within my horizon, Watson. I think, rather, that I am just in time to hear young Master Kennedy's recital at the Pump Room while we are in this handsome city. Will you join me, Watson?"

"Er, no Holmes, if you'll excuse me. I see Mr Rowell's men are entertaining Swansea this evening — and there is one Moriarty in the Welsh team . . .Pass me my muffler, there's a good fellow . . .Holmes, what on earth . . .Why are you tearing up your ticket for the concert? By jove, do you think we should warn the local constabulary?"

OK, it doesn't need a latterday Sherlock to draw the obvious conclusion. But it does look as though the exertion and confidence drawn from victory at Leicester either caused Bath to relax, or assume the next game could not be so tough. Or whatever. The connection is plain.

Doubters or wiseacres should note that, yes, Bath did beat Leicester at Twickenham the week after playing at Welford Road (see below) but they had LOST on that occasion. And they beat Leicester in the league the week before thrashing Gloucester at Twickenham. But that game was NOT at Welford Road. And, contrary to some suggestions, Barnes was in a losing cup side — the home game against Leicester.

Now for the details. Bath have lost twice in the league to Leicester, the first winners of the Courage competition — in the first game either side played in the league — and the following season, when both sides fielded second strings the week before the Final, Bath having already won the league title. Bath lost one of the four cup games between the sides in the decade. Bath's results against Leicester:

Cup: John Player 1985-86 semi-final (a) 10-6; 1987-88 fourth round (a) 13-6; Pilkington Cup 1988-89 Final (Twickenham) 10-6; 1990-91 third round (h) 0-12.

Courage League: 1987-88 (a) 13-24; 1988-87 (a) 12-15; 1989-90 (h) 26-15; 1990-91 (a) 9-3; 1991-92 (h) 37-6; 1992-93 (a) 13-3.

Now Bath should scan the future fixture lists, and watch out for the sequels to tensely-fought victories for Bath at Welford Road . . .

If travels to Leicester are always top-line affairs for the players they are also enjoyable for visiting spectators who are always made welcome (and who can usually find a seat, if they want one, even if it's raining). The atmosphere at The Stoop is hardly the same. Nor have Harlequins, unlike Leicester, won many friends in recent times, beyond the hampers-and-champers covey among the game's followers.

Not much time need be spent here in discussing Harlequins' policy in approaching a season — it comes under some scrutiny in other chapters on the 1992-93 campaign. But Nottingham, Orrell and Bath have not been alone in voicing their opinions. Stuart Barnes suggested their attitude was out of tune with the game in England: "They have done a disservice to league football at times, playing the game by a different set of rules, and some clubs have been badly affected by it.''

His view could hardly be attributed to sour grapes: Bath have won in spite of the Harlequins' diet. It was the prospect for clubs threatened with relegation that was more serious.

Whatever the reasons that drove Harlequins sometimes to refuse to bring their best toys out to play, they never sulked when they played Bath. Even so, they never beat Bath in any competitive game during the decade, losing two cup games, and drawing one of the six league games. It is a record worth stressing given the amount of hype Harlequins' style of (occasional) play can sometimes generate. Gloucester, Leicester, Orrell and Wasps all have a better record against Bath of the top six — only Bristol's is worse.

Details of Bath's games against Harlequins:
Cup: Pilkington 1989-90 third round (h) 9-0; 1991-92 Final (Twickenham) 15-12 (aet).
Courage League: 1987-88 (h) 21-9; 1988-89 (a) 26-9; 1989-90 (a) 32-12; 1990-91 (h) 23-3; 1991-92 (a) 18-18; 1992-93 (h) 22-6.

There has never been any doubt about Wasps' commitment to the league programme: they have twice beaten Bath in the competition. Even when, in 1989-90, they never led the table once until — with Bath and Gloucester slipping up, they took the title — they never ceased to strive.

The memory of those tense John Player Finals, when Wasps led Bath for much of each game still sends shivers down grandchildren's backs at bedtime.

Nor has the rivalry between Rob Andrew and Stuart Barnes when they have faced each other at the Rec marred the matches between the two — a friendship indeed cemented by the game played to mark the death of Raph Tsagane, the Wasps' player killed near Bath. That same season Wasps won at Bath by Fran Clough's late try — but still Bath won the league.

In the 1992-93 season, the game between the two, again at the Rec, was billed as vital to both sides' title hopes. Perhaps the mutual anxiety was too much for the players, with Fran Clough once again making the headlines, this time for his early dismissal. Even so the 14 remaining Wasps were tenacious opponents, before going down and thereby forfeiting their league leadership.

The details of the decade of Bath's games with Wasps are:
Cup: John Player 1983-84 fifth round (h) 26-12; 1985-86 Final (Twickenham) 25-17; 1986-87 Final (Twickenham) 19-12.
Courage League: 1987-88 (a) 15-19; 1988-89 (h) 16-6; 1989-90 (a) 18-9; 1990-91 (h) 15-16; 1991-92 (a) 24-12; 1992-93 (h) 22-11.

Other clubs have taught Bath a lesson in the league from time to time — notably Saracens and Nottingham, who had striven in spite of loss of players to more glamorous clubs, to stay among the best in the game, only to meet with relegation.

Northampton's turn, too, to restore the reputation the club once had, came with major reorganisation plus a steady trickle of imports from all over the land and beyond — the All Black Wayne Shelford being their most celebrated recruit. In three seasons in Division One they lost to Bath narrowly twice, before winning similarly in 1992-93. Bath beat them in the cup in 1991-92.

And then there's Waterloo — with Wasps the only other side to win at Bath in the league in six seasons, albeit on a day when divisional calls still disrupted league sides. No matter: they did it again — this time at Blundellsands in the 1992-93 Pilkington Cup third round.

Results of all Bath's league and cup games since that first trophy-winning success of 1983-84 can be found in the statistical records at the end of this book.

Barnes holds aloft the Pilkington Cup after his extra-time drop goal beat the Harlequins in 1992 and right is the man who led them there, captain Andy Robinson.

The Welsh Clubs

O F ALL the changes in the game in recent years the biggest loss in terms of fixtures for Bath and other English clubs has been the virtual end of the great contests with the leading Welsh clubs.

Given the city's geographical location, it was always well-placed even before the days of motorways to make the comparatively easy rail journey into Wales. The arrival of the Severn Bridge made it even easier for teams and their supporters to consolidate those links.

For most of their history Bath were the underdogs in their games with the Welshmen. Like so much else, that began to change in playing fortune of the 1960s and '70s — Jack Rowell has referred to Bath's 'awful record' in Wales. Instead the expectation of victory became the norm.

Already in Rowell's early years, the hardening of the Bath forwards and their improving skills, allied to the adventurous back-play, meant there were some stirring games at the Rec and in Wales. Bridgend, Llanelli, Swansea, Pontypool and Cardiff, to name but five, could no longer come to Bath expecting a win. Instead they were frequently put to flight. And not only at the Rec. By the mid-1980s, and before the league system began (in Wales even later than in England), Neath and Llanelli were shocked when Bath ran up more than 60 points against them.

It was performances such as these which mocked the querulous complaint from London in particular that Bath were a side of dull dogs. The Welsh, who contributed much in their turn to so many exciting games, could only marvel at such a misreading of Bath's abilities to open up defences with skilful running or vary their game to stifle the opposition's ploys.

No English club side had previously enjoyed such sustained success against the Welsh teams than Bath managed in the early 1980s — and this, remember, was before they started winning trophies.

Notable wins against Swansea and Cardiff at the Rec, mentioned earlier in the book, stay in the memory — along with games at Newport and Pontypool. London Welsh too in their heyday of John Dawes, Mervyn Davies, John Taylor and company also shared in some memorable matches.

Indeed all the great names that subsequently graced Welsh rugby (or, as with David Bishop, disgraced it?) were seen at the Rec from J.P.R.Williams to Jonathan Davies and countless more, including such loyal clubmen as Phil May whose visits with Llanelli were a normal part of each season.

Those historic rag-doll matches against Llanelli were also tough but entertaining games, played home and away each season, for the modest knitted trophy which was slung on the goal-post for each game of whichever club had won the previous encounter. (Arguments about the origin of the rag-doll occasionally surface in the club programme; like the missing no.13 in the Bath line-up, it's a subject that continues to fascinate older memories.)

Now, like so much else, the leagues have virtually swept away the nourishment of the Anglo-Welsh games. The rag-doll games were also at risk and there was even a suggestion that the modest trophy should be offered for games played at youth or junior level between the clubs: it was an indication of the sense that the great days of contests between the full-strength club sides from the two countries were unlikely to return in the near future.

Harry Barstow, writing in the programme for a 1990 rag-doll match, noted how odd it seemed that such an encounter was now officially 'a friendly.'

"Prior to the league emphasis in the English game it would have been perceived as absurd that an Anglo-Welsh match could be anything other than 'needle' stuff of the highest order. How times change."

For Bath players of the Roger Spurrell and John Palmer era, the Welsh fixtures were an essential part of their rugby education that made them all the more valuable in the cup triumphs to come. It was a tough school that gave them an extra edge over some of their English opponents.

Now, perhaps the games don't come harder than top-of-the-table English league clashes against, say, Harlequins or Wasps, or at Leicester or Orrell. But supporters miss their taste of Wales, and so does a new generation of Bath players who have not experienced the contests between the full

Try for Paul Simpson, against Llanelli, 1989.

One of four tries for Guscott, with Swift on the outside, against Llanelli in 1989.

might of, say, Cardiff and Bath in opposition.

(Interestingly, few Welsh players have so far tried their luck at the Rec in Bath's colours — Steve Lewis in the early Rowell days and his nephew Iestyn Lewis in the 1990s are unusual — but few Bath reserve players have moved across the Bridge, Kevin Withey, most notably, to Newport.)

Jack Rowell is in no doubt that Bath must keep their fixtures with the Welsh clubs even if neither side can be at full strength. He has noted, too, that Welsh league games often seem much quicker than the English equivalent, with attacks coming from all directions, which in turn would offer fresh challenges to his own players in similar match conditions.

Interestingly, the idea of an Anglo-Welsh league is mooted; and the Welsh probably need it more than the English clubs. Alternatively an Anglo-Welsh cup has been suggested. But none of these seems to take account of the extra pressures on top players at top clubs, already heavily committed to league, cup, divisional and international demands.

And the calls for a mix of Welsh and English rugby at competitive levels also clamour for attention as other voices ask for English divisional games on a home-and-away basis (the vacant terraces beckon eagerly, presumably) and for the Five Nations' Championship on a similar system.

But of all the conflicting opinions for adding yet more competition to the game, the latter two seem the least likely to have any fire in their boilers.

Abandon the divisional games and replace them with serious Anglo-Welsh encounters, though, and Bath would leap at the chance. So, one day, might England — and Wales. First, though, the clear days would have to be found and England prepared to kick its dismal addiction to the divisionals.

The England Selectors

BATH had numerous international players in their ranks from time to time over the decades, but not many were capped from the club. The distinguished post-war exceptions included those two mighty forwards, the late John Kendall-Carpenter and Alec Lewis (later to become club president) who, indeed, played in the same England pack in several games during the early 1950s. Ian Lumsden was capped for Scotland at fly-half in the late 1940s while with Bath. But post-war caps won by players while at the club were scarce.

Laurie Rimmer won four caps in 1961, and left wing Peter Glover was capped in 1967 and again four years later. David Gay, as a young no.8, played in all the Five Nations' games of 1967, and wasn't even called for the England trial match the following season. Nor did he play for his country again. It was a curious treatment of a young player which was to be repeated by the ever-changing bunches of England selectors over the next 20 years (until the Geoff Cooke era, in fact).

But Bath could have few complaints that their players were largely passed over in the first two decades after the end of World War Two; their play simply didn't warrant international honours.

When Mike Beese was capped in the centre in 1972 it was when he was playing at Liverpool, sandwiched, as it were, between his two spells with Bath. So the club could only share in the honour by proxy. Although he played in England trials later when at Bath, he never won another cap. He has no doubt that he later became a better player than when he won his caps in a losing England side.

John Horton was with Bath when he won his first caps, belatedly as some thought, in 1978.

Although he was a product of that remarkable rugby school Cowley, and played briefly for St Helens and Sale (including half a season partnering Steve Smith), it was as a Bath player that he had polished his game. But after those four caps in 1978 he was passed over the following season and there was speculation that Neil Bennett or Les Cusworth would be permanently preferred to him.

Instead he was restored to be the fly-half in England's Grand Slam side led by Bill Beaumont,

another Lancastrian, in 1980 (Horton was the victim of that high tackle for which Welsh flanker Paul Ringer was sent off). Thereafter, his handful of further caps came spasmodically, and as with John Palmer (with whom he won two caps in South Africa 1984) they came almost at the end of his career instead of earlier, when he and Palmer were at their sharpest and most incisive.

But by then the England selection process was an exasperating mystery to many players, never mind to followers of the game. That Bath players are inevitably mentioned here, for the most part, is not to suggest that they were unusual in the way they were selected — or not selected.

David Trick's bizarre treatment in being played out of position at short notice against Ireland in 1983 ("Who wants to play on the left wing?") has been mentioned in an earlier chapter, for example. But the Northampton second-row forward, Vince Cannon, threw in his boots so far as England hopes were concerned with a cry of a pox-on-the-lot-them or something to that effect after a team to play Romania was announced around the New Year of 1985.

Cannon, on the fringes of selection for some seasons, pointed out that he was one of four locks in the squad for training, but when the team to play the Romanians was announced the two locks chosen — Dooley and John Orwin — weren't even in that same squad.

He pointed out too that John Doubleday of Bristol and Gareth Chilcott had 'flogged it up to Stourbridge last Sunday' and in spite of playing tough Saturday games went through dozens of practice scrums without being given a clue as to who might be loose-head prop against Romania. In the event neither was chosen — instead the choice was Gloucester's Phil Blakeway, who hadn't attended the training session and was not in his club first team at the time.

Players didn't like being dropped, or not being chosen, at any time in the game's history; but they had good reason to object at being picked up by the selectors and then dropped again as if they had some odd contagion, and often without explanation.

That Romanian game was also the one which started the souring of the England relationship with Stuart Barnes, mentioned elsewhere. But

Bath's Jeremy Guscott, an England regular since 1989, charges through for the Barbarians at Welford Road, Leicester, in December 1990.

already Bath had experienced the quirks and foibles of the England selectors when Paul Simpson became the first of their emerging pack of the early 1980s to be selected. He was a star, although at blind-side flanker instead of in his club position of no.8, when he won his first cap, against the All Blacks in 1983. He won one more cap a year later, and his next and last three years later.

Simpson was never an establishment figure in 'Twickers' terms, but that he could be a star in his first international and then discarded, except for one cap, for the next four years was scurvy treatment.

The introduction of Divisional Championships in the mid-1980s was another thicket fence in which Bath players and the selectors soon became entangled.

Bristol, Gloucester and Bath players were the obvious source for most of the South-West XV which would each season play the other divisions, London, Midlands, and North (for whom Simpson played with distinction for a time).

To say the three clubs made up an uneasy amalgam is an understatement; the 'home' players were as likely as not to be derided at Kingsholm if they had been preferred to a local favourite, for example. The mix of talents was always unhappy, whoever was the coach — and in their time Mike Rafter and Jack Rowell all tried their hand.

But the overriding problem was that for a Mike Teague or a Richard Harding, not to mention a Stuart Barnes, playing for their club was a more important occasion than the divisional games, which were seen by smaller crowds who at 'home' showed sound judgement in preferring not to shout, "Come on you South West and South" or whatever the side's correct nomenclature might be.

Nonetheless some players did make their mark even if briefly in the division's colours. Jon Webb, for one, made a considerable early impact, and Alan Buzza in his Cornish persona made an almost physical impression when he tackled Jamie Salmon of London in one game at the Rec — Salmon took no further part in the game. Colin Laity, of Neath, was another who made some useful appearances.

But as captains came and went — Halliday and Robinson among them — so the lack-lustre performance of the divisional side (which only seemed to rise to games against overseas tourists, whether from Romania or Australia) became the despair of both coaches and captains.

The spectators rather shrugged their shoulders and went elsewhere — shopping perhaps — until the dreaded divisionals were over. Players increasingly declared themselves unavailable —

Barnes and Hall famously so. And the England selectors? They behaved towards the errant Bath players rather like public schoolhousemasters confronting small boys caught 'cutting' a cross-country run. Until the culprits learned to behave they wouldn't be considered for treats like the other boys — such as playing for England, perhaps.

By the time Geoff Cooke was running the England show in the late 1980s, the divisionals appeared to matter. He said as much. It was taken as a sign of a player's maturity and potential if he could rise to the challenge of bigger, divisional things.

The trouble with the South-West, and for Bath in particular, was that unlike men playing say, for Wakefield, or Fylde, they were playing First Division league rugby — and usually long cup runs — and felt they needed all their energies as amateurs to do justice to that programme.

Perhaps the Northerners felt the same way. But divisional rugby, like the County Championship before it (and now largely superseded in importance except in Cornwall and the north), was a bigger canvas they needed to demonstrate their skills.

The South-West view looked and sometimes sounded like arrogance, or a determination to undermine a framework apparently carefully constructed to help the formation of the national sides. But it wasn't: winning for Bath was the most important item in the rugby calendar for almost all the Bath players. If they didn't play that way they might not keep their place in the side. And in any case those who England chose were not always in form for Bath when they were selected — and vice versa. That Dick Best coached the successful London Division as well as being involved in the England set-up was a further complication.

And there were dark whispers from some lesser clubs that their young thrusters, brought into the divisional spotlight such as it was, were occasionally seduced into joining more fashionable clubs. (The helter-skelter arrangement which precipitated so many clubs into relegation in order to re-organise the Courage Leagues into home and away games after the 1992-93 season only added to smaller clubs' fears of poaching by the big boys.)

But back to the divisionals. After season after season of lamentable performances the South-West, to most people's surprise and perhaps their own, won the competition in the 1992-93 season. Stuart Barnes, serious about his England ambitions once more, captained the side, and in two games they fought back from positions where in previous seasons they might just have given up the game. They ended by winning two and drawing one — their first unbeaten record since the championship began.

What had happened? For the first time anyone could reasonably remember, Bath, Bristol and Gloucester were all out of the knock-out cup, falling at the first hurdle. (Exeter, briefly, were left to carry the banner for the region.)

For once, perhaps, with nothing on their mind other than a yawning gap where the cup used to be, the players — reinforced by new blood such as Beal of Northampton and Clark of Swansea — decided they had best show what they could do. Green shirts ruled for once. Both the newcomers were rewarded with representative recognition soon afterwards.

Even so when Stuart Barnes lifted the trophy (ADT were the brave sponsors) and admitted that it wasn't quite the same as taking the league or cup for Bath he was again accused of arrogance by one or two critics. It was as if some observers were determined to promote the claimed virtues of the Divisional Championship beyond a point which its tenuous hold on the public imagination could sustain.

Even David Irvine, an experienced rugby watcher in the Midlands and North for the *Guardian* (and one of those irritated by Barnes's comment) spoke of the paying public's 'sad backcloth of indifference' to the divisional games. In the circumstances the call from John Burgess, the North's administrator, for the Divisional Championship to be extended on a home and away basis was surely a forlorn whistle in the wind.

Burgess was understandably concerned for the opportunity it could offer players in the North, given their poor representation in the Courage League's top division. At the same time his plea emphasised the irreconcilable elements contained within the divisional series. With home and away league games imminent, it seemed an ever greater irrelevance for the future for many leading clubs and players outside the North.

Nor finally were its advocates helped when they themselves conspicuously chose their England squad even before the deciding games in the 1992-93 divisional games had taken place. It might have meant the selectors were utterly confident about their selections. But it hardly helped add further confidence in the game's most unloved competition — if the selectors had already made up their minds, what were the divisionals all about?

As for Bath, their cooling love affair with the England selectors in the early and mid-1980s probably reached its nadir with the notorious Wales-England punch-up in 1987. Hill the captain was suspended, and so were Chilcott (an apparent peacemaker on the day) and Dawe together with Dooley who later boasted about his haymaker on a Welsh forward. The following season only Halliday was chosen for his country from a side with a dozen capped players in its ranks.

It was a peculiar snub, and one that did England no favours either. But it was also the last milestone on the uneasy road the club had travelled with the selectors over the Rowell years. Thereafter the Geoff Cooke era — the little difficulty over Barnes apart — gave Bath players a chance of consistent selection.

Whatever the disappointments over the failure of Redman, say, or Robinson to establish a regular international place, supporters and club officials at least knew the players were back in with a chance: Hill, Guscott and Webb all became World Cup regulars in 1991; Barnes, of course, was belatedly reprieved from the sin-bin; Ubogu and de Glanville were blooded. And so on. Even Jack Rowell was at last brought into the field, coaching a successful 'B' tour of New Zealand in 1992, with Barnes as the captain.

There was also the splendid and continuing irony which underlined how apparent irreconcilables were still, on occasion, not to be reconciled, with the continued selection in the 1992-93 season of Bath's Steve Ojomoh as England 'A' team no.8 or blindside flanker when he was — no doubt temporarily — unable to claim a first-team place with his club. But at least John Hall, also back in international action, was his captain on the open-side, and Jack Rowell his coach.

By the end of that season therefore both Bath and England seemed largely to have realised that they could be of mutual benefit at last. It had been a long haul to get there. And if Bath had occasionally shown cussedness towards the England bosses, then it was only matched by the stubbornness of the latter on occasion. From now on perhaps they would live happily ever after.

That same season there was the added and unexpected bonus for Bath of four Scottish caps for the campaign's discovery, the Cornish Scot, Andy Reed. Two other Bath stars, Cronin and Sole, had been capped for Scotland earlier.

And in spite of the problems, and at times mutually inflicted wounds among the selectors and Bath's England contenders, England caps had spread widely around the Bath players since John Horton's isolated honour. By the end of the 1992-93 season, 18 players had been capped by England during Bath's great decade. They were: Barnes, Chilcott, Clarke, Dawe, de Glanville, Egerton, Guscott, Hall, Halliday, Hill, Horton, Martin,

Stuart Barnes.

Richard Hill.

Redman, Robinson, Simpson, Trick, Ubogu, Webb.

In addition Adebayo, Callard, Haag, Knight, Lee, Lumsden, Morrison, and Ojomoh had 'B' or, as it later became, 'A' recognition, without winning full caps.

Only one minor mystery or sadness lingers on. Why wasn't Tony Swift capped during his splendid seasons at Bath? As he neared the end of his career, he told Steve Bale: "I could never understand, why, of all the backs who played for England from Bath, I was never considered at all for anything." Not even for England 'B'.

Fuller details of the caps won appear at the end of the book.

The Critics

AS BATH under Jack Rowell continued to prosper and win so many games and cups so the undercurrent of criticism against the side as being boring in more than one sense, began to surface more widely. It had some prominent followers.

Dick Best, the Harlequins' coach, as mentioned in an earlier chapter, preened himself and reproached Bath (and Gloucester) by boasting that the meeting between his own club and Leicester in the 1989 cup semi-final, would ensure at least one 'good footballing side' played at Twickenham.

Those words, remember, were almost echoed by Tony Russ, coach of Saracens, and later of Leicester, in 1990, when he mourned the prospect of Bath playing Gloucester in what he said would be 'the most boring Final of all time'.

That Best and Russ could feel so confident as to denigrate so publicly the most successful club side in the land might have had just a little to do with envy of that success. Bath's eventual riposte to such criticisms, on the field, to beat Leicester, romp home against Gloucester, and later beat Best's beloved Harlequins, all at Twickenham, may have been as apt as could be imagined. And by the time coaches of club sides from Toulouse to Leicester to Gloucester had publicly praised the style and variety of Bath's brilliant attacking play the earlier critics had almost all packed their tents.

So how did the notion of Bath's 'boring' game and tactical barrenness originate — and why was it sustained for so long?

The 1986 Final between Bath and Wasps is generally cited as the start of the denigration of Bath. But I would suggest its origins are to be found rather earlier — and in a Twickenham Final which did not feature Bath.

The Bath side of the early 1980s played much entertaining, running rugby, but got nowhere in the John Player Cup. In 1983, Twickenham saw one of the most adventurous Finals in its history, when Leicester, and the acknowledged aristocrats of West Country rugby history, Bristol, set the half-full stadium resounding with applause as they exchanged tries in a 28-22 Bristol win.

By contrast, when Bristol returned the following year, they were never allowed to reproduce the kind of play that defeated Leicester, and Bath had won narrowly. After the 1983 Final, it inevitably seemed like anticlimax. And for that, since Bristol were again involved, then perhaps Bath must be rather to blame, muttered some disappointed neutrals, but good luck to Rowell's team — the trophy should go round, they said. And so on.

Bath won the next year in a Final that rarely took fire, Bath's early tries seeing off a London Welsh side heading into decline. That game too was disappointing. It was against that background of comparative letdown that unattached spectators in search of an annual touch of sparkle looked forward to the 1986 game between Bath and Wasps. Instead the match helped spread the canard that Bath had a predilection for dour, dutiful dullness.

The irony was that the Final began with Bath running at Wasps. Spilled passes, and scoring ripostes of inventive opportunism by the Londoners, seemed to have ended the game as a contest within the first quarter. The way Bath then slowly took control by forward strength which effectively wrested initiative and ball from Wasps was a disciplined exhibition of will-power, determination, team spirit, and the technique of a pack at the height of its powers.

Instead of being praised for overturning Wasps' 13-0 lead, Bath found some voices raised which seemed to suggest that somehow perhaps it had been a little unsporting not to let Wasps run away with the game. Fighting back so remorselessly was apparently less acceptable than doing so by running and winning — or at least losing glamorously. That, by implication, Bristol, Leicester, or of course Harlequins might have done. (All three sides later failed to do any such thing when losing to Bath themselves at Twickenham.)

Some of the criticism of Bath's game seemed to stop only just short of wishing Bath's fight-back could be declared invalid as being against the spirit of Twickers. It's not so far-fetched a suggestion as it may seem: the idea that some games Bath have won should in some way be re-run has recurred occasionally in later seasons.

I do not mean to be as absurd or so paranoid as to say the notion has been stated in so many words, but rather that there has sometimes been a fanciful, even wistful seeking for a fresh interpretation of key moments in some key games, even by the odd voice at the game's headquarters.

It was seen the following year, 1987, in the frankly disappointing Final between the same sides, with Bath again coming from behind to win a game they seemed to have lost. The brief and excited pitch invasion Bath supporters merely compounded the club's victory, and again there was the implication in some of the post-match criticism of Bath that the club had somehow played a mean trick on Wasps (who on the day were just as uninspiring as Bath). Worse, Bath had now won four on the trot, which seemed a trifle unsporting. Wasn't it time someone else won?

Next year someone else did — and it seemed to prove the critics' point. Harlequins, catching Bristol cold, ran brilliantly seemingly to win the game by half-time, only for Bristol to come near to overtaking them, but losing 28-22. There, see how much jollier the big club day was at Twickers when those boring Bath chaps weren't to be seen or, happily, heard. Whether Bristol were quite so pleased on the day was doubtful.

But Bath, the spoilsports, were back again the next year, and worse, they didn't let likeable Leicester, dear old departing Dusty and all, win or even score a try. That it was nonetheless a taut and fascinating struggle seemed of lesser importance for such critics (not Leicester-based, by the way) — particularly as Bath won once more.

No wonder some were expecting the bludgeon rather than the rapier, from both sides, as — when would they give up? — Bath returned in 1990 with Gloucester.

The biggest winning score in the knock-out Finals' history should have seen off the snipers; it largely did. But it is worth briefly examining the validity of criticism of the team's play over those years of growing success.

The men in blue, white, and black shirts were capable of dazzling displays of back play, which had won notable victories over those same seasons. In Wales, for example, the criticism of Bath as a dour, nay scurvy, crew, was somewhat puzzling. The fact was that the once-a-year watchers at Twickenham (when Bath, incidentally shed their normal colours for white shirts) had largely seen Bath shed also their capacity for exciting running movements involving backs and forwards.

Heavens above, said the establishment, those Bath chappies just seemed to want to win — and all that ruckin' and maulin', why, it's almost as if they thought they were New Zealanders, what? (There they were on to something.)

But the London brigade had seen, for the most part, only one facet of Bath's game. And tries from Trick, Halliday, or Swift were taken as scant evidence of their three-quarters' capabilities by those who saw the team so rarely.

As the 1988-89 season got under way one of Bath's ardent defenders, Stephen Jones of the *Sunday Times*, extolled and explained Bath's all-round skills:

"They have already shown that in a power game their pack will blow you away. If the game expands, their backs will shred you. If they maintain their early form, then the season will be one long celebration. In Bath that is. Elsewhere, joy will be confined."

Particularly among what Jack Rowell has described to me as 'armchair London supporters': he was no doubt too tactful to mention one or two coaches as well. But he insisted that some occasional watchers of that time did not understand what the team was all about, and what it could do.

For instance, he acknowledged that Halliday, for example, would ideally want to run the ball all the time whatever the situation. But the team's interests did not necessarily coincide with such individual fancies. He recalled the 1989 cup semi-final at Gloucester. "I remember what we said was that . . .you are not going to put the ball in the centre, where Gloucester had a good defensive system, unless you had space to play out wide. For instance, Barnes gives them a ball, they get knocked out, Gloucester get fired up and that's the last thing you want."

On the day, Gloucester were simply frozen out on their own patch, bereft of any tactical answer as Bath closed them down. Inter-active rugby, he called it, where the game plan fitted the occasion, or changed according to circumstances. Three seasons later, it was Bath's brilliant running at Kingsholm so late in the game which ended Gloucester's hopes of another Cup Final appearance.

Was it therefore all a myth, Bath's apparent trudging, grudging game? Or was grudging rather a word to describe Bath's detractors? Stephen Jones had suggested it was difficult to pinpoint 'the exact time when Bath and English rugby fell out of love.' I would suggest that the first pins were put in place after the Bristol Final of 1984, and thereafter used in profusion as Bath, contrary to all precedent, won at Twickenham again and again and again and again. Worse, and crucially, they beat London sides three times in those first four years.

Fresh supplies of pins were sent for when Bath players started saying whether or not they wished to be considered for England, and there was a positive flurry of them when Gareth Chilcott, for some the physical epitome of what was 'wrong' with Bath's approach, was one of four suspended (plus Hill, Dawe, and Dooley) after the Cardiff game between Wales and England in 1987.

The estrangement that followed coincided with the least successful season in Bath's decade of trophies.

There were a variety of other reasons — players returning from World Cup action or inaction, the loss of David Sole, Chris Martin, and of Barnes for much of the league and cup. And there was also an atmosphere of Fortress Bath, with some of the garrison failing to realise the significance of the new league system. With the need to improvise in team selection the side was too often liable to opt for the perceived safety of a forward-orientated game, with back row ball-retention increasingly a safety-first tactic.

The fans grew impatient, and so, we suspected, did the backs — I've earlier mentioned that between them Halliday, Palmer, Guscott and Trick, managed just one try between them in spite of a combined total of 33 league games that opening Courage season. The forwards scored more league tries than the backs, and two of the backs' tries significantly came from Hill at scrum-half. Bath were knocked out of the cup and finished fourth in the league.

Jack Rowell explained it as a transitional stage for the team. Maybe. But by the following season the side was again playing the more expansive game with forwards and backs combining in thrilling passages of attacking play. When the team later occasionally came unstuck — thus misleading Tony Russ — was when they mistakenly concentrated on a forward game as if to compensate for missing key backs. Such displays cost them the league title in 1989.

For the most part, though, Bath have continued to play a mixed entertaining game wherever possible. With such rich, rare combined talents as those offered by Barnes, Webb, Guscott and Swift, to name but four, it would have been folly to do otherwise. It was not an ambition that grew easier as the all-round strength of the top league division increased season by season.

If therefore Bath players and coaches had once and for a short time indulged in keeping it too tight even as the critics circled, it was quickly over. The side, as so often over the seasons, played to its strengths according to the opposition.

One light postscript seems permissible, when even the game's established figures still find their slips are showing on occasion in their head-shaking wonder at Bath's achievements.

Thus Dudley Wood, from his secretary's sanctum of the RFU, wrote in *Rugby World & Post* of Bath having 'stolen' the 1992 Cup Final in the closing moments from Harlequins. Hold it, Dudders, 'stolen'? You mean Harlequins were winning until Barnes's dropped-goal?

Never mind, a couple of Bath fans had some gentle sport with his modest gaffe (see *The Jesters*). And having forgiven Alan Watkins, the fans could also pardon Mr Wood. We just hoped they had also forgiven Bath.

The Sponsors

WHAT had the people of Winsford, on Exmoor, in common with the vicar of a Bristol parish church — and what had either to do with Bath Football Club?

Listeners to BBC Radio Bristol's *Thought for the Day* one January morning in 1989 heard the Revd Neville Boundy, vicar of Cotham, have a go at the £150,000 sponsorship deal between the club and the South-Western Electricity Board announced a few days earlier. "Why were we, whose money is involved after all, not asked first?"

His objections also brought him newspaper headlines ("Vicar calls foul on the big rugby deal") after Mr Boundy said: "Those responsible said although the money belongs rightly to all of us who are paying customers, it will only mean a few pence on everyone's bills — and anyway, if by the publicity more people are encouraged to use more electricity, then the price overall is likely to come down."

Such a response begged a few questions about conservation — "They should be encouraging us to use as little as possible" so as to save resources, he said.

But he probably expected to sound more telling chords with his final point. Why a rugby club, for heaven's sake? "Knowing the needs of many pensioners, homeless and playgroups, couldn't SWEB help them?"

Enter the Exmoor lobby. More than 200 properties at Winsford were still without mains electricity and with no prospect of getting it unless they stumped up the cash for its connection themselves. What were SWEB doing putting cash into a sport instead of helping Winsford gain power?

And if SWEB had money to give away to rugby clubs, said some Cornishmen, then what about giving some to Redruth, say — surely Bath didn't need the money with all the wealthy souls retired there?

To Mr Boundy, to Winsford, and the dissident Cornishmen, SWEB defended its decision; shareholders and customers would benefit from a successful company and that included that company's identification with success on the nation's rugby fields.

From Bristol there came not a peep: but as the headquarters of SWEB was in the city, the bonanza for neighbouring Bath must have been particularly hard to take without a little understandable gritting of teeth. SWEB — like Stuart Barnes a few years earlier — wanted to be associated with success and Bath seemed a better nag to back than the team at the Memorial Ground.

The brokers in the affair were Warwick Sports & Leisure, for whom Chris Rodman, of Rodman Marketing, a subsidiary, set up the deal. He had called Michael Harman, SWEB's public relations manager one day, who immediately thought: "Here's something." It happened that SWEB, on the threshold of privatisation at the time was looking to raise its image. Harman spoke right away to the then deputy chairman, later chief executive, John Seed, a Bath man and rugby enthusiast, who was similarly taken by the notion. Chairman Bill Nicol, by contrast, had some initial reservations.

Nevertheless, within 24 hours, SWEB had responded positively to the approach, which was just as well as others might otherwise have moved in. (Red Star Parcels, who later adopted Harlequins, was thought to be one candidate, for example.) Indeed, the surprise was perhaps that until Warwick Sport & Leisure turned up no one had previously tried 'adopting' Bath as main sponsors.

The Bath deal made good sense for SWEB, with the high profile the club received in the quality and local press, and local and national television. A small group from SWEB, including solicitor and secretary Stephen Marshall, Randoll Meadows representing retail marketing, and Michael Harman, negotiated the details with Bath's chairman Geoff Hancock, secretary Clive Howard, and the captain at the time, Stuart Barnes.

Would the sponsors interfere with the running of the club? No, came the assurance. Instead, for the latter half of that first season, which saw the cup win over Leicester, Bath received £20,000 under the deal, and £45,000 for each of the next three years. Bath would wear SWEB logos on their shirts, and SWEB would also sponsor four games a season, and have some seats reserved for it at each home game. The goalposts, too, have SWEB-inscribed padding.

But not all the SWEB advertising seen at the ground is part of the deal — for some of it the

Bath's record league score: 13 January 1990 – at the final whistle (including three minutes of injury time). The Electricity Board's logo stands proudly above . . .

company pays extra. (And contrary to popular belief, SWEB is not responsible for the floodlighting or the electronic scoreboards.)

Bill Nicol's early caution was not unreasonable, as it turned out. SWEB was not best pleased when four Bath reserve players lifted champagne and other drinks from a Leicester branch of Threshers at the end of the 1988-89 season and were duly fined ("Theft shame of rugby players", went the headline).

A few months later, when Bath had cumulative disciplinary problems whose climax was the sending off of Gareth Chilcott in the league match at Gloucester, SWEB made its dismay clear. Bath assured their sponsors the dismay was mutual. It was a reminder nonetheless that, though the sponsors had no part in the running of the club, as paymasters they could pipe an admonitory tune if necessary.

SWEB's properly-raised eyebrow demonstrated that the acceptance of handsome sponsorship was not simply a question of a club taking the money and running with the ball (or miscreants with the drinks — the four were also suspended by the club:) the sponsors could make their opinions known about misconduct by players on or off the field.

Further, the contract could be 'reviewed and reduced' if Bath were relegated from the Courage League Division One. But there were also hidden extras for success — such as 20 per cent on top of the basic annual fee for winning the cup or league title.

Bath have used the money for financing tours and games against overseas teams, training trips to Lanzarote, and perhaps of equal importance, in developing junior rugby. At the time of the original deal, Clive Howard said: "Like other leading clubs, we are concerned that many schools are no longer playing the game and we need to do our bit to create our own talent."

After those initial alarms, the partners settled down amicably together, and the deal was renewed for the 1992-93 season.

The figures and details of the fresh deal remain confidential, and neither SWEB nor the club will confirm the amounts involved. But basic figures of £65,000 for three seasons, or a basic sponsorship package of £195,000 have not been challenged when quoted. (The only hitch was when the club apparently 'forgot' that it owed 10 per cent to Warwick Sport & Leisure on renewal, and the latter briefly threatened legal action before it got its cut.)

Certainly Clive Howard was happy that the sponsorship, one of the first in the game for individual clubs, was also one of the best. Other clubs may quote apparently larger sums, he said, but they were often hedged in by conditions which meant a full amount was unlikely to be realised.

Michael Harman for SWEB was equally pleased: "It's a very successful sponsorship. We think it's a very good deal for the company and for the club."

Perhaps the only mild surprise for outside observers related to the commercial exploitation of the deal, with neither SWEB nor the club making as much public use of each other, or the players, as might have been expected. That may yet happen.

Even though Bath's early exit from the cup in 1992-93 was in every sense a minus just as the renewed deal was under way, the team's continued run-in for league title honours meant continued exposure on TV and in the press of that SWEB logo — and mutual association with success.

(By early 1993, too, in odd but happy coincidence, not only was Jack Rowell a board member of Dalgety plc, but SWEB also had a new board member and part-time deputy chairman, Maurice Warren, who was chairman of Dalgety plc.)

Other cumulatively useful items of sponsorship also help the club — first Admiral and then Umbro have supplied kit. Individual sponsors take care of match sponsorship, match balls, lucky programme prizes and the like. Of these, the frequent prize of a Scotch salmon, given by Marr of Bristol has become a cult joke in the club fanzine ("Keep your eye out for our friend . . .") and its adventures have been used in ingenious pictures — Hill passing the salmon from the base of the scrum, Webb catching a leaping salmon, and so on.

But perhaps the most unexpected spin-off of other people's sponsorship that has benefited Bath over recent years has been the sports development scholarships at the University of Bath. These mean that an undergraduate who is also a talented sportsman or sportswoman can take their degree in whatever subject they are studying while not losing their sporting chances. This normally means the student does an extra year compared with their contemporaries.

Promising competitors in sports from golf to hockey are beneficiaries. But Bath has enjoyed the services of such sports scholars as Chris Martin, Audley Lumsden, both past recipients of others' benefactions, and more recently Gareth Adams and Iestyn Lewis. The scholarships in 1993 were valued at £6,000 a student to cover their expenses in pursuing their sport and their fees for their extra year.

Key people in the university's sports development programme, of course, have been Tom Hudson, until his retirement, and Ged Roddy, both also associated successively with fitness training of the Bath players.

That Bath themselves might use some of that SWEB money to sponsor a place for a promising sportsman (a rugby player, logically) would seem to be the sensible and likely step for a club which has benefited not only from some of the sports scholars and their tutors, but also from the presence of other fine players who were conventional undergraduates at the city's university, such as David Trick and Greg Bess.

And if they decide not to name the Bath scholarship after the late Jack Simpkins, for so many years a servant of the club, they could name it after Jack Rowell instead. Why not make it two endowments . . .?

The Committees

BATH has another major sponsor of course — the crowd. The club has around 3,000 members, paying a variety of subscriptions, depending on age and whether they stand or sit to watch games. But their contribution can be reasonably estimated at 1991-92 rates at around £80,000. A full house occurs only a few times in each season but match income including a full Pilkington Cup run could bring in around £150,000. That's a lot of money.

Another definition of sponsor in my dictionary is one who contributes towards meeting the costs of an event. On that reckoning Bath's other major sponsors are its dedicated helpers, all volunteers, who do it for free — from gatemen to ground stewards to programme sellers and many more. The club can call on scores of people willing to assist.

By the end of the 1992-93 season only two people at the club were on a regular club payroll — Rob Rowland, the bar steward, and Liz ("Please don't give my full name — I've already discovered I've a million and a half friends wanting tickets when there's a big match here.") who kept the club office ticking over.

Those dedicated volunteers included of course the people who manned the multiplicity of committees associated with the running of a major club: bars, grounds, fund-raising, mini-rugby and more — there were ten such sub-committees in all at the latest count. All were meant to ensure that while coaching staff and players took care of what happened on the field of play, off the field all ran smoothly. Or at least that was the theory.

In truth, so far as the vast majority of supporters, and even members were concerned, they assumed that somewhere behind the scenes people organised the club's affairs but the sign that all was well was, in the best sense, taken for granted. They just wanted to see the rugby. That way everyone stayed happy.

This book is about the club's playing success, and not about the occasional shenanigans that have occasionally ruffled the Bath waters so that even the disinterested onlooker noticed the waves.

Once upon a time behind-the-scenes problems may have been few, or just as many, but they mattered less. When Bath became a major playing success everything that happened at the club was potentially of wider interest and has wider impact on the playing side, too.

With a few notable exceptions not many of the players from the 1960s and '70s era moved into committee work in later seasons. Club stalwarts of an earlier generation, notably the late Jack Simpkins, successively United player, senior referee, secretary, and past president; and Jack Arnold, first-team player, touch judge, management committee member for 19 years, and also a past president, were the kind of men whose service to the club provided a bedrock of continuity and devotion behind the scenes.

But the club that such stalwarts administered and served changed radically as a result of its latterday playing success and the rapid commercial advance in the modern game. These were not changes everyone liked at the time they began, and some still did not like them. A few older members, for example, have complained because they cannot find a comfortable place to sit or stand if they arrive, as they did decades ago, just five minutes before kick-off.

They may be exceptional, in more than one sense. But that unease at how the game was going and where it was taking the club as well as the team (there's a difference) was neatly epitomised in some hand-wringing comments by John Stevens in the match programme for the first Courage League game between Bath and Bristol, in October 1987.

What, he asked, would many who had played in past classics between the clubs be thinking of the way top-class rugby was going — was it a headlong dash towards professionalism?

He went on: "Many people will hope not. Games in the past have always been hard fought . . .but any differences on the field have usually been forgotten in the bar afterwards. One can only hope that such attitudes will exist in a few years' time. If they don't, today's players may miss the long and lasting friendships established by those who have gone before — by for example Tom Mahoney, the current Bristol president, and Jack Arnold, who has held the same office at Bath. They even continued their fierce rivalry as touch-

Secretary Clive Howard in September 1992. He had succeeded Jack Simpkins and was in office for the club's cup-winning years. He died, after illness, in June 1993.

judges for some of the battles of the 1950s of which they were an indelible part.

"They, like many others, will fear for the game they have served so well with such enthusiasm for so long. Where is top-class English club rugby going (when) the old tradition of playing who you want when you want is in danger of being lost by fixed Saturdays, leagues, divisional championships and increasing international demands?

"Many of Bath and Bristol's traditions are under threat. So, I fear, is their strong link with Welsh clubs who have brought them fixture lists which are the envy of the rest of the competition. Do they really understand at Twickenham? Or perhaps they don't care."

It was heartfelt stuff, clearly, and there's no doubt that Stevens articulated the anxieties and the sense of sadness at the passing of club rugby which was felt by many of his contemporaries, and even more so, their elders, at the time.

If there were fears for what was to come in 1987, then the changes that followed even more briskly thereafter meant that most followers of the game were swept forward with them, and in the case of Bath, the consistent and continuing success was heady enough reward for most of the club's supporters. Only the rugby Luddites continued to weep nostalgically in their (nowadays inevitably pricier) pints.

But if Jack Rowell was to be surprised by the success his team was to achieve, the impact on those working on committees, running the club, was no less.

Those who had first known and served Bath as a friendly, always hospitable family club with few ambitions beyond good rivalry and comradely feelings were in a sense transported to being in a gradual but growing world rugby spotlight as the team's fame spread. Modest aims and claims were increasingly expected to expand and perform in keeping with the enhanced image of Bath Football Club and the prestige and added status it conferred on those associated with it.

Inevitably, though, with new people who had perhaps enjoyed considerable business or professional success in their private life also attracted to service at the club, a clash of personalities was inevitable. The players were largely aloof from any little local difficulties, except that for some years some of them sensed a 'them and us' gulf between players and committee.

When so-called rebel members attempted late in 1992 to overthrow the secretary, Clive Howard, and the entire 37-man management committee (which also included Jack Rowell) at a costly emergency general meeting, and also sought public scrutiny of the terms of the SWEB sponsorship deal, the only confident prediction was that there would be tears before bedtime.

So it proved, and it was the rebels who had to call for a handkerchief. (They were soon joined in not-so-silent sobs by their fellow-members and the players when the cup defeat at Waterloo followed a few days later.) But a new executive committee of seven (the club chairman, secretary, treasurer, and chairmen of the fund-raising, grounds, and bars sub-committees, plus a players' representative) promised more streamlined decision-making in the future, Barnes and Robinson having made it clear that the players were 'against' the rebellion but in favour of an end to squabbles that distracted from the club's primary purpose, playing rugby.

It was not the emergence of player power, as some suggested, rather that players were at last making their voice heard in the planning of the club. And it was a voice unlikely to be silenced henceforward.

The Supporters

NO NEWS about committees was good news for the average supporters. That was how they liked it — it meant the committees must be doing a good job.

Although the personalities and the points of view involved in the committee wrangles of late 1992 fall largely outside the purpose of this book, therefore, the brief fracas has been mentioned because the quarrel and the inevitable national publicity perturbed the players — and Jack Rowell — and puzzled the wider membership and regular supporters who simply paid their money to cheer on the team.

Those spectators were a remarkable cross-section, perhaps containing more family groups than any other club's except for Leicester. Michael Ringham, writing in the club's 125th anniversary handbook in 1990, noted the quiet revolution that had taken place at the ground:

"Mums and dads, children, grannies, even babies are here, mellowed by late autumn sun, chilled by winter's nip, and soaked to the marrow in early spring. Yet we still come back for more . . .When the rain pours down . . .your shoes are leaking, and the last try appears more like a 22-metre breast stroke than a touchdown, our spirits are lifted to new heights by the forceful cry of 'Come on me Lovers.' and suddenly Doris, our Lady of the Rec, has filled you with pride and the warmth comes gushing back.

"My children cling to the advertising hoardings, small white knuckles gripping tight when Barnesie takes a kick. 'Why doesn't Damian pull his socks up Dad?' and 'Why does Coochie blow his nose like that?'

Or there's the story from 'the Flowerpot Men' in the club programme who recall Bath unleashing a final onslaught on the Harlequins line in that 18-all draw of 1991:

"A little girl alongside us, about eight years old, whispered out loudly 'Come on Bath, we love you.' Within seconds Phil de Glanville touched down no more than ten yards from her and Webby earned the draw. That whisper did the trick."

Sentimental perhaps but also true in its portrayal of the reality that following Bath is nowadays often as much about parenting as about supping pints — and about the feminine presence.

But strong though the representation of women among the club's supporters may be, anomalies from an earlier, less sensitive era irritate many of them. Unlike most other clubs in the top division, for example, Bath, in company with Wasps and Harlequins, still had a distinctive 'ladies' membership, whose fee was considerably smaller than that paid by what the club officially called (for convenience?) 'gents'.

Some of the old (male) guard have argued this discount was proper because women did so much 'voluntary' work. (Perhaps they had in mind the years of service in providing refreshments given by the redoubtable Mrs Vi Brinkworth and her colleagues; but they too were in time replaced by outside caterers.) But so did many men. Moreover, the differential subscription, said its opponents, simply patronised women and confirmed outdated sexist attitudes. Women, said the critics, should have equal rights in the club which included paying the same subscription as men. Yet there was also a suggestion at one recent annual meeting for a women's committee, which sounded to most of the audience like a barrier rather than a welcome. It was properly dismissed.

But perhaps Abbie Boyle from Atworth, in Wiltshire, summed up the situation best when she wrote to the club early in 1993 to point out that they addressed mail to her as 'Mstr A.E.Boyle." "Fortunately I am not a master, but a Miss!" she said, adding the point that tickets allocated to her and her friends for all-ticket games were printed for 'Schoolboys', not even 'Juniors'. She asked: "Surely it is not uncommon for girls to come and watch rugby?" A small point, perhaps, but it demonstrated how the club had on occasion to run to catch up with social changes it could not always recognise.

But it did meet the challenge of how to entertain the crowds that increasingly came early in order to find reasonable vantage points around the ground for big games.

Two hours before kick-off was a long wait. Occasionally schoolboy (and schoolgirl) rugby

A full house – both inside and out, in 1993.

filled some of the time; and Tony Thresher provided music and talk over the much-improved public-address system. Most enterprising, as the capacity crowd waited for the Wasps game in March 1993, was the engagement, with the help of sponsors, of Pete Martin and the Bath City Jazzmen, including such notable Bristol-based jazzmen as Andy Leggatt and Henry Davies (on Sousaphone!) to play as they perambulated slowly around the ground.

To some diehards music and chat from a club disc jockey, or live jazz, may have seemed frivolity far removed from the pattern of days not so long distant. But like the well-stocked and often crowded club shop, run by Carol Petteford, it was a sign that the club realised it was now in the entertainment business. Although the crowd was there to see top-class rugby a taste of cakes and ale helped pass the time and whetted appetites for the main fare.

In addition there was now the radically altered and improved programme produced by Ken Johnstone, which at last began to be worthy of a club of Bath's stature in its content and presentation.

For many years, in spite of the best efforts of Jack Simpkins, Clive Howard, and the club's history man Harry Barstow, its match programme was put to shame by, for example, Orrell — and even Bristol (misspellings apart, which at the Memorial Ground long had an appeal all of their own: seeing how Bristol could mangle the spelling of a name like Quittenton was itself worth the cover charge).

More progress was promised with the programme for future seasons, and Ken Johnstone also produced an occasional official publication, *The Recorder*.

In all, Bath was filling its coaches with enthusiasts travelling to away games in neighbourly parties, and seeing club scarves decorating cars on the motorways. Faithfully too, hundreds were travelling from Wiltshire and Somerset, Dorset and Gloucestershire to see the side: spectators, like the team, were truly regional. At the Rec, they increasingly found conditions for members and pay-at-the-gate spectators improving by the season — thanks to the committee and their helpers — which is where this chapter started.

But on a few Saturdays from the 1991-92 season a new and unexpected pre-match read was available to first-comers, free of charge. Supporter power, or humour rather, had arrived in the form of Bath's own fanzine, its title already decided, had they but known it, by the bellowing of countless jokers season by season as the ref's whistle shrilled.

The Jesters

IT COULD, I suppose, equally well have been called, "Come on, my lovers," after the faithful Doris on the stand side at the Rec whose heartfelt encouragement pierces the other crowd noises a dozen times a season.

Instead, the title of Bath's own fanzine, *Everytime Ref Everytime* is derived from (and I quote): "The age-old curse at that common enemy of all Bath fans, the referee, when an opposition player has not been penalised for breaking the rules. Regular visitors . . .will be familiar with this chant, usually after about 30 seconds of the game starting; well, let's face it, most referees don't know how to penalise the opposition."

That broad hint of self-mockery, of not taking life too seriously, is perhaps the secret of the modest success of the remarkable fanzine, which calls itself *Ere* for short, and claims to be the 'unofficial publication' for supporters of Bath Football Club.

It is strong on jokes, never nasty or sexist, healthily against racist abuse and booing of goal-kickers ("Absolute silence here at Kingsholm as Stuart Barnes prepares to take the penalty") whether from opponents or Bath voices, and above all thoroughly supportive of the players. (That some of the spelling is only approximate and that it doesn't know its apostrophes from its posses-sives scarcely matters in the circumstances.)

Perhaps *Ere's* most valuable function is to add that important dimension of the faithful mem-bership and beyond: the players are the most important people at the club, and the committees help to run it. But without the supporters Bath would hardly be the same.

In most of its half-dozen issues a season, *Ere* puts down the self-important or plain wrong, too. For example, as I have mentioned earlier, Dudley Wood, secretary of the RFU, no less, reviewing 1992 at Twickenham in his column in *Rugby World & Post* in February 1993, wrote of the Pilkington Cup Final as being 'stolen in the dying moments from the Harlequins by Bath, who also won the league championship by the narrowest of margins'.

Ere tackled him head-on for the inaccurate suggestion that the cup was 'in Peter Winterbot-tom's hands' before Barnes's winning kick. Or had the RFU, it asked, passed a rule without telling anyone during the brief half-time break of the extra 20 minutes? And it speculated on how the rule might have read:

"Should both teams finish level on points after a period of extra time, the team who-

(a) plays nearest to Twickenham; (b) has the terrible misfortune of having two key players missing due to regrettable sendings-off; (c) has the England captain playing for them, shall be awarded the cup."

Not a bad rule, Brian Moore might agree? — and not a bad joke about a gaffe from someone who should have been wiser. *Ere* added that Angry from Bath had written to Mr Wood. There was no reply.

Ere was the idea of two keen fans, Clive Banks from Bath, and Glen Leat from Trowbridge. They began it in the 1991-92 season with 200 copies of their enthusiastic, irreverent first issue which they gave away free outside the ground as spectators turned up for a home game against Richmond.

Clive Banks, admitted: "We were absolutely terrified when we started it — we had no idea what the club's reaction would be." And Glen Leat confessed their worst fears were that the club might ban them or try and take away their membership for their cheek. That fear seemed a bit far-fetched, and indeed the club welcomed the jesters at the gate immediately.

Secretary Clive Howard and Ken Johnstone, who had just taken over responsibility for improving the inadequate club programme, invited them inside the ground to distribute *Ere*. (Soon, indeed, as Bill and Ben, the Flowerpot Men, the pair were also contributing an occasional opinion column to the official programme.)

More, they quickly won modest but essential initial sponsorship from two other members, Harry Wainwright from Waterstone's in Bath, and printer John Roose. Determined to continue *Ere* as a giveaway, Leat and Banks hoped in future to find a few members willing to chip in a couple of quid a season to keep it alive.

Its jokes alone were worthwhile, some of them

against Bath supporters. Like the Bath-scarved man loudly criticising a lad in a pre-match schools game of mini-rugby at Bristol for being selfish, and boasting: "If I was his father I'd give him a clip round the ear." A Bristol supporter, looking at him countered: "If you were his father you wouldn't even be able to catch him."

At a time when Bath had its full share of 'one-eyed' supporters, such gentle put-downs were especially welcome.

But inevitably the jokes were usually on the opposition, particularly Bristol and Gloucester. Thus under the headline 'You Think That's Funny?' there was the one about the two rugby fans stranded in the Sahara on a boiling Saturday afternoon. Says Bert: "Bristol lost again then!" Fred: "How on earth do you know that?" Bert: "It's 4.25." And when Gloucester lost 21-6 at Kingsholm to West Hartlepool, described as 'Result of the Year,' *Ere* added: "Just as well they weren't playing the whole of Hartlepool."

But *Ere* also fishes for its stories in an obvious place, but one seldom written about when Bath Football Club is the subject: the river beside the Rec. Its first issue interviewed 15-year-old Simon Thresher from Crudwell — 'the boy with the net' whose match-day task was to dash off with his net whenever the ball sailed over the stand and into the Avon, an intriguing custom at the Rec over the years.

It was, *Ere* reminded its readers, a tradition even older than the prize salmon, the cry from Doris of "Come on, my lovers" (although she might dispute that), or an ankle injury for John Hall after 20 minutes.

Simon Thresher estimated the ball was kicked over the stand about three or four times in a game, landing in the river about twice, in spite of 'catch' netting on the stand roof. By using his telescopic pole with a net at the end, retrieval was usually fairly easy. But if the ball landed in the further side of the Avon he had to run along the river bank, up the stone spiral staircase, over North Parade bridge and down into the famous Parade Gardens. Despite all these obstacles, said *Ere*,

Simon had 'lost' only one match ball. He said: "There's nothing worse than fishing for a ball and hearing the crowd roar as something exciting happens."

Ere also offered more than comment about the doings of the first team. It urged its readers to visit the Rec on a Sunday morning to encourage the mini-rugby players. The commitment of players and coaches clearly demonstrated that Bath's playing future was in safe hands, it said.

But its self-mockery, rather than its goodwill, saw *Ere* at its best. Its 'comments you won't hear this season' for 1992-93, for example, included "The Gloucester fans applaud the victorious Bath side off the pitch/ and Bath are dominating the line-out/Welcome to this top of the table clash between Bristol and Rugby/Stuart Barnes drove all the way to Heathrow Airport to welcome Rob Andrew back to English rugby" . . .And so on.

In asking for BBC videos of Bath's cup victories to be put on sale *Ere* accurately cited that only then could such questions be answered as, of the two Finals against Wasps: "Were Bath really so awful for over an hour of each game yet still good enough to win?"

And of the 48-6 win over Gloucester in 1990: "Did this game really take place or was it just the most wonderful dream? If it wasn't a dream why did we let Gloucester score?"

Shocked by the 1992 cup defeat of Bath at "W-W-Wa . . .we can't even bring ourselves to write the word," *Ere* faced its editorial responsibilities nonetheless bravely: "As is our normal practice we continue in this issue to jibe at other clubs, but must admit to knowing that all the jibes in rugby at the moment are directed at our great club. Still we can take it. It'll rain at Twickenham on 1 May 1993 anyway." (It didn't. Harlequins were in their third successive Final in the 1990s. And they lost to Leicester.)

Ere's drollery has earned its place in the Rec's gallery of Bath's best supporters — even if it can only match the prize salmon with a tin of sardines for its own lucky prize number.

The Jobs

AS BATH supporters go, Malcolm Pearce — or rather his family — goes back a long way. His mother has been a member for what — "Oh, 60 years" — and he's been a supporter ever since he can remember.

That maternal link apart, the story so far is familiar. What makes Malcolm Pearce rather special so far as the club is concerned is that he is also something of a one-man employment agency for Bath players who may be in need of a job — or even a career. At least seven international players had been through his company's payroll at his last count.

It began when Chris Martin was travelling back and forth from Bedford to play for Bath after he left the city's university. Jack Rowell, knowing Malcolm Pearce's evident interest in the club, asked if he could find Martin a job in the city. Pearce at the time employed around 150 people — he took Martin on for what he admitted to me were probably 'the wrong reasons — they were rugby reasons'. But Martin, a mathematician, was put into the small computer department and turned out to be quite brilliant. By the time he left to go to New Zealand he was, said Pearce, indispensable. Or so it seemed at the time.

"He was a wonderful man as well, and I realised from his success the chemistry is so good with a rugby player in an office organisation. They think in terms of a team."

But Malcolm Pearce was remarkable even as local entrepreneurs go. He was in the wholesale newspaper distribution, dairy farming, the security business, hire-drive, and retail shops for starters, and with international outlets too, his workforce having risen to around 850 by 1993.

The players he employs were not there to go through the motions and pick up the loot. They were there to do a job, even develop their skills further for the days when they were no longer playing. "I make it clear we don't want anyone having to say, look, you're not pulling your weight." Sinecures they were not — and Pearce has not been let down.

And if Martin was his first tentative venture — and a success that encouraged both Pearce and

Jack Rowell to repeat it — then Gareth Chilcott, now running the Chauffeurlink business (a far haul from logging and French polishing) was Malcolm Pearce's longest-running success. Pearce also backed the publication of the Chilcott autobiography of a few years ago.

David Sole, in ice-cream and the dairy business, Damian Cronin — managing a restaurant — and Ben Clarke, marketing Lordswood Dairy's milk to schools, were other internationals who have benefited from the Pearce pay packet. Victor Ubogu and Steve Ojomoh were others. At spring of 1993, forwards Martin Haag (accounts), Colin Atkins (newspapers and magazines), and Mark Crane (milk sales to shops), as well as Chilcott and Clarke were working under one or other of the Pearce companies, whose parent company is Johnsons Central Holdings of Bath. Clarke had left by season's end.

But being the engaging extrovert he is, the boss is not without resource when even the oddest tasks fall into his in-tray. Sorting out past passport problems for Steve Ojomoh was one such; arranging trial modelling sessions for Jeremy Guscott, which opened the player's eyes to his potential and helped persuade him to say 'no' to Rugby League was another. (Guscott, an agent, and British Gas, took it from there.) All apparently in a day or more's work for this unusual rugby follower.

Does Malcolm Pearce ever say 'no'? There was the time Dave Robson, then still at Bath, rang to ask him briskly if Pearce could call up his RAF contacts at Lyneham — three Bath players needed to get back for a big game in time from Tenerife. Could Robson leave it to Pearce? Er, no — even he balked at that one.

The players were eventually flown back — but not, of course, by the RAF (now that would have been a good story for the tabloids and for Questions to the Prime Minister).

More recently, though, when Bath discovered the holidaying Mike Catt from South Africa on their patch with dual British nationality, and a fly-half with considerable potential, Pearce again supplied the money for the rent. No, not a gift.

But to enable Catt to stay until season's end, a temporary job on the till in one of Pearce's retail newsagents' shops in the city centre was found for him.

And so, seemingly, it goes on, with Pearce Players' Club still short of two or three of a full XV of employees over the years but showing every sign of reaching that figure.

If the basic agenda is to enable players to enjoy their rugby with the club free of job worries, the other benefit can be that his job opportunities or other constructive ideas can help counter the occasional sweet talking of Rugby League clubs.

One that got away was Jim Fallon. He was about 18 months short of completing his accountancy qualifications for which he was studying while with Bath (and Pearce's business) when he decided to up pens and go to Leeds. Perhaps if he had been a few years younger he'd have stayed.

Other supporters and players have similarly given genuine jobs to Bath players over the seasons — Dave Robson employed Tony Swift as an accountant, for example. But there's never been anything quite like Malcolm Pearce, successful businessman and creator of openings for Bath players to earn (and learn) as they play.

Is it professionalism in sport? Hardly — unless amateur players are to be denied earning their living. Malcolm Pearce just happened to be a successful businessman with a variety of commercial interests and hundreds of employees who was also a fervent supporter of his home team. Every club should have one; not every club has.

A few heads are shaken in disapproval from time to time around the Bath clubhouse as well as farther afield. But Jack Rowell is in no doubt.

Model centre: Jeremy Guscott's selling power.

Chilcott joins the model set.

"Malcolm Pearce is a marvellous supporter in what he does for the club. What we need is even more like him." He wasn't joking, either.

The Supermarket

WHATEVER Bath's playing future, the club is on the verge of major changes in the property it owns. At the beginning of 1993 it was even contemplating the possibility that it might have to start wondering what to do with millions of pounds, or at least with a sizeable but more modest sum.

The comparatively homely Recreation Ground was not on the market — Bath leases that from the city council. But more of that later. The prize property the club owns is the Lambridge training ground just along the London road beyond the city centre at the junction of the M46.

That ten-acre site has turned out to be one of the best investments the club could have made. It was acquired for around £10,000 in the 1950s as a training pitch. It was also used by Walcot Old Boys as their ground for some years before Bath, with a playing commitment now including the first team, United, Spartans, youth and junior sides, found it needed all the facilities there for training and matches.

Then began a series of planning wrangles that has kept the city of Bath — well used to planning sagas — waiting for some years. Tesco wanted the Lambridge ground for a major supermarket site, and Bath Football Club would benefit by, it is said, around £18 million if the deal went through. But Tesco's planning application was called in by the Secretary of State, together with a rival bid for the bus depot site, a little nearer the city, from Safeway. It seemed unlikely that both would be approved.

If Tesco's proposal was approved, however, the company said it would provide park-and-ride facilities for visitors to the city centre. And if it is not approved, then the likelihood was that the city council would instead acquire the site for its own park-and-ride site (it already had two on other key approaches to the city). In that case the money the Bath club would get, perhaps under a compulsory purchase order, would be very much more modest.

But it should still be enough to enable the club to move to its chosen replacement for Lambridge. In spite of opposition from Wansdyke District Council, in whose area the site lies, the club was granted planning permission for a 60-plus acre site at Bathampton Meadows, with the option to purchase. The money from the Lambridge sale, it was hoped, would finance both the purchase of the Bathampton site and its development.

The club planned five pitches, a dressing room, floodlights and other necessary training facilities. Wansdyke, although not unsympathetic to the club's ambitions, opposed the plan because of what it argued would be unacceptable intrusion to residents caused by the lights, goalposts, and increased traffic.

Throughout the complex and lengthy arguments about the Lambridge and Bathampton sites, the club's principle was simply that it would sell Lambridge only if it could find an alternative which would be an improvement on Lambridge, now effectively outgrown. It was a sensible enough ambition that built on the wisdom of the club's earlier administrators and would ensure an ample facility for future players.

Meanwhile, back at the Recreation Ground the club's plans were more modest but still forward-looking, and in part, revenue-raising — or so it was hoped.

The club came to the Rec almost a century earlier, in the late 1890s. The team had played there ever since, through floods and blitz. But the club did not own the ground. Instead it rented the facilities from the city council, in a series of long leases, for eight months every year (at a cost of around £20,000 in the year ended 31 May 1992).

As any visitor knows, there are hockey pitches beyond the open side of the ground, and (which is where I came in) the cricket square where Somerset played for a week in the year — and probably for less than that.

Curiously, given the properly protected nature of the square, it seemed perverse that the car parking during cricket week covered the rugby ground. Bath — and the council's groundsmen — sighed and put up with it. But if the open side could not be developed, the areas behind the goals were adaptable. The Old North Stand gave way to the present pavilion (and the best lavatory facilities in the Courage Championship?) some years ago.

Regulations covering the safety of sports grounds and the agreement with the city council meant that the Rec's capacity was officially 8,311. But the club always made sure the odd 300-or-so places were never taken up, in order to stay on the side of safety. Hence the members-only and all-ticket games on a few big occasions.

Now the club has received planning approval for its proposed South Stand development. This will have the incidental benefit of masking the ugly elevation of the neighbouring sports centre (and also cut out the free view some enterprising customers find for Bath matches).

But its main purpose was initially announced as providing a number of hospitality boxes and accompanying suite, together with 400 stand seats, or 900 standing room places. Given that the club had a waiting list for stand seat membership, it looked as if that would be the sensible option.

From time to time, the confines of Bath's September to April tenancy of the Recreation Ground irks the visitor and means that many more people than can be accommodated must be turned away.

But for many — and not just Bath supporters — it is at once a handsome setting near to Bath Abbey and the Avon, and the busy Pulteney Bridge and Pulteney Street. No matter either that on certain Saturdays the centre of Bath is choc-a-bloc with shoppers and a few thousand rugby followers. An afternoon at the Rec — a ground so unlike the lower division soccer ground lookalikes that take bigger crowds at Gloucester and Bristol — will do well enough for most supporters. Bath Football Club is firmly at the heart of that great Georgian City.

Press

MY SECOND editor put me right in my comparative youth when I applied for a sports job within the paper. He tore up the application in my presence. "It's a ghetto for life!" he grumped. "You're not going there." And he made it sound like something only slightly up a notch from the Victorian white slave traffic.

So I abandoned the modest ambition to write about sport and played (a little) and watched (a little more). Later, like other, grander sports-dabbling editors of our time (Harold Evans, Peter Preston, Donald Trelford?) I no doubt irritated the sports editors of papers I edited by constantly peering, metaphorically at least, over their shoulders, and exchanging the latest news or gossip with the cricket, soccer and rugby writers.

As time went by I was glad to have such stalwarts as John Stevens working for me, covering Bath rugby, and 20 years later, in Bristol, I was Kevin Coughlan's editor when he moved to a similar patch.

In between, as Frank Keating recalled in his autobiography of 1992, I was the middle man who suggested many years ago that he try for a sports job on *The Guardian*. He tried and got it, and the rest is, well, a thousand or more entertaining columns. Put it down as my one contribution to the sum of British sportswriting.

On *The Guardian*, too, I had valued the work and views of rugby men like the Davids Frost and Irvine in the 1970s, when Bob Armstrong was not then the paper's number-one rugby man — he was not even in the sports department. Instead my relations with him were largely concerned with his role as the tough, but scrupulously fair, father of the journalists' union chapel, and mine as northern editor.

Along the way too I saw Alastair Hignell making tackles for Bristol (and ducks for Gloucestershire) before he became the skilled commentator for HTV. Above all, though, I learned much about cricket in particular and sportswriting in general from my valued friendship with David Foot, one in the best traditions of literate, sometimes literary cricket writers.

Another cricketing man living near Bath, Scyld Berry, latterly with the *Sunday Telegraph*, pointed me in the direction of one of his earlier papers, the brief-lived *Sunday Correspondent*.

Jon Henderson on their sports desk was bold enough to use me as an occasional rugby writer. The snag was that it didn't always take me to see Bath play. But the experience of covering league and cup games at the top level was enough to awaken memories of my lost ambitions of youth, and renew my respect for the writers who must digest the essence of a game and then seek to convey it to their Sunday paper audience, and all within five minutes or so of the final whistle.

Alas, the *Sunday Correspondent* didn't survive. It had a wit or two at the other end of the telephone when one dictated the names of the teams before the kick-off. I remember a cup game at Moseley against Bristol. In spelling out the names of the Moseley forwards I said, "Raymond — as in Raymond's Revuebar."

"This," said my copytaker," is the *Correspondent*, not the *Co-respondent*."

When I came to the Bristol second row, I said "Lear, as in King . . .?"

"You've got it!" she laughed.

All this by way of preamble to say that although there is no great or even modest fund of rugby literature, unlike cricket, the standard of rugby writing in the top end of the newspaper market is of a comparable high quality. The writers love the game, care about its future, and offer some perceptive judgements on trends as well as individual matches.

BBC2's *Rugby Special* is inevitably, given the BBC's exclusive contract for many years for the Five Nations' Championship, heavily wedded to that event. Club rugby, which in Wales and England at least, is the game with the most avid week-by-week participants and followers, is still an afterthought to the BBC's sports planners. Failure to show any highlights from the start of the Courage league programme, for example, became a commonplace. The lapse over the Bath-Harlequins Final is mentioned elsewhere.

In the circumstances, Chris Rea, as in his playing days at the centre of things, has a difficult task. He performs it with panache given the weekly pretence that no one watching can possibly be interested enough to know already the results of the cup or league games of which the programme is about to show highlights — 24 hours after the final whistles have gone.

At the very least the poor lad deserves some modern graphic design — the stuff that pops up on screen to herald 'news' has looked like television's equivalent of a John Bull printing outfit. (Perhaps we should blame their committeemen?)

ITV (with such rugged old hands as Gareth Chilcott and Steve Smith in the team) is breathing ever more hotly down the BBC's neck. The outcome of the eventual maul could be interesting.

As for radio, Ian Robertson is another BBC man whose season is largely bound up with the international scene. But as an admirer — aren't we all meant to be? — of the BBC World Service, my image of its omniscience was dashed horribly when I had to spend the latter half of Bath's great double season in 1992 working in Beijing. I tell you, Rugby Union is a poor relation not just to Rugby League but to weightlifting, ice-hockey, and other curious pastimes. Even on Final day, I picked up progress at Twickenham on a wavering radio at midnight China time only because the World Service sports programme briefly used a slice of the Radio 5 soccer commentary and Ian Robertson (all is forgiven!) occasionally chipped in with the Twickenham score.

Thank heaven for Stephen Jones and Robert Armstrong — the *Sunday Times* and *Guardian Weekly* were the only British papers regularly reaching Beijing and therefore keeping the far-off fans up to date with league surprises and cup excitements, albeit a week or two late.

And indeed it is the press, week in and week out, rather less fickle than national radio and television, that keeps clubs and their followers up-to-date with trends and teams in a sport moving rapidly into big money and all that implies. That dramatic shift in the game was visibly manifest to visitors to the Rec at the start of the 1992-93 season: part of the roof of the main stand was missing. The gap was to be filled by the new press box.

It was a few weeks late arriving, and cost around £80,000, rather more than originally envisaged. But its excellent facilities for press, radio and television meant that few would argue with the boast of the club's ebullient press officer Ken Johnstone: "It is the best press box in the league, as befits a club that has more column inches written about it than any other."

That last point was worth making. Bath benefited from its frequent exposure from BBC *Rugby Special*, and HTV's coverage, and in that extensive coverage from the quality dailies and Sundays in particular, whose column inches and pictures on Bath alone must have equalled the felling of a few forests.

Give or take the odd knock from Alan Watkins in his fitful column when he felt like teasing the Bath folk, the coverage was invariably well-informed and fair to Bath. Indeed, the club had good friends in national and local media, some of them duly quoted in this book. (In the next chapter, many of them also choose their best Bath team of the decade at my invitation.)

In Bath, John Stevens reported the Bath team from thin times to the years of plenty — and was honoured on his retirement from the *Bath Evening Chronicle* by being made a vice-president. "He has become a special part of a special rugby family," said the club. His successor, Alan Pearey, from a notable rugby pedigree, soon showed himself a perceptive writer on the club's often controversial activities.

For its part, the club had always sought to help the press as much as it could over the seasons, even if at times it found itself almost overwhelmed by the level of media interest on big occasions. The new press box was welcome evidence of its continuing bonds with the media — and it also freed more space for extra spectators in the stand below.

Best of the Decade

SO WHO have been the 'best of Bath' in their decade of success? It may seem invidious to choose the best XV — under rules old or new — but it's also, surely, the kind of enjoyable diversion indulged in by followers of any sport.

Picking Richard Hill at scrum-half is easy enough — he had no real rival. But as his partner? Stuart Barnes may have become apparently indispensable to the side — but John Horton was the keystone of much of the club's initial successes. And in the centre: how to choose between Halliday and Palmer, and their successors Guscott and the emerging de Glanville?

In the pack too the options are rich. Ben Clarke was preceded by the redoubtable Simpson, so essential to cementing that formidable back row of the early 1980s, and then by Egerton whose impact on opponents was only dented by injury. And who dare choose between Spurrell and Robinson?

It's a fascinating challenge. But for Bath past or present players, committeemen or club members for that matter, to play that game publicly is probably not risking friendships — but at least a pint or two. Instead, therefore, I asked some distinguished national and West Country rugby writers and commentators to choose their own best Bath team. As experienced observers of Bath's performances over the seasons — away as well as at home — they are reliable judges. Three of them are also former internationals.

The brief I offered them was simply to choose from the players who started in any of Bath's seven Cup Finals from 1984 to 1992 — with two additional names — Lumsden who would have appeared in the 1989 Final side but for his injury, and the Scottish international lock, Reed, who emerged as a first-choice player after the 1992 Final, and was also chosen for the Lions' tour.

A reminder — there was no choice other than Hill for scrum-half, and Egerton, Hall, Ojomoh, and Simpson had all played for Bath and for representative England sides both as flankers and no.8 forwards. And if my selectors were sometimes spoiled for choice, for example in the centre or back row, other areas were perhaps thinner for

definitive candidates, as one or two of my guests pointed out.

The players the journalists had to choose from were, in alphabetical order, as follows:

Full-back: Callard, Lumsden, Martin, Webb
Right-wing: Swift, Trick
Centres: de Glanville, Guscott, Halliday, Palmer, Rees
Left-wing: Adebayo, Fallon, Sagoe, Trevaskis (also Swift)
Fly-half: Barnes, Horton
Scrum-half: Hill
Props: Chilcott, Lee, Sole, Ubogu
Hooker: Bess, Cunningham, Dawe
Locks: Cronin, Gaymond, Haag, Morrison, Redman, Reed
Back row: Clarke, Egerton, Hall, Ojomoh, Simpson, Spurrell, Robinson, Withey

Now for the teams they chose, given in alphabetical order of the correspondents' names, and with the no.8 forward as the penultimate name in the lists. Some named two replacements, as asked, others more generously listed six, and some none.

Robert Armstrong (*The Guardian*) named: Webb; Swift, Guscott, Halliday, Fallon, Barnes, Hill, Chilcott, Dawe, Ubogu, Haag, Redman, Hall, Clarke, Robinson. (Repl: Palmer, Egerton.)

Steve Bale (*The Independent*) named: Webb; Trick, Guscott, Palmer, Fallon, Barnes, Hill, Sole, Dawe, Chilcott, Morrison, Redman, Hall, Clarke, Spurrell. (Repl: Halliday, Simpson.)

Bill Beckett (sports editor, *Western Daily Press*) prefaced his selection with the thought: "It's like a menu at a really first-rate restaurant . . .there are so many superb choices your taste buds won't allow you to pass one over."

He chose: Webb; Swift, Guscott, Halliday, Fallon, Barnes, Hill, Sole, Dawe, Chilcott, Redman, Reed, Hall, Clarke, Robinson. (Repl: Lumsden, Egerton.)

Mick Cleary (*The Observer*) selected: Webb; Swift, Guscott, Halliday, Fallon, Barnes, Hill, Sole, Dawe, Chilcott, Cronin, Redman, Hall, Clarke, Robinson. (No repl. named.)

Kevin Coughlan (*Bristol Evening Post*), like some others, goes off the master list for a replacement

Contemplative Victor Ubogu, 1990.

Another contemplative prop, Gareth Chilcott.

which is legitimate as his choice appeared as such in one Final. He named: Webb; Swift, Guscott, Palmer, Fallon, Barnes, Hill, Sole, Dawe, Chilcott, Cronin, Redman, Hall, Egerton, Robinson. (Repl: Knight, Ubogu.)

Barrie Fairall (*The Independent*) chose: Webb; Swift, Guscott, Halliday, Fallon, Barnes, Hill, Sole, Dawe, Chilcott, Cronin, Redman, Hall, Clarke, Robinson. (Repl: Palmer, Simpson.)

David Hands (*The Times*), who said "I regret being unable to find a place for as good a player as John Palmer," chose: Webb; Swift, Guscott, Halliday, Fallon, Barnes, Hill, Sole, Dawe, Chilcott, Redman, Cronin, Hall, Egerton, Robinson. (No repl. listed, but by implication Palmer would be one)

Alastair Hignell (HTV) named: Webb; Trick, Guscott, Palmer, Halliday, Barnes, Hill, Sole, Dawe, Chilcott, Cronin, Redman, Hall, Clarke, Robinson. (Repl: de Glanville, Horton, Knight, Ubogu, Cunningham, Egerton.)

Stephen Jones (*Sunday Times*) added the rider: "It is almost a random selection in the sense that de Glanville and Ubogu are brilliant players and there is no genuine middle of the line-out jumper of top class . . ." He selected: Webb; Swift, Guscott, Halliday, Fallon, Barnes, Hill, Sole, Dawe. Chilcott, Morrison, Redman, Hall, Clarke, Robinson. (No repl. listed.)

John Mason (*Daily Telegraph*) added: "Sadly, no room for Horton or Spurrell . . ." and chose: Webb; Trick, Guscott, Halliday, Swift, Barnes, Hill, Sole, Dawe, Chilcott, Cronin, Redman, Hall, Egerton, Robinson. (Repl: Lumsden, Palmer,

In the wars again – Egerton against Saracens, 1990.

Knight, Ubogu, Cunningham, Clarke. "At a pinch, Chilcott could hook, allowing Spurrell to be on the bench.").

Chris Rea (BBC *Rugby Special* and *The Independent on Sunday*) named: Webb; Trick, Guscott, Halliday, Fallon, Barnes, Hill, Sole, Dawe, Ubogu, Redman, Reed, Hall, Clarke, Robinson. (No repl. listed)

John Stevens (formerly *Bath Evening Chronicle*) chose: Webb; Swift, Guscott, Halliday, Trevaskis, Barnes, Hill, Sole, Dawe, Chilcott, Gaymond, Redman, Hall, Clarke, Robinson (Repl: Callard, Fallon, Palmer, Horton, Ubogu, Morrison.)

John Taylor (*Mail on Sunday*) remarked: "Isn't it strange? With all those great players no outstanding middle jumper or left wing? . . .I'd play Tricky on the left rather than leave him out." He added by way of further caveats to his selections: "I'm a great fan of de Glanville," and that he thought Sole played his best rugby after he left Bath. He named: Webb; Swift, Guscott,

Halliday, Trick, Barnes, Hill, Chilcott, Dawe, Ubogu, Morrison, Redman, Hall, Clarke, Robinson. (Repl: de Glanville, Sole, Egerton.).

Seven players were in each of the teams selected by the press — Webb, Guscott, Barnes, Hill, Dawe, Redman and Hall. They might reasonably qualify as a certain seven in any Bath team of the decade, therefore, to play against The Rest of England.

Chilcott and Robinson appear in every choice bar one, and Clarke, Halliday and Sole in all but two of the 13 selections.

And I promised not to identify the man who said with a chuckle, "Spurrell or Robinson . . . that's difficult — I'd better say Andy or he may never speak to me again."

The rest of the score I leave the reader to count at leisure. But old hands will be pleased to see first-choice mentions of retired stalwarts such as Palmer, Trevaskis, Gaymond, and Spurrell — it's perhaps inevitable that more recent performances stay in the memory to the exclusion of older ones.

Centre Philip de Glanville, 1991.

That said, it's also fair to add that more than one of my selectors made the point that some players were still making their reputation — de Glanville and Ubogu were cited in particular.

My apologies, too, to all my diligent respondents (and to the player) for omitting Ojomoh from the master list I sent them (he played in the 1992 Final, of course). But as no one pointed out the omission, I have assumed he wasn't a first-choice for anyone; he is, though, in the category of younger players whose best is perhaps yet to come.

To make up a full side of 15 'selectors', I also invited the editors of Bath's fanzine, *Ere*, to join the fun by naming their best Bath team — perhaps they, unlike other club members, don't mind losing friends by going public?

Fly-half Stuart Barnes, preferred to John Horton.

Prop Richard Lee, 1989.

Clive Banks and Glen Leat chose the same 14 in their team: Webb; Swift, de Glanville, Guscott, Fallon, Barnes, Hill, Sole, Dawe, Ubogu, Gaymond, Redman, Hall, Clarke . . .

. . .but Banks chose Spurrell to complete his side, and replacements Knight, Halliday, Robinson, Bess, Horton; Leat chose Egerton as his last name. With replacements Callard, Halliday, Haag, Robinson, Simpson.

Their bold selection of de Glanville will raise an eyebrow or two, no doubt, plus their bold omission of Chilcott and Robinson. But like the reporters, they too chose the famous seven.

As for my own selection, well, I couldn't forget Horton, Palmer or Trick, and wouldn't be able to decide between Simpson and Egerton, never mind Clarke. So, as a natural coward, and on the basis that the temptation is to forget the older names too readily I'm choosing two Bath sides — the John Player Cup team against the Pilkington Cup XV.

To qualify, players must have played in one of the relevant Finals; but those who played under either sponsorship I can choose for either side. It's called literary licence — and as well as avoiding awkward choices it also gives a deserved game to such worthies as Richard Lee and Chris Martin. (Reed and Lumsden I excluded, like Hakin and Ralston, because I chose only from those who took part in a Cup Final.)

My teams: John Player Special Cup XV: Martin; Trick, Palmer, Halliday, Trevaskis, Horton, Hill, Sole, Cunningham, Lee, Gaymond, Redman, Hall, Simpson, Spurrell (capt).

Pilkington Cup XV: Webb; Swift, de Glanville, Guscott, Fallon, Barnes, Knight, Chilcott, Dawe, Ubogu, Cronin, Morrison, Egerton, Clarke, Robinson.

Replacements for either team: Callard, Bess, Knight, Haag, Ojomoh.

Referee (no argument): Fred Howard.

As for choosing your own best Bath team of the decade — you've probably done so already, several argumentative paragraphs ago. But what about that best Rest of England side to play them . . .?

Hare; Underwood . . .(No, that way madness surely lies).

QUIZ QUESTIONS

1. Only two Bath players appeared in each of the club's seven Cup Finals. Name them.

2. Either Trick or Swift played on Bath's right wing in the seven Cup Finals. During the same period five players were chosen for the left wing in a Bath Cup Final side, including Adebayo, Fallon, Sagoe and Trevaskis. Who was the fifth?

3. In two Cup Finals two seasons apart, Trevaskis (left wing) and Swift (right wing) had to be replaced during the games. The same replacement was used on each occasion. Who was he?

4. Two players who took part in Cup Finals involving Bath later moved to Rugby League. Who were they?

5. Five of the following six players appeared in two Cup Finals for Bath. Who is the odd man out — Cronin, Cunningham, Gaymond, Horton, Trevaskis, Ubogu?

6. Two of the Bristol team which lost to Bath in the 1983-84 Final later played both cup and league matches for Bath. Who were they?

7. In successive Pilkington Cup Finals, Bath faced teams each of whom included a player with the same first name and surname, but they were not related. What is the name and which clubs did the two play for?

8. In Bath's four John Player Cup Finals, who kicked the most conversions for Bath, Stuart Barnes, John Palmer, or David Trick?

9. Who has kicked the highest total of dropped-goals for Bath in Twickenham Finals?

10. Wasps fielded two players at fly-half in Finals against Bath later to play for their countries in the World Cup finals of 1991. One was Rob Andrew for England. Who was the other?

11. Four of the following five players were at Bath University. Who is the odd man out: Adebayo, Bess, Martin, Trick, Lumsden?

12. John Horton played how many Courage League games for Bath: (a) 11; (b) 0; (c) 4?

13. Who played fly-half for Bath when they lost cup games (a) at Moseley in 1988; (b) at home to Leicester in 1991; (c) at Waterloo in 1993?

14. Bath fielded four different full-backs in Twickenham Finals, including Martin, Callard and Webb? Who was the other?

15. Name three Bath players who won full Scottish international caps while at the club during the Jack Rowell era?

16. Which Bath player who appeared in three Cup Finals for the club later moved to Bristol?

17. In the seasons since Bath's first Cup Final win, what has been the club's heaviest cup defeat?

18. Which player has scored the most points in a Cup Final against Bath?

19. Bath scored 82 points in one cup game. Were their opponents (a) Lichfield; (b) Hereford; (c) Oxford?

20. Bath's highest score in a Courage League game was against (a) Liverpool St Helens; (b) Rugby; (c) Bedford?

Answers on Page 246

International Caps

England

Barnes S. (1984 Australia, while at Bristol); 1985 Romania (r), New Zealand (2); 1986 Scotland (r), France (r); 1987 Ireland (r); 1988 Fiji; 1993 Scotland, Ireland.

Chilcott G. 1984 Australia; 1986 Ireland, France; 1987 France (r), Wales; World Cup, Japan, United States, Wales (r); 1988 Ireland (r) Fiji; 1989 Ireland (r), France, Wales, Romania.

Clarke B. 1993 South Africa, France, Wales, Scotland, Ireland.

Dawe G. 1987 Ireland, France, Wales; World Cup, United States.

de Glanville P. 1993 South Africa (r), Wales (r).

Egerton D. 1988 Ireland, Australia, Fiji (r), Australia; 1989 Fiji; 1990 Ireland, Argentina (r).

Guscott J. 1989 Romania, Fiji; 1990 Ireland, France, Wales, Scotland, Argentina; 1991 Wales, Scotland, Ireland, France, Fiji, Australia; World Cup, New Zealand, Italy, France, Scotland, Australia; 1992 Scotland, Ireland, France, Wales; 1993 Canada, South Africa, France, Wales, Scotland, Ireland.

Hall J. 1984 Scotland (r), Ireland, France, South Africa (2), Australia; 1985 Romania, France, Scotland, Ireland, Wales, New Zealand (2); 1986 Wales, Scotland; 1987 Ireland, France, Wales, Scotland; 1990 Argentina.

Halliday S. 1986 Wales, Scotland; 1987 Scotland; 1988 Scotland, Ireland (2), Australia (2); 1989 Scotland, Ireland, France, Wales, Romania, Fiji (r); 1990 Wales. Scotland. (Seven later caps when with Harlequins).

Hill R. 1984 South Africa (2); 1985 Ireland (r), New Zealand (2, r); 1986 France (r); 1987 Ireland, France, Wales; World Cup, United States; 1989 Fiji; 1990 Ireland, France, Wales, Scotland, Argentina (3); 1991 Wales, Scotland, Ireland, France, Fiji, Australia; World Cup, New Zealand, Italy, United States, France, Scotland, Australia.

Horton J. 1978 Wales, Scotland, Ireland, New Zealand; 1980 Ireland, France, Wales, Scotland; 1981 Wales; 1983 Scotland, Ireland; 1984 South Africa (2).

Martin C. 1985 France, Scotland, Ireland, Wales.

Redman N. 1984 Australia; 1986 Scotland (r); 1987 Ireland, Scotland; World Cup, Australia, Japan, Wales; 1988 Fiji; 1990 Argentina (2); 1991 Fiji; World Cup, Italy, United States.

Robinson A. 1988 Australia (2), Fiji; 1989 Scotland, Ireland, France, Wales.

Simpson P. 1983 New Zealand; 1984 Scotland; 1987 Ireland.

Swift A. (Seven caps when with Swansea, before coming to Bath.)

Trick D. 1983 Ireland; 1984 South Africa.

Ubogu V. 1993 Canada, South Africa.

Webb J. (16 caps, including one as replacement, when at Bristol); 1991 Fiji, Australia; World Cup, New Zealand, Italy, France, Scotland, Australia; 1992

Jonathan Webb.

Scotland, Ireland, France, Wales; 1993 Canada, South Africa, France, Wales, Scotland, Ireland.

Scotland

Cronin D. 1988 Ireland, France, Wales. England, Australia; 1989 Wales, England, Ireland, France, Fiji, Romania. (16 later caps when with London Scottish.)

Reed A. 1993 Ireland, France, Wales, England.

Sole D. 1986 France, Wales; 1987 Ireland, France, Wales, England; World Cup, France, Zimbabwe, Romania, New Zealand. (32 further caps when with Edinburgh Academicals.)

British Isles (Lions)†

Guscott J. 1989 Australia (2).

(Note: Chilcott and Robinson toured with 1989 Lions but did not play in Tests).

Barnes, Clarke, Guscott and Reed were also selected to tour with the 1993 British Lions.

(†They are the only Bath players in the club's history to go on a Lions' tour.)

Progress to Finals

John Player Special Cup

		1983-84			1984-85			1985-86
Third round	(h)	17-0 Headingley	(h)	24-3	Berry Hill	(a)	16-16	Orrell
Fourth Round	(a)	41-12 Blackheath	(h)	37-3	Blackheath	(a)	22-4	Moseley
Fifth round	(h)	26-12 Wasps	(a)	25-15	Sale	(a)	18-10	L Welsh
Semi-final	(a)	12-3 Nottingham	(a)	12-11	Gloucester	(a)	10-6	Leicester
Final	(T)	10-9 Bristol	(T)	24-15	L Welsh	(T)	25-17	Wasps

		1986-87			1987-88
Third round	(h)	32-10 Plymouth A	(a)	43-3	Lichfield
Fourth round	(h)	30-4 L Welsh	(a)	13-6	Leicester
Fifth round	(h)	12-3 Moseley	(a)	3-4	Moseley
Semi-final	(a)	31-7 Orrell			
Final	(T)	19-12 Wasps			

Pilkington Cup

		1988-89			1989-90			1990-91
Third round	(h)	82-9 Oxford	(h)	9-0	Harlequins	(h)	0-12	Leicester
Fourth round	(a)	48-3 Hereford	(h)	25-3	Headingley			
Fifth round	(h)	14-12 Bristol	(a)	35-3	Richmond			
Semi-final	(a)	6-3 Gloucester	(a)	21-7	Moseley			
Final	(T)	10-6 Leicester	(T)	46-6	Gloucester			

		1991-92			1992-93
Third round	(h)	52-0 Nottingham	(a)	7-9	Waterloo
Fourth round	(a)	13-9 Northampton			
Fifth round	(a)	15-6 Bristol			
Semi-final	(a)	27-18 Gloucester (aet)			
Final	(T)	15-12 Harlequins (aet)			

Cup Final Teams

John Player Special Cup

1983-84

Bath 10 (Simpson, try; Palmer, pen; Horton, drop goal)

Bristol 9 (Harding, try; Barnes, con, pen)

Bath: Martin; Trick, Palmer, Rees, Trevaskis, Horton, Hill, Chilcott, Cunningham, Lee, Gaymond, Redman, Hall, Simpson, Spurrell (capt).

Bristol: Cue; Morley, Knibbs, Hogg, Carr, Barnes, Harding, Doubleday, Palmer, Sheppard, Pomphrey, Stiff, Rafter (capt), Chidgey, Polledri.

Referee: R.Quittenton

1984-85

Bath 24 (Trick, Chilcott, tries; Palmer, 4 pens, 2 drop goals)

London Welsh 15 (Price, 5 pens)

Bath: Martin; Trick, Palmer, Halliday, Trevaskis (rep: Guscott); Horton, Hill, Chilcott, Bess, Lee, Gaymond, Redman, Hall, Simpson, Spurrell (capt).

London Welsh: Ebsworth; Hughes, Ackerman, Fouhy, Rees (capt); Price, Douglas, Jones, Light, Bradley, Lewis, Collins, Watkins, Bowring, Russell.

Referee: R.Quittenton

1985-86

Bath 25 (Swift, Spurrell, Hill, Simpson, tries; Trick, pen, 3 cons)

Wasps 17 (Stringer, Pellow, Balcombe, tries; Stringer, pen, con)

Bath: Martin; Trick, Palmer (capt), Halliday, Swift, Barnes, Hill, Chilcott, Dawe, Lee, Redman, Morrison, Hall, Simpson, Spurrell.

Wasps: Stringer; Smith, Cardus (capt), Pellow, Bailey, Rees, Bates (rep: Balcombe); Holmes, Simmons, Probyn, Pinnegar, Bonner, Pegler, Rose, Rigby.

Referee: F.Howard

1986-87

Bath 19 (Redman 2, Halliday, tries; Barnes, pen, 2 cons)

Wasps 12 (Davies, try, pen; Andrew, con, drop-goal)

Bath: Martin; Swift (rep: Guscott); Palmer, Halliday, Trevaskis; Barnes, Hill (capt); Sole, Dawe (rep: Bess), Chilcott, Morrison, Redman, Hall, Egerton, Robinson.

Wasps: Davies; Smith, Simms, Lozowski, Bailey, Andrew, Bates; Rendall, Simmons, Probyn, Pinnegar, Bonner, Pegler (capt), Rose, Rigby.

Referee: F.Howard

Pilkington Cup

1988-89

Bath 10 (Barnes, try, 3 pens)
Leicester 6 (Hare 2 pens)

Bath: Palmer; Swift, Halliday, Guscott, Sagoe, Barnes (capt), Hill; Chilcott, Dawe, Lee, Morrison, Cronin, Hall, Egerton (rep: Simpson), Robinson.
Leicester: Hare, Evans, Dodge, Bates, R.Underwood, Cusworth, Kardooni, Redfern, Thacker, Richardson, Foulkes-Arnold, T.Smith, I.Smith, Richards, Wells.

Referee: F.Howard

1989-90

Bath 48 (Swift 2, Withey, Guscott, Callard, Dawe, Redman, Ubogu, tries; Barnes, 2 pens, 4 cons; Halliday, con)
Gloucester 6 (Dunn, try; T.Smith, con)

Bath: Callard; Swift, Halliday, Guscott, Adebayo, Barnes (capt), Hill (rep: Knight); Ubogu, Dawe, Chilcott, Redman, Cronin, Withey, Egerton, Robinson.
Gloucester: T.Smith; Morgan, Caskie, Mogg, Breeze, Hamlin (capt), Hannaford, Preedy, Dunn, Pascall, Scrivens, Brain, Gadd, Teague, I.Smith.

Referee: F.Howard

1991-92

Bath 15 (de Glanville, try; Webb 2 pens, con; Barnes, drop-goal)
Harlequins 12 (Winterbottom, try; Pears 2 pens, con) (after extra-time)

Bath: Webb; Swift, de Glanville, Guscott, Fallon, Barnes, Hill, Ubogu, Dawe, Chilcott, Haag, Redman, Ojomoh, Clarke, Robinson (capt).
Harlequins: Pears; Wedderburn, Halliday, Carling, Davis, Challinor, Luxton, Hobley, Moore, Mullins, Edwards, Ackford, Russell, Sheasby, Winterbottom (capt).

Referee: F.Howard

Cup Appearances & Scorers

John Player Special Cup

1983-84, winners: 5 - Gaymond (2t), Horton (1t, 1dg), Lee, Martin (1t), Rees, Simpson (2t), Spurrell, Trevaskis, Trick (5t); 4 - Cunningham (1t), Hall, Hill (1t), Palmer (8p, 5c); 3 - Chilcott, Hakin; 2 - Lilley, Redman; 1 + 1 as rep - Bess, Ralston (3p, 2c); 1 as rep - Morrison.

1984-85, winners: 5 - Chilcott (1t), Hall (1t), Halliday, Hill (2t), Horton (3dg), Lee (1t), Palmer (1t, 10p, 5c, 2dg), Redman, Simpson (1t), Spurrell, Trevaskis (3t), Trick (3t, 3p); 4 + 1 as rep - Bess; 4 - Gaymond, Martin (1t); 1 - Cunningham, Hakin; 2 as rep - Stanley; 1 as rep - Guscott.

1985-86, winners: 5 - Barnes (8p, 3c), Chilcott, Dawe, Halliday (1t), Hill (2t), Martin, Morrison (1t), Redman, Spurrell; 4 - Trevaskis, Egerton (2t); 3 + 1 as rep - Lee; 3 - Hall, Simpson (2t), Swift (2t), Trick (1p, 3c); 2 - Sole.

1986-87, winners: 5 - Barnes (2t, 6p, 10c), Chilcott, Dawe, Hall (2t), Halliday (1t), Hill (1t),
Martin, Palmer (1t), Redman (2t), Robinson, Swift (2t); 4 - Egerton (2t), Morrison (2t), Sole; 3 - Trevaskis; 1 - Blackett, Cronin, Lee, Sagoe (1t), Simpson; 1 as rep - Bess, Guscott, Knight.

1987-88, lost in fifth round: 3 - Chilcott, Cue (4p), Dawe (1t), Egerton (1t), Guscott (2t), Hall, Halliday, Hill (2t), Lee (1t), Palmer (1dg), Redman, Robinson (1t), Swift (2t), Trick (2c); 2 + 1 as rep - Morrison; 2 - Cronin; Scores include 1 pen try.

Pilkington Cup

1988-89, winners: 5 - Barnes (1t, 6p, 12c), Chilcott (1t), Dawe, Egerton, Guscott (2t), Hall (2t), Halliday (2t, 1c), Hill (2t), Lee, Robinson, Swift (6t); 4 - Lumsden (5t), Morrison (1t), Redman; 3 - Sagoe (7t); 2 - Cronin, Trevaskis; 1 - Palmer; 1 as rep - Simpson.

1989-90, winners: 5 - Barnes (6p, 13c), Callard (2t), Chilcott (2t), Cronin (1t), Dawe, Egerton (1t), Halliday (1c), Hill, Redman (2t), Robinson, Swift

(4t); 4 - Blackett (1t), Guscott (3t); 3 - Hall (3t), Lee; 2 - Adebayo, Ubogu (1t); 1 - Withey, Simpson. 1 as rep - Knight 2.

1990-91, lost in third round: Team Webb; Swift, Guscott, Adebayo, Blackett, Barnes, Hill, Ubogu, Dawe, Lee, Haag, Redman, Ojomoh, Hall, Robinson.

1991-92, winners: 5 - Barnes (1t, 7p, 2c, 1dg), Clarke, Dawe, de Glanville (3t), Fallon (5t), Guscott (2t), Haag, Redman, Robinson, Swift (2t), Ubogu (1t), Webb (1t, 4p, 8c); 4 - Chilcott, Hill, Ojomoh; 1 - Egerton, Knight, Mallett.

1992-93, lost in third round: Team - Webb (1p); Swift (1t), Guscott, de Glanville, Adebayo; Raymond, Hill; Chilcott, Dawe, Mallett; O'Leary, Redman, Hall, Robinson, Egerton.

Appearances in KO Finals
(John Player Special or Pilkington Cups)

7 - Chilcott, Hill (1984, 1985, 1986, 1987, 1989, 1990, 1992).
6 - Redman (1984, 1985, 1986, 1987, 1990, 1992).
5 - Barnes, Dawe, Swift (1986, 1987, 1989, 1990, 1992); Hall, Palmer (1984, 1985, 1986, 1987, 1989); Halliday (1985, 1986, 1987, 1989, 1990).
4 - Lee (1984, 1985, 1986, 1989); Martin (1984, 1985, 1986, 1987).
3 - Guscott (1989, 1990, 1992 + 2 as rep (85, 1987); Egerton (1987, 1988, 1990); Morrison (1986, 1987, 1989); Robinson (1989, 1990, 1992); Spurrell, Trick (1984, 1985, 1986).
2 - Gaymond, Horton, Trevaskis (1984, 1985); Cronin (1989, 1990); Ubogu (1990, 1992).
1 - Bess (1985) + 1 as rep (1987); Adebayo, Callard (1990); Clarke (1992); Cunningham (1984); de Glanville, Fallon, Haag, Ojomoh (1992); Rees (1984); Sagoe (1989); Sole (1987); Webb (1992); Withey (1990); 1 as rep - Knight (1990).

Courage Clubs' Championship
Bath – Division One results

1987-88: Leicester (a) 13-24; Moseley (h) 14-0; Nottingham (a) 15-25; Bristol (h) 15-9; Wasps (a) 15-19; Coventry (a) 9-9; Gloucester (h) 16-9; Waterloo† (h) 10-17; Orrell (h) 23-18; Harlequins (h) 21-9; Sale (a) 46-17.
P 11, W 6, D 1, L 4, F 197, A 156, Pts 30. Position: Fourth (†Divisional day)

1988-89: Harlequins (a) 26-9; Gloucester (h) 19-9; Rosslyn Park (a) 19-6; Bristol (h) 16-9; Moseley (a) 38-0; Orrell (h) 36-12; Wasps (h) 16-6; Liverpool St Helens (a) 21-7; Nottingham (h) 22-16; Waterloo (h) 38-9; Leicester† (a) 12-15.
P 11, W 10, D 0, L 1, F 263, A 98, Pts 20. Position: champions.

(†Each side fielded second team week before Cup Final.)

1989-90: Harlequins (h) 32-12; Gloucester (a) 6-13; Rosslyn Park (h) 34-6; Bristol (a) 14-13; Moseley (h) 27-9; Orrell (a) 9-6; Wasps (a) 18-9; Bedford (h) 76-0; Nottingham (a) 9-12; Saracens (a) 7-9; Leicester (h) 26-15.
P 11, W 8, D 0, L 3, F 258, A 104, Pts 16. Position: third.

1990-91: Liverpool St Helens (h) 46-3; Northampton (a)16-10; Orrell (a) 17-9; Bristol (a) 10-3; Harlequins (h) 23-3; Leicester (a) 9-3; Moseley (h) 11-6; Wasps (h) 15-16; Nottingham (a) 22-9; Gloucester (a) 17-15; Rosslyn Park (h) 45-21; Saracens (a) 49-6.
P 12, W 11, D 0, L 1, F 280, A 104, Pts 22. Position: champions.

1991-92: London Irish† (a) 26-21; Northampton (h) 15-6; Orrell (a) 9-10; Bristol (h) 9-4; Harlequins (a) 18-18; Leicester (h) 37-6; Gloucester (h) 29-9; Wasps (a) 24-12; Rugby (a) 32-0; Nottingham (h) 25-15; Rosslyn Park (a) 21-13; Saracens (h) 32-12.
P 12, W 10, D 1, L 1, F 277, A 126, Pts 20†. Position: champions. (†Point deducted for playing unregistered player)

1992-93: Harlequins (h) 22-6; London Irish (h) 42-19; Northampton (a) 8-11; Orrell (h) 39-3; Bristol (a) 31-8; Leicester (h) 13-3; Rugby (h) 61-7; Gloucester (a) 20-0; Wasps (h) 22-11; West Hartlepool (a) 38-10; London Scottish (h) 40-6; Saracens (a) 19-13.
P 12, W 11, D 0, L 1, F 355, A 97, Pts 22. Position: champions.

Courage Clubs' Championship
Bath - Appearances & Scorers

1987-88 (Fourth; 11 games played): 11 - Lee (1t); 10 - Guscott (1t, 5c), Hill (2t); 9 - Dawe, Egerton (2t), Trick; 8 - Chilcott (1t), Cue (5p, 3c, 1dg), Redman (2t), Robinson (1t) Swift (3t); 7 - Halliday, Palmer (2c, 1dg), Morrison; 5 - Simpson; 4 - Barnes (7p, 1c), Lumsden + 1 as rep (1t); 3 - Cronin (1t), Withey (2t); 2 - Deane, Hall, Jones, Miles, Martin, Maslen + 1 as rep, Sagoe (1t); Bamsey (1t), Blackett, Davies + 3 as rep, Janes, Kipling, Knight, Lilley, Stevens, Whitehead; 1 as rep — Harris, Hoskin.

1988-89 (Champions; 11 games played, second team fielded in game week before cup final); 10 - Chilcott (1t), Dawe (1t), Lee, Robinson (1t); 9 - Barnes (17p, 14c, 2dg), Egerton (5t); Lumsden (3t); 8 - Guscott (10t), Halliday (1t), Hill (2t), Morrison (2t); 7 - Hall (2t), Redman (1t), Swift (3t); 6 - Sagoe (1t); 5 - Cronin (2t), Trevaskis (1t); 3 - Knight + 1 as rep, Palmer, Simpson (1t), 2 - Cue, Westcott (1t); 1 - Bamsey, Bick, Crane, Cundy, Deane, Haag, Hoskin (1t), Jones, Kipling, Maslen + 2 as rep, Sparkes, Trick, Weekes. (Also 1 pen try.)

1989-90 (Third; 11 games played): 11 - Callard (6t, 1c), Dawe (1t), Swift (10t), Robinson (1t); 10 - Barnes (5t, 7p, 2dg), Cronin, Hill, Lee; 9 - Blackett (2t), Egerton (2t), Guscott (4t), Halliday (2t); 7 + 1 as rep - Chilcott; 6 - Hall (3t), Morrison, Redman; 5 + 1 as rep - Ubogu (2t); 3 - Adebayo (2t), Simpson; 2 - Maslen, Withey (1t); 1 -. Bamsey, Haag, Hoskin (1t), Knight + 1 as rep, Walklin, Westcott.

1990-91 (Champions; 12 games played); 12 - Dawe, Robinson (1t), Swift (5t); 11 - Barnes (3t, 7p, 9c, 2dg), Guscott (5t), Haag (2t), Hall (3t), Hill (1t), Webb (3t, 17p, 14c); 9 - Ubogu (2t); 8 - Bamsey (1t), Redman (1t); 6 + 1 as rep - Lee (1t), Ojomoh; 5 - Adebayo (4t), Chilcott (1t), Fallon (1t), de Glanville (1t); 4 - Egerton; 3 - Crane (1t), Cronin, Maslen; 2 - Blackett, Callard, Reed; 1 - Knight + 1 as rep; 1 as rep - Deane.

1991-92 (Champions; 12 games played): 12 - Barnes (3t, 20p, 12c, 2dg), Fallon (7t), Hill (2t), Robinson (2t), Swift (8t); 11 — Clarke (1t), Dawe, Redman (1t); 10 - Chilcott, de Glanville (3t), Haag, Ubogu; 9 - Webb (12p, 7c); 8 - Ojomoh; 7 - Guscott (1t, 1dg); 4 - Egerton (1t); 3 - Bamsey, Lewis, Mallett + 1 as rep; 1 - Atkins, Heatherley†, Lee, McCoy, Maslen, Reed; 1 as rep - Beddow, Crane, Knight. (†Unregistered player)

1992-93 (Champions; 12 games played): 12 - Dawe, de Glanville (2t), Swift (4t); 11 - Adebayo (3t), Barnes (7t, 2c, 1dg), Clarke (4t), Hall (2t), Hill (1t), Redman (3t); 10 - Chilcott, Guscott (3t), Robinson (1t), Webb (3t, 24p, 19c); 9 - Ubogu (3t); 8 - Reed; 4 - O'Leary (1t); 3 - Callard (5t, 2c), Ojomoh; 2 - Hilton, Lewis; 1 + 1 as rep - Mallett, Sanders; 1 - Catt, Egerton, Haag; 1 as rep - Atkins.

Courage Clubs' Championship

Division One

1987-88

(Not all clubs played each other; 4 pts awarded for win, two for draw, one simply for playing)

	P	W	D	L	F	A	Pts
Leicester	10	9	0	1	225	133	37
Wasps	11	8	1	2	218	136	37
Harlequins†	11	6	1	4	261	128	30
Bath	**11**	**6**	**1**	**4**	**197**	**156**	**30**
Gloucester	10	6	1	3	206	121	29
Orrell	11	5	1	5	192	153	27
Moseley	11	5	0	6	167	170	26
Nottingham	11	4	1	6	146	170	24
Bristol†	10	4	1	5	171	145	23
Waterloo	10	4	0	6	123	208	22
Coventry	11	3	1	7	139	246	21
Sale	11	0	0	11	95	374	11

(Sale and Coventry relegated; †Cup final between these teams also counted for league points

1988-89

	P	W	D	L	F	A	Pts
Bath	**11**	**10**	**0**	**1**	**263**	**98**	**20**
Gloucester	11	7	1	3	215	112	15
Wasps	11	7	1	3	206	138	15
Nottingham	11	6	1	4	142	122	13
Orrell	11	6	1	4	148	157	13
Leicester	11	6	1	4	189	199	13
Harlequins	11	5	0	6	188	117	12
Rosslyn Park	11	5	0	6	172	208	10
Moseley	11	3	0	8	113	242	6
Waterloo	11	1	1	9	120	235	3
Liverpool St Helens	11	1	0	10	116	254	2

(Waterloo and Liverpool St Helens relegated)

1989-90

	P	W	D	L	F	A	Pts
Wasps	11	9	0	2	250	106	18
Gloucester	11	8	1	2	214	139	17
Bath	**11**	**8**	**0**	**3**	**258**	**104**	**16**
Saracens	11	7	1	3	168	167	15
Leicester	11	6	0	5	248	184	12
Nottingham	11	6	0	5	187	148	12
Harlequins	11	6	0	5	218	180	12
Orrell	11	5	0	6	221	132	10
Bristol	11	4	0	7	136	144	8
Rosslyn Park	11	4	0	7	164	243	8
Moseley	11	2	0	9	138	258	4
Bedford	11	0	0	11	70	467	0

(Bedford relegated)

1990-91

	P	W	D	L	F	A	Pts
Bath	**12**	**11**	**0**	**1**	**280**	**104**	**22**
Wasps	12	9	1	2	252	151	19
Harlequins	12	8	0	4	267	182	16
Leicester	12	8	0	4	244	131	16
Orrell	12	7	0	5	247	115	14
Gloucester	12	6	0	6	207	163	12
Rosslyn Park	12	6	0	6	216	174	12
Nottingham	12	6	0	6	128	194	12
Northampton	12	5	1	6	197	206	11
Saracens	12	5	0	7	151	228	10
Bristol	12	4	1	7	135	219	9
Moseley	12	1	1	10	113	244	3
Liverpool St Helens	12	0	0	12	88	349	0

(Moseley and Liverpool St Helens relegated)

1991-92

	P	W	D	L	F	A	Pts
Bath	**12**	**10**	**1**	**1**	**277**	**126**	**20†**
Orrell	12	10	0	2	204	95	20
Northampton	12	9	1	2	209	136	19
Gloucester	12	7	1	4	193	168	15
Saracens	12	7	1	4	176	165	15
Leicester	12	6	1	5	262	216	13
Wasps	12	6	0	6	177	180	12
Harlequins	12	5	1	6	213	207	11
London Irish	12	3	3	6	147	237	9
Bristol	12	4	0	8	192	174	8
Rugby	12	2	3	7	124	252	7
Nottingham	12	2	1	9	133	204	5
Rosslyn Park	12	0	1	11	111	258	1

(†Bath deducted one point; Nottingham and Rosslyn Park relegated)

1992-93

	P	W	D	L	F	A	Pts
Bath	**12**	**11**	**0**	**1**	**355**	**97**	**22**
Wasps	12	11	0	1	186	118	22
Leicester	12	9	0	3	220	116	18
Northampton	12	8	0	4	215	150	16
Gloucester	12	6	0	6	173	151	12
Bristol	12	6	0	6	148	169	12
London Irish	12	6	0	6	175	223	12
Harlequins	12	5	1	6	197	187	11
Orrell	12	5	0	7	175	183	10
London Scottish	12	3	1	8	192	248	7
Saracens	12	3	0	9	137	180	6
West Hartlepool	12	3	0	9	149	236	6
Rugby	12	1	0	11	104	368	2

(London Scottish, Saracens, West Hartlepool and Rugby relegated)

Quiz Answers

1. Chilcott and Hill
2. Swift, 1986
3. Guscott
4. Ackerman (London Welsh) and Fallon (Bath)
5. Cunningham, one Final
6. Cue and Barnes
7. Ian Smith (Leicester) 1989, and Ian Smith (Gloucester) 1990, both back-row forwards. Each side also fielded a T.Smith (Tom, Leicester; Tim, Gloucester).
8. Trick, with a total of three, all in the 1986 Final. (Barnes's later conversions came in the Pilkington Cup Finals)
9. John Palmer, two, both in the 1985 Final.
10. Gareth Rees, who later appeared for Canada.
11. Adebayo
12. None
13. a. John Palmer b. Barnes c. Raymond
14. John Palmer, 1989
15. Cronin, Reed, Sole
16. Morrison
17. Beaten 12-0 at home by Leicester, 1990-91
18. Colin Price, 15 points, all penalty-goals, for London Welsh, 1985.
19. Oxford, 1988-89
20. Bedford, 1989-90

Players' Appearances

Cup games from 1983-84 and League games from 1987-88
Figures following oblique indicate appearances as replacement

	League	Try	Pen	Con	DG	Cup	Try	Pen	Con	DG		League	Try	Pen	Con	DG	Cup	Try	Pen	Con	DG
ADEBAYO	19	9	0	0	0	4	0	0	0	0	KNIGHT S	6/4	0	0	0	0	1/2	0	0	0	0
ATKINS	1/1	0	0	0	0	0	0	0	0	0	LEE	38/1	2	0	0	0	26/1	0	0	0	0
BAMSEY	14	2	0	0	0	0	0	0	0	0	LEWIS I	5	0	0	0	0	0	0	0	0	0
BARNES	57	18	65	38	9	26	4	31	40	1	LILLEY	1	0	0	0	0	2	0	0	0	0
BEDDOW	0/1	0	0	0	0	0	0	0	0	0	LUMSDEN	13	3	0	0	0	4	5	0	0	0
BESS	0	0	0	0	0	5/3	0	0	0	0	McCOY	1	0	0	0	0	0	0	0	0	0
BICK	1	0	0	0	0	0	0	0	0	0	MALLETT	1/1	0	0	0	0	2	0	0	0	0
BLACKETT	12	2	0	0	0	6	1	0	0	0	MARTIN	2	0	0	0	0	19	2	0	0	0
CALLARD	16	11	0	3	0	5	2	0	0	0	MASLEN	9/3	0	0	0	0	0	0	0	0	0
CATT	1	0	0	0	0	0	0	0	0	0	MILES	2	0	0	0	0	0	0	0	0	0
CHILCOTT	50/1	3	0	0	0	36	4	0	0	0	MORRISON	21	2	0	0	0	15/2	4	0	0	0
CLARKE	22	5	0	0	0	5	0	0	0	0	OJOMOH	17	0	0	0	0	5	0	0	0	0
CRANE	4/1	0	0	0	0	0	0	0	0	0	O'LEARY	4	1	0	0	0	1	0	0	0	0
CRONIN	21	3	0	0	0	10	1	0	0	0	PALMER J	10	0	0	2	1	15	2	18	10	3
CUE	10	0	5	3	1	3	0	4	0	0	RALSTON	0	0	0	0	0	1/1	0	3	2	0
CUNDY	1	0	0	0	0	0	0	0	0	0	RAYMOND	0	0	0	0	0	1	0	0	0	0
CUNNINGHAM	0	0	0	0	0	5	1	0	0	0	REDMAN	51	8	0	0	0	36	2	0	0	0
DAWE	65	2	0	0	0	30	1	0	0	0	REED	11	0	0	0	0	0	0	0	0	0
DAVIES	1/3	0	0	0	0	0	0	0	0	0	REES	0	0	0	0	0	5	0	0	0	0
DEANE	3/1	0	0	0	0	0	0	0	0	0	ROBINSON	63	7	0	0	0	25	1	0	0	0
de GLANVILLE	27	6	0	0	0	6	3	0	0	0	SAGOE	8	2	0	0	0	4	8	0	0	0
EGERTON	36	10	0	0	0	23	6	0	0	0	SANDERS	1/1	0	0	0	0	0	0	0	0	0
FALLON	17	8	0	0	0	5	5	0	0	0	SIMPSON	11	1	0	0	0	15/1	5	0	0	0
GAYMOND	0	0	0	0	0	9	2	0	0	0	SOLE	0	0	0	0	0	6	0	0	0	0
GUSCOTT	56	24	0	5	1	19/2	9	0	0	0	SPARKES	1	0	0	0	0	0	0	0	0	0
HAAG	24	2	0	0	0	6	0	0	0	0	SPURRELL	0	0	0	0	0	15	0	0	0	0
HAKIN	0	0	0	0	0	4	0	0	0	0	STANLEY	0	0	0	0	0	1/3	0	0	0	0
HALL	37	10	0	0	0	35	9	0	0	0	STEVENS	1	0	0	0	0	0	0	0	0	0
HALLIDAY	24	3	0	0	0	28	4	0	2	0	SWIFT	62	33	0	0	0	28	19	0	0	0
HARRIS	0/1	0	0	0	0	0	0	0	0	0	TREVASKIS	5	1	0	0	0	19	3	0	0	0
HEATHERLEY	1	1	0	0	0	0	0	0	0	0	TRICK	10	0	0	0	0	16	8	4	5	0
HILL	62	8	0	0	0	38	10	0	0	0	UBOGU	33	7	0	0	0	8	2	0	0	0
HILTON	2	0	0	0	0	0	0	0	0	0	WALKLIN	1	0	0	0	0	0	0	0	0	0
HORTON	0	0	0	0	0	10	1	0	0	4	WEBB	30	6	53	40	0	7	1	5	8	0
HOSKIN	2/1	2	0	0	0	0	0	0	0	0	WEEKES	1	0	0	0	0	0	0	0	0	0
JANES	1	0	0	0	0	0	0	0	0	0	WESTCOTT	3	1	0	0	0	0	0	0	0	0
JONES	3	0	0	0	0	0	0	0	0	0	WHITEHEAD	1	0	0	0	0	0	0	0	0	0
KIPLING	2	0	0	0	0	0	0	0	0	0	WITHEY	5	2	0	0	0	1	1	0	0	0

Index

Index of names in main text but excluding team lists.